THE FAUSTBALL TUNNEL

JOHN HAMMOND MOORE

Random House
New York

THE FAUSTBALL TUNNEL

German POWs in America and Their Great Escape

Library of Congress Cataloging in Publication Data

Moore, John Hammond.
The faustball tunnel.

Includes index.
1.   World War, 1939–1945—Prisoners and prisons,
American.   2.   Prisoners of war—Germany.   3.   Prisoners
of war—United States.   4.   Escapes.   I.   Title.
D805.U5M6   940.54′72′730979173   77–90291
ISBN 0–394–41158–7

Manufactured in the United States of America

9 8 7 6 5 4 3 2

FIRST EDITION

To the men of Compound 1 A, Papago Park . . .
they did the digging

faustball (*fistball*)—a form of volleyball of Italian origin, introduced into Germany in the 1890s.

tunnel—a subterranean passage through or under an obstruction, such as a fence.

Foreword

This book, like many, has its origins in yet another book. While doing research for a bicentennial history of Thomas Jefferson's Albemarle County in Virginia, I discovered that during World War II about three hundred German prisoners of war were quartered in a small camp near White Hall, a tiny crossroads community nestled in the eastern foothills of the Blue Ridge Mountains. For some twenty-four months they picked apples and peaches, cut pulpwood and performed a variety of chores for local farmers hard pressed to find wartime labor.

I knew that other Germans had picked potatoes on my father's farm in northern Maine, and wondering how widespread POW labor might have been, I began digging into records at the National Archives in Washington, D.C. Before long I learned that nearly half a million POWs housed in five hundred camps worked and lived in the United States (1942–1946), yet in the midst of momentous events and the onrush of peace, their presence on American soil, for the most part, has been forgotten.

Fortunately, my quest got under way shortly after three thousand boxes of material from the Provost Marshal General's Office were declassified; that is, all restrictions relative to national security matters were removed. This step, part of a systematic review of thirty-year-old files, meant that researchers now could see the great mass of POW records gathered by the PMGO, the office in charge of prisoners of war during World War II; nevertheless, some restraints remained. Only the agency that originated certain items could authorize publication of material less than fifty years old if disclosure might constitute unwarranted invasion of personal privacy, reveal confidential sources and investigative techniques, or endanger the life or personal safety of enforcement personnel.

At first these rules posed no special problems. Then one day I opened Box 1373 of the PMGO files on prisoner-of-war-camp operations containing information relating to escape attempts in 1944. The first folder consisted of miscellaneous data from all parts of the country, none of them especially interesting. But the next three folders, two of them unusually fat and complete with diagrams, are the basis of the story that follows: how twenty-five German naval officers and seamen dug a 178-foot tunnel and escaped from their compound at Papago Park, Arizona, in December 1944.

These reports, compiled by three groups of U.S. Army officers who investigated various aspects of this daring exploit, reveal that these inquiry boards sat for twenty-three days between December 25, 1944, and January 27, 1945, examined forty-four exhibits, heard from eighty-three witnesses and compiled 307 pages of testimony. Since this is precisely the type of record—the work of special inquests—that comes under the fifty-year restriction, I applied to the Department of Defense for permission to use these reports, and after some months it was granted.

Meanwhile, research continued on other fronts. I began looking for additional files related to the prisoner-of-war camp at Papago Park (designated as Security Unit # 84 by the United States Army) and for information on naval warfare in general, since all of the POWs held at that installation on the outskirts of Phoenix were from U-boats, merchant ships, blockade runners and coast-artillery companies. And I also started hunting for the men involved in the escape.

Tracking down former German prisoners of war after three decades of peace became a fascinating pasttime, sort of a transatlantic detective game governed by airmail, hunches and considerable luck. Thanks to the work of the three inquiry boards, I knew names, but I had few addresses. National Archives files sometimes cited the birthplace of a POW or the residence of next of kin, but changes since 1945 often made such information obsolete. A records center in West Berlin (Deutsche Dienststelle—WASt) kindly reviewed a list of thirty names and forwarded the addresses of ten ex-POWs. Some of this information, more than twenty-five years old, turned out to be useless, the men having died or moved elsewhere; however, five of them answered my letters, astonished to learn that anyone remembered their Arizona adventure after so many years.

One or two of these correspondents provided leads to other men, but for the most part, close association within (and outside of) barbed-wire compounds had not blossomed into lasting friendships. West German telephone books at the Library of Congress also were helpful. Comparing a list of names with the voluminous pages of fifty directories is tedious work, yet it occasionally paid dividends, especially if an individual had a unique or unusual name.

Within a year I had located seven men who went out through the Papago Park tunnel, the widow of another escapee, and four other former POWs who, although they did not participate in the escape, could shed some light upon that remarkable exploit. Only one man who was contacted declined to be interviewed.

Armed with these addresses, an English-German dictionary and a Eurailpass, in the fall of 1976 I set out on a six-week tour which took me all over West Germany from the breathtaking splendor of the Alps south of Munich, through the historic Rhine country and the industrialized Ruhr, to centers such as Kiel, Bremerhaven and Heiligenhafen in the far north. These visits, enlivened by fine food, wine, superb hospitality and much conversation and laughter, sometimes led to others, and before I returned home I had talked with seventeen people associated with Papago Park and the story of German POWs in America during World War II.

Tracking down Americans who were involved in this wartime episode was, strangely enough, a more formidable task, but since their version of what happened is clearly delineated by scores of memos, letters, photographs, the findings of inquiry boards, reports issued by U.S. and Swiss diplomats who routinely inspected POW camps, even transcripts of telephone conversations (especially those of generals and colonels intent upon "setting the record straight"), most of them could do little more than add interesting detail or occasional bits of insight . . . and several former servicemen did just that. A trip to the Phoenix-Tucson area gave me an opportunity to see Papago Park, vestiges of the POW camp itself and the wild desert country through which twenty-five Germans tried to make their way to Mexico and to freedom.

This tunnel escape story, a bizarre twist on America's homefront during World War II, could not have been told without the assistance of numerous individuals, among them three former U-boat commanders, Fritz Guggenberger (now a retired admiral), Hans Werner Kraus and August Maus, and the widow of another, Ruth Quaet-Faslem. Others who helped piece this narrative together include Wolfgang Clarus, Berndt von Walther und Croneck, Hans F. Johannsen, Walter Kozur, Reinhard Mark, Emmerich von Mirbach and Heinrich Palmer, all of West Germany; Bill Cunliffe and Marilla Guptil, National Archives, Washington, D.C.; Cecil Parshall, Glendale, Arizona; and William M. E. Rachal, Richmond, Virginia.

I also am indebted to Bob Loomis of Random House for his advice, guidance and patience. As a youthful GI he saw hundreds of German POWs in Arizona; as an editor he now knows what at least a few of them were doing.

J. H. M.

Contents

THE FAUSTBALL TUNNEL

Port of Spain, Trinidad—September 10, 1942

Just one week ago today three British destroyers, the *Path-finder*, the *Vimy* and the *Quentin*, had closed in on the *U-162* and sent it to the bottom of the sun-soaked Caribbean. Maschinengefreiter Walter Kozur, compact, sturdy product of the Ruhr Valley city of Dortmund, chuckled as he gazed at the lush green hills rising behind a single strand of wire separating him from the rest of Port of Spain. This certainly was not his idea of what a prisoner-of-war camp would be like.

He and his comrades often shook the towers to wake up their guards. The drill held yesterday by this ragtag colonial force and its British officers was a farce from beginning to end, punctuated by much uproarious laughter from the compounds. After the officers departed, the blacks, instead of pulling off their bayonets and using them as giant toothpicks as was customary, needled the entire crew with angry taunts: "If you can march better, you goddamn Germans, then show us! Show us how you goose-step! Show us your strut!" Several prisoners said they really could not perform without rifles resting on their shoulders, so two barefoot natives, one with a great knife scar across his left cheek, actually urged the Germans to take their guns, and smiling broadly, thrust those old World War I rifles across the wire into the hands of the men they were supposed to be guarding. Incredible!

Turning his head slightly, Kozur looked toward the officers' area. No one could mistake the towering six-foot-three form of Fregattenkapitän Jürgen Wattenberg for anyone else. Austere, correct, perhaps at forty-two a bit too old to be on a submarine, nevertheless a fine captain. A native of Lübeck, Wattenberg had been navigation officer on the pocket battleship *Graf Spee*. Some said Berlin was not pleased when Wattenberg was among those advising Captain Hans Langsdorff to scuttle the ship after it was damaged off Uruguay in December 1939; yet, when Wattenberg escaped from Argentina and made his way home to Germany, he easily secured command of the *U-162*.

Wattenberg was talking with Berndt von Walther und Croneck, a young Prussian-born Leutnant zur See whom Kozur didn't know, although his friend, Johann Kremer, also a fireman third class like himself, said this ramrod aristocrat was a fair, considerate man. Johann also reported that, according to rumor, Walther was somehow related by marriage to the "Red Baron."

Two days after they arrived in Trinidad, enemy naval officers had questioned each of the forty-nine survivors but learned little, for Wattenberg had warned his crew not to talk if captured. In fact, he had always gathered the men together before each patrol, and reading directly from a copy of the Geneva Convention, pointed out that all they had to tell any captor was their name, rank "and, or else" serial number.

Officers, of course, were interrogated first, and even before Kozur's turn came, he had heard how Walther amazed those questioning him. He evidently began his interview in a sullen "arrogant Junker" mood, then became expansive and described how he used to go ashore from the *U-162* on previous patrols and have drinks at the bar of the Queen's Park Hotel in Port of Spain. He also told of walks around Woodford Square and visits to South Quay night clubs. "It is quite boring at sea so long," Walther noted in a matter-of-fact tone. "When shipping activity is not expected we occasionally put on civilian clothes, climb into a rubber boat and visit various ports for a night of fun."

Each crewman subsequently was asked if this was true, did their officers really go ashore evenings? Some said yes, some said no, which only added to the confusion in the minds of the interrogators. What they did not know was that Berndt von Walther had vacationed in Trinidad early in 1939, the trip a twenty-first-birthday present from an uncle.

The *U-162*'s three cruises had not been what one would call exciting. The first outing was in the North Atlantic, where they sank a single British freighter. The second cruise, sixty-three days long, took them to the Caribbean. There was one ineffective air attack; Kozur still remembered the chaos that first dive caused in the engine room. Before returning home, the *U-162* sent nine lone vessels to the bottom, an estimated 49,000 tons of enemy shipping. One ship, the *Florence M. Douglas*, had yielded up unexpected booty: three pigs. Two ended up on the table amid heaps of sauerkraut, but the smallest, named "Douglas," lived in the engine room for nearly two weeks. When they got back to Lorient in Brittany, "Douglas" was presented to their flotilla chief with much ceremony. "A prize of war for you, sir, a British pig."

Even the sinking of the *U-162* on their third time out had somehow lacked drama. Not planes but surface ships did them in, and it was not violent, movie-screen action but a slow, almost predictable five-hour game of cat and mouse with the mouse facing ever increasing difficulties.

Bands had played on July 7 when they departed from their French base on their last cruise. Four days out, and again in mid-August, enemy planes gave them trouble. The second onslaught was an especially close call. Their 750-ton craft was cruising on the surface in daylight while several men cleaned companionway mats. Kozur heard later that mats and crew came tumbling through the hatchway in a heap, but since the plane's three bombs were way off target, in retrospect it was more fun than danger. Officers said there was no damage, although they later discovered that some of the technical gear attached to the hull had been knocked askew.

Meanwhile they sank four small ships near the South American coast, their operating area for a second time. On the afternoon of September 3 the *U-162* was patrolling about forty miles offshore. Nothing had happened for several days, no contacts, no sightings of anything worth wasting torpedoes on. Shortly after supper there was a rush to action: a British destroyer was cutting through rolling seas and soon would be a near-perfect target as it crossed their path.

This was the first opportunity for a real prize in nearly two weeks. In the engine room Kozur and Kremer smiled grimly at each other, mouthing short, silent prayers for luck. At 1807 a single torpedo shot out toward the *Quentin*, but (as Kozur learned later) it surfaced, betraying their position, and skittered off harmlessly into blue-green waters.

Within minutes, depth charges were tossing the *U-162* this way and that as the crew struggled to elude the bone-shattering blasts. At first Kremer joked about their troubles, but soon the situation was no longer funny. Supper dishes, still on the table, crashed in a pile in one corner, only to race foolishly toward another a few seconds later. Several engine-room pipes spewed oil; lights flickered and flashed, went out, then settled for a weak, unsteady glow. One could see around the engine room, but just barely. More important, when the *U-162* tried to get under way Kozur was alarmed by the unsteady throb of the engines, too loud at times, then sputtering and coughing like an old man puffing on his first morning cigar.

At 2327 the crazy depth-charge dance began once more. Within seconds their captain made his decision: they must surface, they had no other choice. Their only chance, and a slim one, was to make for shore. However, as soon as they surfaced, the engine-room gang too was ordered up on deck. Kozur nervously adjusted the straps of his life jacket and followed Kremer's big feet out through the hatch into the open air. To his surprise, in fact to the astonishment of everyone, flares and searchlights from *three* destroyers, not one, made night into day. Escape was impossible, although the *U-162* was still cutting through rough seas at a respectable six or seven knots.

Without waiting for further orders, Kozur and Kremer jumped free and quickly swam away from the boat. A few moments later they looked back as the *Vimy* rammed into its starboard side. Within less than a minute the *U-162* sighed as its conning tower, bearing a black sword on a gray shield, a motif copied from the flyleaf of *Mein Kampf*, disappeared below the surface for the last time. Only two men were lost: the engineering officer, Stierwalt, while trying to release scuttling charges, and Ernst Dettmer, a Maschinengefreiter recovering from a minor operation. The destroyers soon plucked the rest of the crew out of the warm ocean waters and headed for Trinidad, and now they had been behind barbed wire for seven hot days and six steaming nights.

Moving a foot or so in order to remain in the shade, Kozur's attention was caught by strange voices rising from a nearby compound. In it were about forty Finns, members of a crew captured by the British. Beyond them was a sad, ragtag collection of German Jews, also internees, with a tragic tale to tell. In the summer of 1939, during the last weeks of peace, they had somehow got hold of a vessel and made their way into the Atlantic. Kremer said this pitiful band sought refuge at more than a dozen ports, only to be turned away. Shortly after World War II broke out they arrived in Trinidad, and being German citizens, were locked up. For more than two years they had languished in near-destitute conditions. These people were civilians. They had nothing to do with war. It was not fair. Even Jews should not be treated that way.

This was, thought Kozur, a very strange war. Here he was, resting on a warm tropical island doing absolutely nothing. Fat black girls served as cooks and orderlies for captured U-boat officers. Guards either slept at their posts or tried to give prisoners of war their guns. Finns argued and laughed a few yards away, and Jews who had fled from Germany to avoid

incarceration ended up in prisons run by enemies of the Third
Reich.

Atlantic Ocean, two hundred miles west of the Azores—November 19, 1942

"You stupid little fool, Horstig, can't you do anything right?
You can't remember to requisition ammunition, you keep a
diary when you know that is forbidden, you leave your
watch to take a goddamn piss, you fail to destroy that diary
and let it fall into American hands—and God knows, Horstig,
you *cannot* play cards!"

Quaet-Faslem was furious. His balding forehead glowed
with anger beneath thinning blond hair. He threw down his
hand, kicked back his chair and stalked to a covered porthole.
They were all edgy, he knew that. Three days cooped up on
the high seas going somewhere, probably to America, was
nerve-racking. The other men—Mirbach, Kaiser and Horstig—
stared at the table. This argument was endless, only it really
wasn't much of an argument—more of a tirade, since young
Horstig rarely answered his U-boat commander. Much of
what their Kapitänleutnant, a very self-confident Prussian,
said was indeed true, but during the last few days he had
been repeating it over and over and over . . .

Their last patrol, the third in little more than four months,
had started off on a sour note when twenty-one-year-old
Leutnant zur See Horst Eberhard von Horstig, baby-faced
son of a major general from Hamburg, forgot to order
charges for the submarine bubble target (SBT, or *Pillen-
werfer*), a device designed to confuse enemy sonar. Horstig
scurried about in panic and borrowed a few charges from
nearby boats, but the U-595's departure from Brest in Brittany
was delayed for nearly an hour. Quaet-Faslem gave the entire crew a severe dressing down before they were out of sight
of land.

After they got through the Gibraltar Straits into the Mediterranean they had some luck, sinking two enemy transports. Then, as they were cruising on the surface early on the morning of November 14—as Quaet-Faslem seemed unable to forget or forgive—Horstig, shortly before his watch was over, went below to the head. At that moment a British plane appeared out of the sun and quickly released four bombs. One, to the amazement of those topside, dropped on the deck, bounced twice and then quietly rolled into the sea. The others, although missing the hull, exploded close-by, causing severe damage to the guts of the craft. Instruments, lights, pumps, vents all became erratic and virtually useless. In less than thirty seconds, as Oberleutnant Emmerich Freiherr von Mirbach said later, their ship became a semifloating junk heap.

The U-595 dove deep but had to surface within a few minutes. For the next four hours, as the crew struggled to reach shore, planes flitted in and out like angry bees, but gunfire kept them at a respectable distance and they did no more damage. None was necessary. The U-595 was already mortally wounded.

Because of faulty compass readings the submarine ran aground on shoals about seventy miles northeast of Oran, off the Algerian coast. It made little difference, except that Quaet-Faslem had hoped, with the aid of a skeleton crew, to sink his doomed craft in deeper water. So the men got off, Mirbach set scuttling charges and a few moments later the light gray cylinder simply rolled over and disappeared. All forty-five men were saved, although one youngster was swept out to sea and later picked up by a British destroyer which, scenting blood, had closed in needlessly for the kill.

Within minutes after they were ashore a British plane swooped low over the crew, dropping a garbled note in a mixture of Italian and German: "Halt, or I will spray you with machine-gun fire." The men ran for cover along the beach, and the ensuing shower of bullets hit no one. As they walked toward the little village of Picard, Horstig suddenly blurted out an unexpected question, yet even then he displayed a thinly veiled, if strained respect: "Why, Herr Kapitän, were we cruising on the surface at 0800?" There was no answer.

In Picard, Quaet-Faslem sought out a local police official, a Frenchman with a German-speaking wife. The Frenchman received him in a correct manner, neither friendly nor unfriendly. Yes, he could put them up for the night if they didn't mind sleeping on straw. Yes, it would be best if men and officers remained together. They could use the schoolyard a short distance from his office. No, they could not keep their pistols. Vichy French, Free French, British, Americans, now Germans! He threw up his hands. This was too much for him to handle, a mere country policeman. Yes, he would get them soup and coffee. Yes, he would speak to his superiors if he could reach them at this hour; if not, in the morning. Yes, if they said it was correct to do so, he would return their pistols to them.

Where could they go from here? "Well, Herr Quaet-Faslem," replied the Frenchman, a bit exasperated and hesitant to mention the first destination that came to mind, "you must remember we have a war here in Algeria. I cannot, I regret, answer that question. Let me talk to my superiors, please. You and your men get food and rest. I am sure you need both. Please permit me to see what can be done."

After supper in a barren schoolyard scuffed dry by hundreds of reluctant feet, the U-595's crew stretched out on straw provided by the policeman and went to sleep. Shortly after one o'clock they heard the unmistakable rumble of vehicles as a large American tank, its single white star glistening in the cold moonlight, came down the road toward the schoolhouse. In its wake was a covey of jeeps manned by thirty or so well-armed GIs. A few of the men had to be awakened forcibly with rifle butts; they were now prisoners of war. For the first time in history a ponderous tank, elephant of the battlefield, had captured the crew of a U-boat, shark of the ocean depths.

The Americans hustled them into a nearby building, searched them carefully, officially informed them of their new status, gave them cigarettes and wine, then separated the four officers from their crewmen. Quaet-Faslem, Mirbach, Horstig and Friedrich Kaiser, the U-boat's navigation officer, a quiet youth of twenty-two who rarely spoke if not spoken to, were immediately interrogated by a U.S. major. By sunrise this perfunctory "first briefing" ended and the four men were permitted to wash and clean up.

While Quaet-Faslem and Mirbach were in the toilet the French policeman strolled in, expressing his regrets at what had happened. "I had no choice, really. The Americans, they are everywhere in this area. I'm sorry. I had to do it." The two officers thanked him for his comments and his hospitality, assuring him they hardly could hold him responsible for their fate. Both British planes and ships knew where the U-595 was scuttled. It would merely have been a matter of time before they were found. This was, after all, enemy territory.

At about nine o'clock four armored cars appeared. Each officer, accompanied by two guards, was driven to an Oran hotel where much more detailed questioning lasted throughout the day and on into the night. It was during these sessions that the existence of Horstig's diary was disclosed. As usual Kaiser said nothing; Mirbach was incredulous; Quaet-Faslem, predictably, flew into a rage.

Early the next morning these officers and the rest of the crew were driven to docks a short distance away where a huge troopship, the U.S.A.T. *Brazil,* awaited their arrival. They were hustled below deck, sealed off from the world and closely guarded as a convoy was organized to put to sea. To Mirbach's amazement, within a very short time, perhaps an hour, they actually were under way. These Americans, true to their reputation, certainly did not waste time.

And here they had been for three, now almost four days. This card game, about all they had to do, seemed to be going the way of the others. Once more Mirbach decided to put on his jovial act and try to be peacemaker. "Look," he said quietly, being careful not to address either adversary by name, "we're all in this together. God knows how many days we may be locked up in this cabin. Each of us knows how we got here —why talk about it? For all we know there may be microphones hidden behind or even in these pipes. Squabbling can only comfort the Americans, not us."

A few minutes later, just as Kaiser picked up his third trick, an American officer knocked on their door and informed them that a lifeboat drill was in progress. Would all of the gentlemen please put on their life jackets and follow him to lifeboat station number seven?

Mirbach stepped out on deck, exhilarated by the first really fresh air he had breathed in seventy-two hours and stunned by the panorama which greeted him. An aircraft carrier, a cruiser, a galaxy of tankers and transports, and several destroyers cutting smartly through the Atlantic on each flank. There must be a dozen, perhaps even as many as twenty ships in their convoy. He almost emitted a low whistle but caught himself just in time. Instead he glanced at Quaet-Faslem, who also looked stunned. So many ships, so much power!

Twenty minutes later the drill was over. The four officers went back to their prison below deck. Somehow this unexpected outing had broken the tension of recent days. Mirbach, first out and last back, jokingly told the GI guarding their quarters he had nothing to fear: "No U-boat captain is stupid enough to attack such a large convoy with such air and fire power. No, never." To his astonishment the husky youth, a red-haired youngster from Idaho named Bill, dropped his rifle with a clatter, let out a cry of very obvious relief and threw his arms around Mirbach's neck.

The other officers burst out laughing, Horstig holding his sides as he collapsed in his bunk. "The expression on your face—if I only had a camera!" sighed Kaiser. Quaet-Faslem, sinking into a chair, agreed that perhaps the life of a POW would not be so bad, after all, especially if the enemy proved to be *that* friendly! Mirbach's only comment as he picked up his cards was: "These Americans, they most certainly are a strange breed."

Mateur, Tunisia—May 13, 1943

Wolfgang Clarus, his slim six-foot figure slumped, carefully tailored tunic awry, clashing absurdly with rolled-up dungarees, sat dejectedly in a Tunisian onion field. He was sick of their odor and would, he swore, never again eat an onion, garlic, leek or any member of that obnoxious family as long as he lived. Boots of several hundred prisoners of war had crushed bulbs and shoots into a slimy mass now mixed with dust, dirt and urine. Dirt, dust, flies, heat, onions, watery soup, stale bread, the heady smell of sweaty bodies and excrement. Defeat was a miserable existence.

It would be easy to say that the German offensive in Tunisia, an age-old battleground, was doomed from the outset, but Clarus did not believe that to be true. At least his part in the affair seemed to have its ups and downs.

Late in 1942 the marine artillery unit he had commanded on the Dutch coast for nearly a year and a half had packed up and headed south. In Rome, Clarus learned they were going to Bizerte, where new gun emplacements awaited them, installations guarding the entrance to that important harbor. Shortly after he received these orders, an admiral summoned Leutnant Wolfgang Clarus to his quarters and hinted broadly that a substantial promotion might be forthcoming if he volunteered for duty near Leningrad.

The admiral backed up this attractive offer with hard facts. Because of Allied air power, only one Axis supply ship was crossing the Mediterranean each week. In short, if Clarus chose to go on to North Africa, there was every possibility that he would end up dead or in an Allied prison camp. Well, he sighed, the admiral had been right. All he left out was the onions.

Clarus and his men had pushed on to Naples, where they spent a desolate Christmas and waited six weeks for transport, finally securing passage on an Italian destroyer. During that time Clarus tried unsuccessfully to get emergency leave to see his wife and father back in Bavaria.

After two nights at sea, more frustration and disappointment. Although ordered to do so, the Italian captain adamantly refused to take them to Bizerte or even to Tunis. Instead he put three hundred men and their equipment ashore by small boat somewhere along the Tunisian coast. After a miserable twenty-four hours spent sorting out men and gear, Clarus and the other officers learned from Arab natives that they were about twenty-five miles west of Tunis. There was nothing to do but walk, so they set out on foot.

Tunis proved to be a maddening whirl of mindless confusion and bedlam. No one seemed to be in charge, no one could tell Clarus how to get to Bizerte, forty miles to the northwest by road, at least eighty by rail. Then a strange stroke of luck. Three of his men found an abandoned railway engine at the station, and after much hammering and swearing, the trio proudly announced that, yes, it might take them to Bizerte.

Early the next morning Clarus and his coast artillery unit set out, accompanied by scores of foot soldiers clinging to every conceivable part of the engine and the caboose. This ragtag express puffed past olive trees, bewildered natives and swamps, through Djedeida and Sidi Athman. The trip was almost enjoyable at times.

Just past Mateur the engine suddenly slowed, shuddered and blew up. The soldiers jumped to safety, their officers quickly deciding they would proceed on foot. Some months later Clarus learned that nearly all of these men were captured by U.S. forces within an hour; meanwhile, with the ominous staccato of gunfire in the distance, the three mechanics went to work once more. Soon, to the surprise of everyone, the engine gasped and lunged forward, and within a short time they sped along the shores of Lac de Bizerte and into the port itself.

No one was more astonished than Kapitän Wilhelm Günther, the commanding officer to whom Clarus reported in Bizerte. "How on earth did you do it?" he asked, laughing. "Why, you passed right through the front lines, right through enemy-held territory. According to all we know here, that railroad was cut by the British near Mateur three days ago!"

This moment of triumph was brief. Allied generals soon gave approval for Operation Vulcan, the final assault in Tunisia, and day by day the Americans, British and French pushed the Germans and their Italian comrades in arms toward the sea. On May 8 Günther ordered Clarus and his men to the northernmost tip of the African continent, a point eight miles from Bizerte jutting out into the Mediterranean as if trying to touch Sicily and link up with Europe. There an Italian warship would pick them up and take them to Salerno or Naples. Once more Benito Mussolini's navy proved wanting; the vessel never showed up.

After twenty-four hours, desperate, Clarus commandeered a small coastal boat, which promptly sank a few yards from shore. Those abroad were able to swim to safety, but Clarus lost his pants and boots. They spent a wretched night huddled on the beach, hungry, cold, helpless. The next morning there was a rumble of tanks and vehicles, an American officer appeared on the heights above, smiling as he called out to them, "Come on, boys, this is it!" (In a report of battle activity for that day the New York Times noted that "north of Tunis only minor mopping up operations were recorded.")

These new POWs, a mere handful of nearly 250,000 rounded up during those weeks, clambered up the steep dunes to waiting trucks and headed off toward impromptu enclosures. As they bounced along, a black soldier, using unmistakable sign language, informed Wolfgang Clarus that he wanted his wristwatch and the handsome Iron Cross hanging from his neck. When Clarus failed to respond, the black youth reached for his throat, but this young German officer moved first and got a firm grip on the GI's rifle.

The American soldier looked shocked, smiled weakly and withdrew his hand, and Clarus did the same. The confrontation was over. Leutnant Wolfgang Clarus had learned his first basic lesson as a prisoner of war, one which would prove invaluable in months and years ahead: play dumb and move fast.

Bethesda, Maryland—July 28, 1943

He opened his eyes slowly, very slowly, tried to move his head and couldn't. The operation. The American doctor named Travis had told him he would be immobile for at least ten days. A complex grape arbor of metal bars interlaced with wires loomed over his head. Kapitänleutnant Fritz Guggenberger, twenty-eight years of age, with blond curly hair and more than his share of medals and decorations, could not see the guard at the door but knew he was there. If it was morning, then it was Corporal Davis talking with a nurse; if afternoon, Sergeant Reese.

There was no need for guards. He was going nowhere. Both of his ankles were encased in plaster casts, a large padded collar encircled his neck, his wrists still throbbed occasionally, and now that the doctors had tinkered with his fractured spine, he was a modern Gulliver trapped by a dozen weights and pulleys.

Dozing off, he began to dream about some faraway places where he had been not so long ago: an Italian coastal city bright with sunshine, the snowy wastes of East Prussia, and then in the warm clear waters of the South Atlantic . . .

Three Italian dock hands, chattering and laughing, grabbed lines tossed to them as the submarine eased toward its berth. A few moments later Kapitänleutnant Guggenberger was ashore talking excitedly with a group of German naval officers.

Then it was true. The *Ark Royal* went down, after all! Only one hit. An aircraft carrier. What incredible luck! Guggenberger wheeled, raced back to the boat, shouting as he ran. Soon the entire crew was in a state of ecstasy. Beer and wine and laughter flowed as each man recounted his version of what happened. During the afternoon all of the men, their uniforms showing creases where rolled and folded but their faces all smiles, lined the deck as photographers' bulbs popped. Some years later Guggenberger found a picture of them in, of all places, the New York *Times*. Date: February 4, 1942 . . .

General Alfred Jodl, Chief of Operations for the German General Staff, looked first at Guggenberger, then out across the bleak plains of East Prussia as wind and snow chased each other past the frost-covered windows of the officers' mess. "I understand that you are to be decorated by the Führer, Kapitänleutnant Guggenberger. My congratulations." But the conversation was brief indeed. Within a few moments Jodl muttered something about Stalingrad, then he and his aides abruptly excused themselves and left Guggenberger and another U-boat commander alone.

Three hours later, boots polished, their uniforms brushed and pressed, the two young naval officers stood proud and erect before Adolf Hitler. "On behalf of a grateful German people—it is my great privilege—to award you, Kapitänleutnant Friedrich Guggenberger—in recognition of your exploits . . ." Hitler droned on, a halting, brusque delivery sliced into precise segments by long pauses and sprinkled with Austrian inflections which, even though a native of Bavaria, Guggenberger found puzzling. An orderly handed Hitler the coveted Oak Leaves, gleaming as they lay on a bed of satin. Guggenberger bowed his head slightly, felt the wide black, red and white ribbon caress the back of his neck, and then glanced down at his chest: Oak Leaves, an Italian crest with emeralds, Knight's Cross of the Iron Cross. It was impressive, and a little sobering too.

The ceremony over, Hitler motioned the small party toward the other end of the great hall at Wolfsschanze ("Wolf's Lair"), where hot chocolate and cakes were set out before a roaring fire. After a few pleasantries the host posed several quick questions: "These American B-17s, as you gentlemen must know, are causing considerable damage to our cities. Would it be possible, perhaps, for our planes to fly even higher and bomb them before they bomb us?"

Guggenberger's companion, a young man who had once sunk an incredible eleven ships in the Indian Ocean in less than three weeks, replied that air defense really was Reichsmarschall Göring's business; he was merely a submarine officer. Guggenberger nodded in agreement, wondering if German bombs that missed enemy B-17s might not, in a very short time, fall on German soil.

"Would it be possible," Hitler continued, "to develop a bomb which, even if it did not score a direct hit on a destroyer, would roll the vessel over . . . capsize it perhaps?"

Guggenberger knew he must handle this one. "Mein Führer, with all respect, as U-boat men we believe only torpedoes, not bombs, sink ships."

For a few moments Hitler studied the blazing logs and stroked the head of Blondi, his handsome Alsatian bitch, as young Guggenberger, from a distance of less than four feet, quietly studied the head of one of the most controversial figures of the twentieth century. The face radiated good health, his reactions were quick and decisive. Seen in profile, without those dramatic eyes riveted on you, this actually was a rather ordinary-looking man, not of heroic proportions at all. But, strangely, the hairs in his mustache were gargantuan, twice as big as they should be, and his tongue, too, seemed abnormally large, swollen and distended.

Hitler sighed deeply and in a thin, tired voice which shocked the small fireside group asked no one in particular, "My friends, what should a leader do if he thinks he may be losing a great struggle? Can we rely upon our technology to provide us with new weapons? Can our scientists do it?"

Guggenberger joined everyone present in an instant chorus of reassurance: "German research is the best in the entire world . . . Victory is not only possible, it is inevitable . . . We will win, *mein Führer* . . . Do not be distressed by minor setbacks. We . . . all Germany will do its part . . ."

The American plane came in fast, very low. The pilot was indeed a brave man. His bombs fell a short distance from the *U-513*. Guggenberger was elated. It was a narrow escape, a very close call. Drenched with spray, he turned to yell words of encouragement to the forward gun crew, but the men had disappeared. Instead, a shimmering sun greeted his eyes.

He drifted upward as if drawn by some giant magnet on a pleasant journey to nowhere. Time seemed to stand still. Everything was languid, quiet, peaceful. After what seemed an eternity Guggenberger burst through the veil of water to discover he was on the surface of the ocean, being pulled this way and that by idle currents. The stern of the *U-513* floated awkwardly far in the distance, silhouetted against a bank of gray-white clouds, then disappeared from view.

Closer, almost within arm's length, was a small rubber raft. A seaman named Mohr and a dark-haired youth whose name he couldn't recall pulled and rolled him to safety. Only then did the throbbing pain start. Kapitänleutnant Fritz Guggenberger suddenly realized he was seriously hurt, the *U-513* was sinking, most of his crew was dead; the American bombs had not missed their target, after all.

Getting aboard the *Barnegat* was the worst part, an experience he would never forget. Enemy hands lifted his useless limbs from the drifting, bobbing raft, up the side of the ship, over the rail, and then carried him to the dispensary. There, at last, those hands stretched him out and undressed him like some large helpless baby. Although somewhat confused, Guggenberger decided to play for time.

"*Sprechen Sie Deutsch?*" he asked, very pale, but smiling as he looked up at the ship's doctor.

"No."

"Do you speak English?"

"Yes."

"This bed feels good. Thanks for the blankets. That is very practical," Guggenberger said, nodding toward a Syrette of morphine which had just been administered to him. "Is this an aviation ship?"

"Yes."

"English?"

"No."

"American?"

"Yes."

"Was the plane American too?"

"Yes."

"The pilot showed great courage in attacking us."

The doctor clearly thought he was addled. And well he might. His submarine was attacked by American planes, he floated for four hours in a raft clearly marked "United States Navy," was taken aboard a ship flying an American flag by sailors speaking American English, and . . . Well, perhaps they would think he had been knocked in the head too, which wasn't so far from the truth.

The *Barnegat*'s dispensary . . . a hospital bed on an American air base in Brazil . . . another in Miami. White beds, white walls, they all looked alike. And now he was in . . . Guggenberger wasn't sure. As soon as the airplane had taken off from Florida, the Americans became very secretive. They had flown for about five hours, then traveled in a closed ambulance for at least another hour. When the doors swung open he was already inside what appeared to be a huge hospital.

They immediately wheeled him to a basement cell and probably he was still there. Before the operation he had studied every tiny line in a drab retaining wall about five feet from a window covered with heavy iron bars. One section vaguely resembled an outline map of Corsica. His quarters looked and smelled new . . . occasionally jackhammers stuttered in the distance, trucks rumbled by . . . apparently construction still was going on.

Guggenberger thought he was near Washington, D.C. He was quite certain the flight from Miami had been in a north-easterly direction. Several days ago he heard the words "Penta-gon" and "Annapolis" mentioned in the hall outside of his room. One meant U.S. Army, the other U.S. Navy. Both were close by the national capital. So, if . . .

"Hello, Dr. Travis. Good morning—that is, if it's morning. How do I feel? Fine. How soon are you going to unhook these lines and set me free?"

Recife, Brazil—January 8, 1944

Two men, both blond, slim, muscular, about six feet tall, one perhaps twenty-five, the other a youth of twenty, crouched near the fence and absent-mindedly drew designs in the sand with short sticks. Heinrich Palmer, the older of the pair, raised his head to watch a U.S. Navy plane taxi along an air-strip and begin to turn only a short distance away. Because of the intense heat the side doors remained open. Palmer nudged Reinhard Mark as the aircraft roared its engines, gathered up speed, took off and disappeared into the almost cloudless sky over Recife.

Mark, a Fähn zur See, or midshipman, spoke first. "I don't think it will work, but God knows you're right. We must try to escape as soon as possible and at least make the effort. Once these Americans get us in a permanent enclosure our chances of success will be less, much less."

Palmer, an experienced boatswain's mate, went over the plan again, scratching the ground as he talked. They would go it alone, just the two of them. It was safer that way. They would cut through the fence, dash to the plane just as it was turning, jump through the open door, overpower the pilot and fly to either Argentina or Chile. Mark listened thoughtfully, then nodded toward an armed guard a short distance away. "That," whispered Palmer, "is a risk we must take. There's only one man on this side of the compound, no towers. We may never get a better chance. As for the pilot, I've already begun to carve a wooden pistol. It will be finished soon."

Palmer stood up, threw down his stick and strolled casually toward the barracks. Their high-level conference was over. What a clever man, thought Mark as he watched him join a large group of seamen, most of them deck hands from the *Weserland* standing about doing nothing. He had laid mines off the English coast, almost drowned when his ship went down in frozen waters off the Norwegian coast at Narvik, hunted for whalers in the Antarctic, helped capture enemy vessels in the Indian Ocean, and like Mark himself, ended up on a blockade runner in the Far East.

Mark had met Heinrich Palmer for the first time shortly after the great Yokohama harbor *"Katastrophe"* of November 30, 1942. Mark's ship, the famous *Altmark* (renamed the *Uckermark*), as well as the *Thor-Raider 10* and the *Leuthen*, went up in smoke after a fuel-tank explosion. Flames burned for nearly three days. Mark was walking along a pier when the blast shook the entire harbor. Within seconds he took refuge behind a warehouse. He blamed the Russians.

A few days later the survivors were divided up among various blockade runners. Mark was assigned to the *Weserland*, which arrived in port shortly after the explosion. During his first meal on board he expounded his sabotage theory, only to be cut short by Palmer. "Russians, hell, sheer stupidity. Chinese workers cleaning those tanks on the *Leuthen* were at fault. Russians aren't that smart."

It was an inauspicious beginning for friendship. Bootsmann Palmer seemed so confident, so sure of himself. Only later did Mark realize Palmer wasn't even in Yokohama when the blast erupted. And to his surprise, he also discovered that this petty officer, seemingly so much a part of the *Weserland,* had joined the crew only two weeks before in Batavia.

During the months that the *Weserland* remained in port the two men got to know each other well. They climbed Fujiyama, drank at special bars near the wharves, the few where the Japanese permitted them to congregate, and occa-

sionally visited museums and theaters, also under the watch-
ful eyes of their suspicious hosts. Late in 1943 they set out
for home. By December 12 the *Weserland* was proceeding
very cautiously seven hundred miles south of the Cape of
Good Hope.

Mark and Palmer both were optimistic, unaware that Kapitän Friedrich Krage, the ship's commander, had received
somber words of warning: "Follow a zigzag course near Natal-
Freetown to avoid U.S. planes and ships. It will not be possible, we regret, to provide U-boat escort as hoped."

Shortly after noon on New Year's Day, as they were giving
Ascension Island wide berth, an American plane appeared,
part of an air blockade across the South Atlantic between
Brazil and West Africa. Taking no chances, Krage had
painted a British flag on the roof of the wheelhouse and attached signboards reading "Glenbank" to its sides. Mark and
his aft gun crew, already in khaki shorts, slapped British hel-
mets on their heads and raced to battle stations, waving and
smiling as the American pilot circled and scrutinized the good
ship "Glenbank."

After following the vessel for ten minutes and sending a
radio message to his base, the pilot left. A half-hour later he
returned, to be greeted by a messed-up line of signal flags,
carefully tangled, soiled and hauled down before they could
be read, if that was even possible. Not satisfied with what he
saw, the pilot opened fire. Mark says the bullets cut through
one of the *Weserland*'s funnels; U.S. sources report the
salvo was across the ship's bow, merely a routine warning. In
any case, Mark's gun crew responded in kind, knocking out
one of the plane's engines. Unable to continue the contest,
the wounded aircraft limped off toward home.

The *Weserland* immediately changed course, but the following afternoon a much larger American plane appeared. The
masquerade over, gunners at once opened fire, scoring a number of direct hits. The aircraft veered sharply and crashed into
the sea several miles to port. The *Weserland* investigated but
found nothing. That evening Krage ordered all those aboard—

an exotic mix of regular navy, merchant marine, Italian seamen and assorted civilians—to be prepared to abandon ship if necessary. He was certain the two days of air activity were the prelude to a surface attack the *Weserland* could not possibly cope with.

At 2302 the anticipated assault began as the American destroyer *Somers* lobbed shells toward the helpless vessel. Krage decided it was useless to reply. The crew and passengers immediately went into the lifeboats, and despite some confusion, few lives were lost. As soon as it was light the *Somers* began scouring the Atlantic, picking up survivors as it went. The following day, in the same general area, American planes and ships sank another blockade runner, the *Rio Grande,* and on January 5 yet another, the *Burgenland.* A triple-header. The *Burgenland* tried unsuccessfully to convince its attackers that it actually was the "Floridian," a U.S. merchantman.

The skipper of the *Somers* said the Italians from the *Weserland* were a dirty, unkempt lot. They were barefoot, crowded into rubber rafts; the Germans all wore shoes and put to sea in sturdy lifeboats. The Italians swore they had been treated "like dogs." On board the *Somers* the Germans adamantly refused to drink coffee from pots used by the Italians. Now all of the survivors from the three ships were crammed together in hot, dusty pens on the outskirts of Recife.

On January 10, as they were eating noon chow, Palmer reported that the pistol was finished. In the afternoon the two conspirators met at their usual conference spot. The gun was beautiful, truly beautiful—black, shiny, perfect. "How on earth did you do it? Where did you get the paint?" Mark asked, giggling with excitement as he carefully turned it in his hands.

Palmer started to answer but paused when he saw three American officers about to enter the compound. A few moments later they were told to pack whatever gear they had; they were moving on. Palmer carefully wrapped the pistol

in a sweater, but decided that was stupid; they certainly
would be searched at their new quarters, perhaps even as they
left now as well. Instead he stuffed the weapon under a
mattress, grabbed his sea bag, and walked out into the searing
sunshine.

As they marched through the gates Mark quipped quietly,
"You see, all of your work for nothing. We didn't have to cut
the fence to get out, after all."

"Don't worry, smart ass," replied the boatswain's mate with
a confident grin. "There will be more fences to cut. And, you,
Herr Fähn zur See Reinhard Mark, *you* will have a chance
to help too!"

Papago Park, Arizona—January 12, 1944

Captain Cecil Parshall, Papago Park's provost marshal, looked
down from the guard tower and out over the camp. Only
one compound had any POWs in it, a group of thirty Germans
who had arrived a few days before from Louisiana. Parshall,
a World War I veteran and a seasoned campaigner, was a
brusque, toe-the-line type, always neatly dressed, shoes
shined, a razor-sharp press in his trousers. In the months that
followed, he sometimes would be the only American officer at
Papago Park who really exhibited any military bearing at all.
Part German, American and Texan, he had begun his Army
career with Pershing in Mexico in 1916, was gassed in France
two years later, and shot by a German prisoner he stopped to
chat with. As a result of these adventures he collected a
Silver Star and two Purple Hearts.

During the next two decades Parshall was in and out of the
service from time to time. While on a ninety-day furlough
south of the border, he became a general in the Mexican army
and participated in a highly profitable bank robbery
($350,000). Upon his return north, he was promptly court-

martialed. The judge who gave Parshall a suspended sentence allegedly encouraged him to re-enlist. He did so the following day.

In the 1930s this man was an undercover agent in the Canal Zone, and using a forged Mexican passport, fought with the Loyalists in Spain. For a few years, out of uniform again, Parshall was a police detective in Wichita, Kansas, where he became something of a matinee idol as the leading man with a local little theater group.

This veteran of one, two, three, perhaps four wars had been in the Phoenix area for nearly two months, hard at work creating secure compounds for these German navy men and hundreds of their comrades who soon would join them. But Parshall was far from happy with the results. The terrain of the northeastern corner of Papago Park, the area the U.S. government had chosen for the camp, was much too rough. It was impossible to put guard towers precisely where they should be according to Army regulations. And more important, it was utterly impossible to see at least one section of Compound 1 from where he stood. That area, the eastern border of the camp, was adjacent to the Arizona Crosscut Canal. It would have to be watched very closely at all times from other towers and by patrols outside of the double wire fence that enclosed the POW stockade.

Parshall slowly circled the small platform. The brown waters of the canal flowed sluggishly a few hundred yards away. To the south lay the Papago Buttes, two huge globules of red rock. The skyline of Phoenix was barely visible six or seven miles away along the western horizon, glistening in the morning sun. Picturesque Camelback Mountain with its distinctive humps dominated the view to the north.

Once more his eyes came back to the canal and Compound 1. If only the land were flat like the camp down at Florence, where for nearly fourteen months he had guarded several thousand Italians with virtually no difficulty. Papago Park, Parshall feared, was going to be quite different. Years of experience told him there was going to be trouble. These Germans were a keen, aggressive lot, completely unlike their Italian comrades.

The guard company and the new camp commander, Colonel A. H. Means, also made Parshall uneasy. They seemed somewhat unsure of themselves. More GIs and officers would arrive shortly and perhaps the situation would improve; but, thought Parshall as he started down the ladder to the ground, for every American at Papago Park there soon would be ten Germans.

In microcosm, the experiences of Kozur, Mirbach, Clarus, Guggenberger and their comrades, even those of Captain Parshall to a degree, mirror the problems of Hitler's thousand-year Reich as its war machine began to cough and sputter. The Führer's introspective query in the isolated splendor of Wolfsschanze ("What should a leader do if he thinks he may be losing a great struggle?") reveals the problems Germany faced by the opening weeks of 1943.

Kozur's *U-162* was caught hunting prey along the rim of the Caribbean. Although this was an important route from Detroit and Gary to the Middle East, it certainly was less vital than the North Atlantic run to Britain. However, after the summer of 1942, thanks to a better-organized Allied war effort—escorted convoys, coastal blackouts, more patrol planes—fewer and fewer U-boats were able to operate there.

The wonderful, carefree spring of that year—halcyon weeks German submariners called "the American shooting season" as they sank at will along the East Coast—was over. June of 1942 had been their peak month: 145 vessels torpedoed in vital shipping lanes to beleagured Britain, an average of almost five a day. With the aid of carefully laid mines, German undersea craft even bottled up the Chesapeake Bay for several weeks.

Submarine crews considered the Mediterranean, setting for the demise of the U-595, especially hazardous. They had to run the Gibraltar gauntlet, sharp-eyed pilots could spot submarines at greater depths than in the Atlantic, and every watch nervously scanned the heavens for land-based aircraft.

Guggenberger's U-513 was part of a "sub blitz" of Brazilian waters, and the manner in which he and his friends were waging war caused considerable concern, yet most of these offensive maneuvers were born of frustration. To counter rising Allied strength they had to take chances which a year before would have been considered foolhardy. For the first time, sporting heavier fire power and improved technical equipment, their craft cruised close to South American ports, and instead of diving, often remained on the surface and squared off with attacking airmen, shot for shot.

Wolfgang Clarus, the coast artillery officer who became a prisoner of war during the final days of fighting which saw Rommel and Montgomery chase each other back and forth across the sands of Libya, was, like the crews of Wattenberg, Quaet-Faslem and Guggenberger, a casualty of mounting enemy strength. As for Mark and Palmer, the reckless dash their blockade runner had made north through Atlantic waters betrays the truly desperate state of the German home front by the end of 1943.

Although all of these men had much in common—being young Germans associated with the navy, regular or reserve, the merchant marine, coast artillery, and so on, who ended up as prisoners of war in the United States of America—their first days on enemy soil could differ greatly. Some were sent to Fort Hunt, an interrogation center located in Alexandria, Virginia, just across the Potomac from the nation's capital. Others were not. And this distinction could cause considerable difficulty for a prisoner who spent time there, for no German was quite sure how much any of his comrades had told those who questioned them. For one young seaman, Werner Dreschler, these tensions proved fatal.

Fort Hunt had its origins in the realization of the United States Navy that the first enemy to be captured undoubtedly would be German merchant seamen and U-boat crews. In mid-1941 the Office of Naval Intelligence (ONI) sent a thirty-five-year-old reservist, Lieutenant Harry T. Gheradi, to London to study British interrogation methods. Gheradi returned from England much impressed with what he had seen, especially the luxurious quarters in lovely old mansions where selected prisoners, those thought to possess vital information, were treated like visiting potentates in the belief that the contrast with stark combat conditions might loosen their tongues.

Meanwhile, a joint Army-Navy committee agreed that the U.S. Army would be responsible for the final custody of all POWs; the Navy would deliver enemy personnel to military authorities as soon as the men reached port. Then, on December 18, 1941, as a staggered nation assessed the devastation at Pearl Harbor, the Secretary of the Navy approved the creation of special interrogation centers; three weeks later his Army counterpart concurred. They decided that joint facilities should be set up, one near Washington, D.C., the other in California. At these installations, to be operated by the Army, the Navy would be able to grill naval POWs independently; however, once either branch of the service finished questioning a man, the other could interrogate him if it wished to do so.

Gheradi and his ONI pals immediately began searching for imposing estates appropriate to their special needs—something isolated, yet possessing sufficient stateliness to impress any visitor from the Third Reich. Their first choice was Swannanoa, a marble mansion on the crest of the Blue Ridge Mountains near Charlottesville, Virginia. Erected in 1912 by a Richmond philanthropist named James Dooley at a cost of $1 million, this Italianate structure had been sold for $350,000 in 1926. Two years later Calvin Coolidge spent Thanksgiving weekend there. "Cal" briefly even considered the estate as a retreat for his successors.

For a short time Swannanoa was the center of an ill-fated country-club scheme and now, stark and vacant, could be purchased for a mere $175,000. According to an inspection report of January 19, 1942, "The entire impression regarding the Mansion is one of grandeur comparable to the world's show places and movie settings." Several officers were especially pleased with a stained-glass-window portrait of Mrs. Dooley, a "Tiffiney" [sic] masterpiece.

Within a month, however, the price of purchase, renovation, fences, barracks and guard posts rose to nearly half a million, and the joint Army-Navy committee backed off. No one dared ask Congress for $500,000 with which to buy a marble palace. The group then looked at other palatial homes north of the Potomac in Maryland. The Navy, it appears, wanted as grand a structure as possible. The Army was less interested in splendor, and eventually, perhaps by design, word of this search reached the highest levels of the Pentagon. With a quick snort, General George C. Marshall ended this farce: "Tell them to go get an empty hotel. There are plenty of them."

In May 1942 the Army's intelligence arm (G-2) and ONI agreed to set up shop on both coasts: at Fort Hunt, seventeen miles from Washington close to Mount Vernon, and at Byron Hot Springs, an isolated spot near Tracy, California, fifty-four miles from San Francisco. The nucleus of the Western installation was, as Marshall had suggested, a hotel. It was owned by Mrs. Mae Reed, an elderly lady whose husband once ran a health resort there. This Contra Costa County site was, according to one Army officer, not only isolated, it was desolate.

Fort Hunt, developed in the late 1890s as a coastal fortification and named for a Union general who served as commandant of the Old Soldiers' Home in the nation's capital, had an undistinguished, even drab history. In 1923 it was abandoned as a fort, but five years later became a subpost of a nearby military installation. In the early 1930s Negro Reserve

Officer Training Corps (ROTC) units, "Bonus Marchers" in need of hospitalization, and in time, young men enrolled in the Civilian Conservation Corps (CCC) were housed at Hunt. In June 1939 the King and Queen of England, accompanied by the President and Mrs. Roosevelt, visited the site, said to be a model of CCC and New Deal efficiency and planning.

Fort Hunt was on National Park Service land, but the Army and Navy promised to return it to the Interior Department soon after hostilities ceased. Within a short time the depleted CCC unit moved to nearby Fort Belvoir, and federal authorities appropriated $221,000 for new construction at Hunt.

Architectural plans used by workers were labeled "Officers' School," although those men must have wondered why officers needed a maze of electrical wires, eight-foot fences, "conference" rooms and rows of cells, and pondered what wag gave streets names such as Nathan Hale Drive and Pinkerton Road. In the East, temporary "holding stations" for POWs were developed at Fort George G. Meade, Maryland, and Pine Grove Furnace, Pennsylvania, and in the West, at Camp Stoneman at Pittsburg, California, and Angel Island in San Francisco Bay.

By August 1942 Fort Hunt was ready to receive "guests," as they were euphemistically called, and early in 1943 Byron Hot Springs also began operation. Both could hold forty or fifty men, depending upon how many were quartered to a room. Byron was intended for Japanese prisoners, but so few were captured during the early years of World War II that it soon was host to Germans and Italians instead, sort of an overflow facility or "guesthouse" for Hunt.

Strictly speaking, intelligence activity of this nature contravenes or at least "bends" a dozen articles of the Geneva Convention of 1929 relating to the treatment of prisoners of war. As soon as possible after capture a prisoner's name was to be reported to an intermediary power (during World War II this was Switzerland) and an address given to which his family could write. His captors were required to provide a canteen, infirmary and all other basic facilities furnished their own troops. POWs were to have an opportunity for daily exercise, at least two hours in the open air, and within a week of arrival at a camp, be permitted to write home. Throughout World War II U.S. officials stoutly maintained that Fort Hunt, Byron Hot Springs and temporary interrogation centers developed in North Africa, Europe and the Southwest Pacific were not *true* camps. Prisoners were merely being "processed," hence such international regulations did not apply.

Except for the mental anguish of captivity, long hours of boredom, uncertainty as to what was happening or would happen next, life at Fort Hunt and Byron Hot Springs actually was relatively pleasant. Food was good, question sessions often featured relaxed, informal conversation and copious quantities of beer and whiskey, and cigarettes and reading materials (especially newspapers) were readily available. Interestingly, the New York *Times* and the *Christian Science Monitor* were favorites, since the Germans thought both reported battle news and communiqués with a minimum of distortion.

Yet Major General Allen W. Gullion, Provost Marshal General at the outset of the war and the man in charge of all POWs, was far from happy because Army Intelligence (G-2) really ran Fort Hunt and sometimes acted in a high-handed manner. When Swiss authorities complained that men lodged there were not allowed outdoor exercise each day, Gullion declared he had no jurisdiction over the *inside* of that facility and forwarded those protests to the U.S. Army's Deputy Chief of Staff.

Interrogation procedures developed slowly and were subject to constant change and experimentation. The first German seamen to be interned by the United States were from the *Odenwald,* a blockade runner seized by the U.S.S. *Omaha* near Brazil in November 1941 because it ostensibly was masquerading as an American merchantman, the *Willimoto-Philadelphia,* but perhaps of greater importance, its cargo included 4,000 tons of crude rubber.

A blistering radiogram from the Chief of Naval Operations

on January 5, 1942, to the captain of the *Omaha* indicates exchange of souvenirs and visiting cards between crewmen and officers of the two vessels, no segregation of those interned, and little effort made to obtain papers, photos and other materials of "extremely great value." A Georgia ensign even signed a card he gave to an *Odenwald* officer: "A good American friend." The Chief of Naval Operations conceded that hostilities did not then exist, but now that war had been declared, the men of the *Omaha* were ordered to surrender Nazi party buttons, flags and anything else they had received. Of course, Germany and the United States had been shooting at each other on the high seas for several months, but only after December 11 did a state of war exist. Early that morning (Washington time) both Berlin and Rome informed U.S. officials that they were joining Japan in its fight with America, and before the day ended, Congress reciprocated with formal declarations against Hitler and Mussolini.

Five months later, on May 19, 1942, the Vice Chief of Naval Operations instructed all ships and stations concerning the capture and detainment of POWs. Enemy officers, noncoms and enlisted men were to be placed under armed guards and separated into three groups. There was to be no fraternization with U.S. personnel; only interpreters were to talk to prisoners. Each man was to be "minutely searched." "EVERYTHING" was to be taken from him except necessary clothing. His effects were to be bundled and marked, and a receipt given if demanded. (A fine opportunity, it was noted, to obtain name, rank, serial number.) After segregation and search, and only then, POWs could be given warm clothing, medical attention, cigarettes and food. "*Our first interest* is in obtaining all information of value to *us* and any humanitarian considerations must be subordinated to this interest."

There was to be no formal interrogation at sea unless a seriously wounded man who might die wished to give information. When a ship bearing prisoners reached port, enemy seamen and their possessions were to be handed over to local naval district representatives who, in turn, would deliver them

to the U.S. Army. "NO SOUVENIRS OF ANY KIND WHAT-
SOEVER ARE TO BE RETAINED." The Vice Chief said he
appreciated that "an understandable desire" for such existed
and assured all captains that ONI would endeavor to return "articles of no value" to crewmen involved in the capture
of enemy sailors.

On April 14, 1942, the U.S.S. *Roper* sank the *U-85* off
Cape Hatteras. There were no survivors, but intelligence experts were able to gain considerable information from twenty-
nine bodies, debris and diaries found at the site. The first live
submariners to be captured by U.S. forces were from the
U-352, sunk off the North Carolina coast on May 9, 1942. Interrogators were especially interested in finding out what
damage British commandos had wreaked on the German
U-boat base at St. Nazaire in Brittany a few weeks before,
since they suspected that these men had been there. They
learned little except that the crew liked to drink at La
Belle in Gotenhafen (as they called the Polish port of Gdynia
near Danzig), and that the men were distressed because a
bottle of champagne now cost six marks or more at the
Maritza Bar in St. Nazaire's beachfront community of La Baule.
This antisubmarine war and interrogation were, of course, a
joint American-British effort. Survivors usually were interned
in the nearest nation, and to facilitate intelligence gathering,
Lieutenant Ralph W. B. Izard of the Royal Navy worked with
Gheradi and others throughout 1942.

Since neither Fort Hunt or Byron Hot Springs were yet
ready for "guests," the men of the *U-352* were questioned at
their point of entry (Charleston, S.C.) and shipped to temporary enclosures at Fort Bragg, but by the latter part of 1942,
members of several U-boat crews were in residence at "P.O.
Box 1142," code name for Hunt. Byron Hot Springs was "P.O.
Box 651."

Fort Hunt's first visitor was Horst Degen, age twenty-nine,
captain of the *U-701*, caught off Cape Hatteras on July 7,
1942. Lodged briefly in Norfolk Naval Hospital, Degen later
claimed he was drugged, questioned rudely and forcefully by

two officers and a civilian, and accused of espionage. Subsequent investigation indicated there was some substance to these charges. Without informing ONI, the Fifth Naval District commandant had permitted a Duke University psychiatrist to "interview" Degen, although Norfolk authorities denied that any "rough stuff" occurred.

At Hunt this U-boat captain talked quite freely. He told how he operated with Wattenberg's U-162 for several weeks in the autumn of 1941 and said he understood that the Fregattenkapitän soon would get a shore post as a flotilla commander. The record for diving, with four men scrambling to safety from the bridge, was, Degen thought, twenty-eight seconds. Yes, he told his inquisitors, each submarine skipper reported directly to Admiral Dönitz after returning to Lorient from a patrol, and the admiral questioned them sharply, very sharply indeed. What happened here? Why were you cruising there? What was your speed? Yes, they did listen to British radio while at sea. American, too. The jazz was very good. The men enjoyed it. Listening was no sin; telling what you heard was.

Crewmen of the U-701 had more prosaic comments. Like all German prisoners who later came to America, they detested commerical white bread and asked for sturdy black loaves instead. "It is nothing but air. Look, you take two hands and you can squeeze it into nothing, hardly a single slice in it. This is not bread, this is cake, and it is bad for our teeth, very bad."

In September 1942 several men from the U-94 appeared at Hunt. This submarine, sunk off Cuba on August 27, was commanded by Otto Ites, a daring, nerveless young man of twenty-four, much admired by his crew. These survivors were joined a few weeks later by a select delegation from Wattenberg's U-162. Walter Kozur and his comrades had traveled by plane from Trinidad to Miami, where scores of guards escorted them to lofty quarters in a Miami Beach hotel. At the request of a U.S. sergeant, Berndt von Walther stood by as translator while roll was called. "Decker, Dietrich, Hartmann,

Hiller, Kremer, Schmidt, Weber . . . Hell," barked the sergeant with a grin, "they all got American names!" Twenty-four
hours later these POWs climbed aboard a train bound for
Washington, a trip which precipitated an interservice flap.

Within days ONI dispatched a stern memo to G-2. These
nineteen Germans, the Navy complained, were accompanied
by nineteen MPs, both groups in khaki uniforms, the only difference being that the prisoners wore tennis shoes. They read
U.S. magazines en route and traveled from the Washington
train station to temporary quarters at Fort George Meade in
open buses. In the future, POWs must not wear U.S. uniforms
unless conspicuously marked, and those destined for special
interrogation should not be given reading materials or have an
opportunity to survey the countryside.

The Army retorted that the Navy itself was at fault. Its officers approved the magazines in question and provided clothing given to the prisoners. Also, train windows *were* closed at
all times. After a brief sojourn at Meade, *U-162*'s officers proceeded to Hunt in large, windowless buses, the enlisted men
remaining at that Maryland base for several more weeks. Despite such precautions most prisoners of war sent to Fort
Hunt figured out that they were close to the nation's capital.
On occasion they were told they were at Fort Belvoir, although one seaman knew exactly where he was: he had once
lived in Washington and he and various girl friends used to
park along the banks of the Potomac.

"Guests" lodged at Fort Hunt lived under strict rules. They
had to obey all orders promptly and were forbidden to speak
to other prisoners in the latrine, through open windows or to
resident staff without permission of U.S. officers; gambling,
betting and writing on or smearing of windows were *verboten,*
as were (naturally enough) attempts to escape. Enlisted
men were responsible for the cleanliness of their rooms, but
efforts to force officers to police their quarters failed miserably.
The last rule, number 16, stated that transgressions of any order would mean loss of "buying privileges," a rather hollow
threat, since these were virtually nonexistent.

Interrogators never used their true names when facing POWs and usually wore uniforms outranking their adversaries, although sometimes they posed as professors or businessmen familiar with the German scene. Those playing at superspy at first kept survivors of various U-boat crews apart but soon concluded that 90 percent of information of any value came not from interrogation sessions *per se,* but from "judicious mixing" of POWs and recording their informal conversations. This departure from established regulations precipitated yet another angry memo skirmish between Army and Navy officers.

As a result of this change, Berndt von Walther found himself quartered with Rolf-Kurt Gebeschus, a young Oberfähnrich (senior midshipman) and second officer on the *U-94.* Wattenberg was placed with Ites in the cell above. Exhausted by air, train and bus travel, Walther merely nodded as he entered the room, shook hands without speaking, dropped his bag on a table, flung himself on the unoccupied bed and stared at the acoustic ceiling, which, according to an Army report, "served admirably for microphone concealment and, at the same time, proved to be adequate as a sound conductor." A hot afternoon sun cast sharp shadows throughout the neat but stuffy cubicle.

Walther suddenly motioned to Gebeschus. Just as he thought. There were three distinct depressions up there. Sloughing off his shoes, he quietly moved a chair to the center of the room. Climbing up on it he pried cautiously with a nail file and there they were. Not wasting an instant, he lunged toward the window and yelled as loud as he could, *"Mikrophon! Mikrophon!"*

Walther smiled and tried to look confident. Five days had elapsed. This was his third session with Captain Blind. (He was sure that must be a phony name.) Each had opened with a stern reprimand for shouting out of the window. However, his interrogator could not quite bring himself to say the word "microphone."

The first meeting was a barrage of questions, one on top of another. Sometimes the American did not even seem to expect a reply as he raced along: What is your home port? Could the *U-162* lay mines? How? When did you leave port? Speed? Course? Were you escorted by any craft? How far? When were you due to return? Have you refueled at sea? How? What sort of radio equipment did you have? How did you avoid enemy aircraft? What was the general nature of air attacks? Did the *U-162* usually operate alone? How were you captured? Why?

Walther answered some questions in a hit-or-miss fashion, ignored others. The second time they met the captain changed his technique completely. There were long silences and very few questions—in fact, little conversation. What Walther found alarming was how much, *how very much*, these Yanks already knew, not just about his submarine but about German naval secrets in general. On the desk between them lay a series of *original* code books. The captain did not mention them until the end of their talk, then only in an offhand manner. The Allied spy network within the Third Reich must be extremely effective. This was shocking, truly shocking.

Their interrogation methods might be crude and unprofessional, but they certainly had tons of information at their fingertips. The only vital fact about U-boats the Americans didn't seem to know was how deep they could dive when necessary. It actually was two hundred meters or more. The captain seemed to be convinced it was much less. Good.

Also, he didn't seem to know about Code Irland. Blind had not mentioned it so far, and since he had discussed codes for several minutes on Tuesday, perhaps he was ignorant of this simple means by which U-boat officers could relay vital information home from prison. (Walther would subsequently discover that Code Irland worked well indeed, at least until late in 1944, perhaps even longer.) Based on the international Morse code—dots and dashes—the only requirements were that each officer keep how it worked in his head, not write it down, and that his wife, parents or some family member be on the lookout for "strange" letters and immediately send them on to the navy.

The recipient merely took the first letter of each word and interpreted it as a dot or a dash. A through I equaled a dot, J to R a dash (both in words being spelled out by means of the Morse code), and S to Z represented a space between those letters. A sentence such as "Any *m*an *w*ho *m*akes *t*hat *m*achine *o*perate *q*uickly *w*ould *r*eap *r*iches" could convey the word "atom" (in Morse code $A = \bullet -$, $T = -$, $O = ---$, $M = --$). It was tricky, sometimes cumbersome and time-consuming to compose a letter smooth enough to get past a suspicious American censor. But one thing any POW had plenty of was time.

Once more Captain Blind was pressing for specific technical details. "We now know . . ." He usually began with these words, indicating new information acquired since their last confrontation. "We now know from talking with some of your crew—"

Damn. Those idiots would be swayed by some of the information these Americans spewed out.

"—that SBT charges are carried to the U-boats in small bags. How many at a time? What do they weigh?"

Walther could see those small silver containers clearly enough in his mind and started to form an answer when a buzzer rang, interrupting his thoughts. Blind pressed a button on his desk. The door opened and in came Gebeschus accompanied by two guards, one of them carrying a large oval tray on which there were cigarettes, ice, glasses, a fifth of liquor, and several bottles of beer.

"We thought," the captain said, "that we might have a little celebration. Leutnant von Walther has been with us nearly a week now, Oberfähnrich Gebeschus a bit longer, right? We've gotten to know each other quite well. That will be all for now, Corporal. Beer? Not our best perhaps, but good. Or do you prefer bourbon . . . ice and branch water. Branch water, that's what folks in the South call it. Just plain ole tap stuff, though. Help yourselves, gentlemen. There's plenty of everything. We can get more if we need it. Drink up."

Walther giggled and stumbled as he struggled with his pants, finally falling heavily on the bed in a heap. "Well, Rolf, how do you like American beer?"

"It tastes like tar."

"You can't say that. It tastes very good to me."

"Berndt, if you compare this to German beer, you can readily see that the beer in Germany is much more substantial than this. This is only an imitation of beer. It gives me a terrific headache. I've got a headache now. I can't really say much for it. I rate it as inferior German beer or lager."

"Yes."

"Yes. It is only an inferior imitation."

"Rolf . . . I should say that with my befuddled head?"

"They're probably taking a recording of what we're saying right now. Very probably, since those three pear-shaped chromium-plated microphones with paper cones are up there. What we ought to do is take off the covering tomorrow, take the things apart and lay the parts on the bench. When the captain comes in, we'll say, 'What's this? We found it up here in the ceiling.' We'll do the same with the two in the partition wall and in back of the corner. We'll say, 'What's this? It fell out of the wall. There's something hanging there.'"

"We'll do it."

"I sure would like to see the expression on their faces, wouldn't you?"

"They'll say, 'Why did you take the ceiling apart?'"

"We'll say, 'There's nothing in the camp regulations against it.' Then they'll have to insert a new paragraph into the regulations: 'It is forbidden to tamper with the microphones.'"

"Ha ha ha."

"Yes, lad, they certainly won't get anything out of me. No matter how many sessions we have or how much beer they give us."

"Nor out of me either."

"Not even if they kill me."

"They won't get anything out of us. Once you're dead, you're dead. That is a lot simpler than being alive. If we had drowned, we would have the matter of dying weeks and weeks behind us. Most humans don't understand that. It must be rather pleasant, don't you think?"

"I don't know just how it is. Perhaps one is happy at the prospect of going to heaven."

"One just doesn't know . . ."

When Walther woke up it was not yet nine o'clock, but the room was stifling. His eyes throbbed, or something somewhere behind them did. His throat was bone-dry. He clearly did not feel well. Two breakfast trays, both untouched, were on the table. He hadn't heard anyone come in. Turning his head slightly, he stared unconcerned as Gebeschus vomited into a small bowl, neatly, slowly, methodically.

"Hey, my friend, there's a puddle on the floor."

"So? It'll take a long time," Rolf gasped, "before I fill up this room."

Walther smiled, lay back. A wave of nausea and heat passed over him. He rolled over with a sigh, pulled a pan on the floor closer to the bed and stuck two fingers down his throat. He gagged slightly, then louder, much louder, but nothing happened. "Oh, God," he said, laughing, "triple *heil, mein Führer*, triple *heil*, triple goddamn *heil!*"

Questions, questions, questions. Too much beer. Too much time to do too much nothing. Truth, half-truths, half-lies, complete lies. The line between fact and fiction, truth and falsehood, was becoming blurred. Captain Blind, Herr Kapitän Blind. How much did he really know? Hot days, hot nights, hot mornings, hot afternoons. And he had been there for only a few days. When would it all end?

Gebeschus was drinking cold coffee and eating cold eggs. How could he do it? The room seemed even warmer than before, if that was possible. Two large cockroaches skittered across the floor and out under the door into the hallway. Just think, those miserable little creatures were free and he was trapped. He must have dozed for an hour or so.

Gebeschus tossed part of a newspaper on Walther's sweaty, hair-matted chest. He opened it slowly, then pointed at a small picture. "There, Gebeschus, *that's* what I'd like to have in here with me instead of you."

Gebeschus glanced at the open page. "But she's a Negress!"

"That doesn't make any difference to me. Say, could that aunt of yours in Jersey City arrange for us to meet some girls?"

"So, Berndt, you want to start spoiling American women. After all the damage you claim you've done in France, Germany and the rest of Europe! No, no, no."

Inspired by this unexpected exchange and already feeling somewhat better, Walther winked at Gebeschus and motioned him closer so both of them would be directly under a microphone. What followed was no-holds-barred sex talk, each of them recounting vivid bedroom exploits interspersed with raucous, ribald jokes and much laughter. For nearly an hour they discussed thirty-nine positions of intercourse in great detail, each trying to outdo the other in vulgarity. The whole episode ended with a spirited debate over how many orgasms a healthy male might have in a lifetime. They concluded the number was 3,400.

Suddenly a guard was banging on the door and it was time for lunch. Time had passed so quickly. Amusing the Americans plugged into your cell was fun. Also, it certainly helped one forget a bad hangover. In the days that followed, this high-spirited pair produced news broadcasts, plays, songs, more obscene stories, and additional recollections of performances past. On one occasion they staged an imaginary interrogation session with Walther playing the role of Captain Blind.

"We treat prisoners of war very good, right? We give them a large room—and a phone."

"A phone? How's that?"

"Why, those microphones! You people in Germany have no

microphones. No, no, no. In America we give you real service. And we lock the door tight so nobody will come in and kill you. We give you shelter for your safety. Yes, yes. Do you perhaps know France?"

"Yes. I have been there often."

"I don't believe it, but I have heard from German officers and prisoners that French girls make very good love."

"Sir, I cannot tell you about that. It is a military secret."

"The Americans make all the best motorcars, the best in the world, the best airplanes, the best killing . . ."

"Yes, yes, yes. That is certainly true."

"Oh, yes, the most planes, but perhaps not the best."

"I would agree."

"But I do think we have the best battleships. You can see them on the ground at Pearl Harbor."

Whether these uninhibited young officers chattered on to wile away the long hours or to keep U.S. personnel busy, they clearly achieved both goals. Army clerks, shrewdly egged on by a potpourri of occasional wit, sarcasm, crude sex and rare bits of seemingly important information, were dutifully transcribing, translating and collating one outrageous statement after another for weeks after these two POWs had left Fort Hunt. To add to their problems, these youths carried on in four languages: German, French, English and Spanish. French, they noted on one occasion, was the language of music and love, English merely "chewing-gum talk."

As long as they were in residence, Berndt von Walther und Croneck and Rolf-Kurt Gebeschus made certain they were the stars of Fort Hunt. Gebeschus departed after forty-two days, on October 13, 1942. Fregattenkapitän Wattenberg and Walther left three days later.

During November, Walter Kozur and Johann Kremer were "guests" for seventeen and seven days, respectively, having remained at Fort George Meade while their officers were at Hunt. Questioned on the ninth, Kozur praised the "new" government (Hitler) for creating jobs, stopping street crime and ending civil disorder. "I've been in prison for eight weeks. When," he asked, "will I be permitted to write home?" Kremer, once a lathe operator at the Humboldt Works in Cologne, was extremely uncooperative, even belligerent. Interrogators once called him "a stupid little boy," but Kremer continued to remain silent or sometimes argue rapidly in a loud voice, almost shouting. On another occasion they threatened him but to no avail: "We'll send you to a bad camp if you won't talk . . . How do we know you are not a saboteur? You know what happens to them . . . they get the electric chair!"

Early in December the card-playing officers of the U-595 arrived after a dreary, cold bus ride from Newport News, where the *Brazil* had docked. Quaet-Faslem, Mirbach, Kaiser and Horstig were driven directly to Hunt. Emmerich von Mirbach recalls they already were inside a building before the doors of the vehicle opened. Eighteen of their crewmen also came north to Hunt, the rest going to Fort Bragg in North Carolina.

Controversy marred this trip at the outset when these POWs objected to handcuffs, citing specific provisions of the Geneva Convention. Eventually their captors loosened the manacles somewhat but refused to take them off. Whenever handcuffs were reported to the Swiss, the War Department expressed regret and said it would not happen again. The Pentagon issued specific orders against handcuffs from time to time, but GIs continued to use them freely throughout the war. The Army's defense, at least as far as Quaet-Faslem's crew was concerned, was that these were very dangerous men, some guards had poor eyesight and wore glasses, and these GIs really had no choice but to handcuff POWs when they were in transit from place to place.

Mirbach and Quaet-Faslem were assigned to the same cell. Like those who preceded them, they were suspicious, cautious, careful. What was going on? Why such secrecy? Without speaking, they examined the acoustic ceiling, the walls, beds and chairs. On the window sill Mirbach found a nail left by a carpenter. Taking off his shoe, he quickly pounded it into a depression that caught Quaet-Faslem's eyes. Within two minutes guards appeared and hustled them off to the latrine, where they had to remain for half an hour. When they returned, the nail was gone and the hole plugged with fresh putty. So there were microphones, after all!

Kaiser, a slender, red-haired youth born in Westphalia in 1920, son of a school principal, said little when he faced his interrogators. Mirbach, a native of the Baltic region, two years older than Kaiser, blond, of medium height, rather stocky, proved to be affable, chatty, gregarious. The Americans at Hunt thought him "only moderately security-conscious." Their opinion of Quaet-Faslem was quite different, for in this gentleman they more than met their match.

Jürgen Quaet-Faslem, descendant of a Flemish road builder who went to Moscow with Napoleon and settled near Hanover during the disastrous retreat of 1812, was a slender man with thinning blond hair, an intense, dedicated individual but hardly devoid of wit and humor. Born in Göttingen in 1913, he first entered the navy in the late 1920s, but then served as a Luftwaffe pilot before turning to submarines. His wife and two children lived on a substantial estate near Weimar. As those who knew him on both sides of the Atlantic soon realized, this U-boat commander possessed a trigger-sharp mind and usually was in the thick of things.

A typical Quaet-Faslem interrogation session featured innumerable "Yes, sir's" and many questions by the man who was supposed to be answering, not asking them. On December 16 an American officer began by apologizing for losing his temper the day before; however, he chose not to preserve transcripts of that outburst for posterity. Then, in an inept overture, this interrogator described how mad Adolf Hitler really was. "He's fanatic, utterly fanatic, given to tantrums and fits of depression, howling like a dog and weeping for hours. At times he even falls on the floor and starts chewing the carpet!"

Drawing quietly on a cigarette, Quaet-Faslem appeared un-

moved by this startling revelation, finally uttering the brief-
est of comments: "Really? I didn't know that."

A few moments later the American turned to Poland. "But
why should Poland be part of Germany?"

"Poland belonged to Germany before the Middle Ages, since
the year 1200."

"And before that?"

"Before that, it was Poland."

"There, you see . . ."

"But you did the same thing to the Indians in this country. You kicked them out, killed them and took the country
away from them. You can't deny that. It is the same story over
there."

"In between we gave them recognition as Indians and declared them to be real Americans."

"Yes, now after there are not any of them left!"

The American, sensing he was not doing too well, tried to
shift away from politics, but Quaet-Faslem was on the offensive and would have none of it. "Last time you asked me
about the Communists in Germany. Of course they caused
trouble, they were a threat to civil and domestic order, just as
Huey Long and Father Coughlin were in this country. And
look what happened to Long!"

"But the government did not shoot Long. A crazy man
did that."

"Do you know he was not hired by men in Washington?
Why are you and your country so interested in the internal
politics of Germany? Does not the United States stand for the
independence of nations above all else? Was that not
Woodrow Wilson's program at Versailles? Why this pressing
concern for Germans and Germany?"

"Because, as you well know, Captain, a madman like Hitler
threatens the very existence of our nation."

"How? How in hell does he threaten the United States of
America? This is a powerful country, much bigger than
Germany. It has many more people. Has Hitler landed armies
on your soil? Has he bombed your cities? Has he—"

"That will be all for today, Captain Quaet-Faslem. I must talk with other men now. Perhaps we can get together again in a day or so. Guard, please show this gentleman to his room."

On December 21, 1942, after twenty days at Fort Hunt, Quaet-Faslem, Mirbach, Kaiser and Horstig packed their belongings and left for Crossville, Tennessee, home of most of these U-boat officers throughout 1943. Enlisted men from their crews, however, were sent to a variety of internment centers throughout the country.

After these groups of enemy seamen departed, the Navy sifted, digested and finally published what it had learned in small classified booklets called "Post Mortems," each one analyzing the life and death of a U-boat. These were distributed to various wartime offices and departments, as well as to Allies concerned with naval warfare. The U.S. Navy insisted, however, that purely technical knowledge was not to be shared with the U.S. Army. This caused another rhubarb, but captains and admirals were adamant and on this point they finally prevailed.

It is no surprise that Jürgen Quaet-Faslem received an unfavorable rating in the "Post Mortem" of his U-595. He was pictured as bitter, taciturn, barely civil, gloomy, hate shining in his eyes. "A typical Nazi." His crew, the Americans reported, thought him shiftless, inefficient, cowardly, ineffective as an officer.

Raw interrogation files now at the National Archives in Washington, D.C., tell a quite different story. Quaet-Faslem certainly was assertive, abrasive, capable of posing more questions than he answered, but in the process he was a spirited conversationalist with a keen sense of humor. His characterization of Goebbels as "the stud goat of Babelsberg," a sly reference to the propaganda chief's well-known nocturnal carousings with movie folk at his showplace on the Wannsee outside Berlin, precipitated an outburst of universal laughter during one interrogation session. It appears that those who chatted with Quaet-Faslem, as they reviewed transcripts of their conversations, realized they'd been "had."

Fort Hunt had not heard the last of Kapitänleutnant Jürgen Quaet-Faslem. Within a month, at his insistence, the Swiss government was pressing the U.S. Department of State on the subject of daily exercise at Fort Hunt. (Quaet-Faslem of course did not know the name of the camp but could identify it as being close to Fort Belvoir.) State, in turn, demanded an explanation from the War Department. Army brass hedged. The weather was bad in December when Quaet-Faslem was a "guest." Also, the Geneva Convention regulation requiring two hours in the open air each day really applied, they said, only to men in disciplinary confinement.

Eventually Quaet-Faslem won, the United States Army lost. In May 1943 the Secretary of War informed the Assistant Secretary of State that it was regrettable, but at the time of the captain's visit to Fort Hunt, "military expediency did not permit free access to air and exercise." He hastened to add that adequate measures were being implemented to rectify this unfortunate deficiency.

During 1942, 175 prisoners of war from eight U-boats and one blockade runner passed through Fort Hunt, their visits tending to become shorter and shorter as their interrogators became more proficient. On January 4, 1943, the first army POW appeared and before that year was over, several more submarine commanders who would end up at Papago Park also faced intelligence experts stationed there.

The most important of these were Hans Werner Kraus (*U-199*), August Maus (*U-185*) and Fritz Guggenberger (*U-513*), still recovering from his injuries after a month in Bethesda Naval Hospital and walking with the aid of a cane. For their wartime exploits all of these men had received the Knight's Cross of the Iron Cross; Guggenberger had received Oak Leaves as well.

The *U-199*, the first 1,200-ton craft from which survivors were taken, was sunk by aircraft near Brazil on July 31, 1943. Shortly after seven o'clock in the morning an American bomber flying out of Rio de Janerio began the attack.

During a series of strafing runs, the boat and plane exchanged fire. For a time the *U-199* seemed erratic, out of control; then, after an unsuccessful dive attempt, regained trim, and although its stern was awash, resumed course, only to encounter two Brazilian aircraft and still more gunfire. As Kraus was trying desperately to change course, with only his bow breaking the surface, the American plane closed in for the kill.

This entire engagement, from the first radar contact to sinking, lasted sixty-two minutes, and during that time the *U-199* traveled eight miles. The *Barnegat,* the same ship that had rescued Guggenberger and six members of his crew twelve days earlier, picked up a dozen men out of a crew of sixty-one and took them to Recife.

These individuals included Kraus, once executive officer on Günther Prien's famed *U-47,* the craft with the snorting-bull emblem which did the impossible by sneaking into Scapa Flow in October 1939 and sinking the *Royal Oak,* and Leutnant zur See Helmut Drescher, his dark-haired second watch officer. Drescher, twenty-one years old, was from Berlin; Kraus, a popular, efficient skipper, twenty-eight years of age, was married and had two children. His wife and family resided in Erfurt.

Kraus and Drescher were at Fort Hunt from August 18 to September 6. The Americans thought Kraus pleasant, well-mannered, an attractive personality. Drescher, in their opinion, was a convinced Nazi. Both responded in some measure to questions, but interrogators learned little from them.

Guggenberger, who arrived at Hunt on September 25, was put in the same cell as August Maus, an experienced, twenty-eight-year-old native of Döbeln-Grossbauchlitz in Saxony. Like Kraus and Guggenberger, Maus was an aggressive commander and stern disciplinarian who led an intensely loyal crew. Only one youth, a Communist, provided any useful information.

The third and last patrol of Maus's *U-185,* hair-raising drama from beginning to end, encompassed not one but *three* submarine sinkings and enough excitement to last most seamen for an entire war. On June 4, 1943, the undersea raider, its dragon-head insignia glistening in brilliant sunlight, sailed from Bordeaux. Six miles out, serious engine trouble developed. Maus immediately returned to port and discovered, as he suspected, that French workmen had put dirt and steel splinters in the main bearings.

On the ninth the *U-185* set out again and rendezvoused with three other submarines, but three days later British bombers severely damaged one of the craft and Maus decided to shepherd it back toward Bordeaux for a meeting with a destroyer. En route another enemy onslaught finished off the crippled U-boat. Maus rescued eighteen men, all of them later transferred to the destroyer. Once more, for a third time, the *U-185* turned its bow to the southwest, heading for Brazilian waters.

Two months later, after a reasonably successful outing, ten enemy ships sent to the bottom, Maus was homeward bound. On August 11, just south of the equator, he met yet another damaged submarine, the *U-604*, commanded by an unpredictable madcap named Höltring, a man whose two passions in life seem to have been liquor and firearms. (His crew called him "the gunman.") Maus agreed to take half of his men and supplies; the *U-172*, which was also on the scene, would take the rest. Exchange finally completed, Höltring's ship was scuttled and the *U-185* continued on its way.

Shortly after dawn on August 24 two aircraft from the American carrier *Core*, patrolling at a height of seven thousand feet southwest of the Azores, spotted the *U-185* about four miles away. The submarine, its slim form reflecting the rays of a bright early-morning sun, was proceeding at ten or twelve knots, course 330 degrees. The attack was brief, chaotic, and for Maus and his men, disastrous. This is how the action report submitted by the *Core* described what happened.

The planes sought cloud cover and turned to starboard for an approach. Planes emerged from clouds astern of submarine and F 4 F immediately started strafing run. Shortly thereafter T B F followed in 15° angle dive, attacking astern on starboard quarter. Two Mark 47 depth charges were dropped from 250 feet. They straddled the U-boat, one charge exploding underneath the hull near the conning tower, the second on the port bow. Water thrown up by the explosions nearly enveloped the U-boat. Submarine turned 90° to port with dense, black, low-lying smoke trailing aft as the stern of the U-boat began settling. F 4 F made slight turn to left and completed second strafing run. At that time pilot noticed a heavy list to port and some wrecked railing near conning tower. Sub made no further evasive turns nor was any AA fire experienced.

In the midst of this confused melee, *U-604's* seriously injured captain, now a passenger on the *U-185*, decided he could not make it through the hatchway to safety. Drawing his pistol—a constant companion, which he had once used to shoot off his big toe while lying in a drunken stupor in a bunk in Gotenhafen—Höltring committed suicide, but not before killing an ill seaman who begged him to do so. Within three hours an American destroyer picked up three officers and thirty-one sailors, who soon were transferred to the *Core*. Only later, despite the admonitions of Maus, did the Americans learn that some survivors were from the *U-604*, not the *U-185*.

Interrogators at Fort Hunt found both Maus and Guggenberger friendly and intelligent—in fact, too intelligent. They talked easily, drank liquor, smoked cigarettes, but said little of any consequence. An ONI officer noted Guggenberger was "so smooth and intelligent that it is impossible to obtain any trustworthy and useful information from him." On October 4, 1943, after only brief visits at Fort Hunt, these U-boat commanders also were sent on to Crossville.

Most of the German POWs taken to Fort Hunt thought it a rather inept operation, somewhat naïve and bumbling, but none underrated the stunning array of intelligence information the enemy seemed to have at his fingertips. "It was truly incredible," Hans Werner Kraus remarked in awed tones three decades later. "The Americans had plotted my last cruise with pinpoint accuracy. They almost knew where I was going before I got there myself."

Nearly every "guest" soon learned of the microphones, or suspecting they might exist, spoke guardedly and with great caution. In 1943 the Americans renovated and enlarged Hunt, recessing listening devices to make them less obvious. But word of this installation, thanks to Code Irland, soon got back to Germany, and those who had been at Hunt indoctrinated hundreds of other POWs who might, under certain circumstances, be transferred there for questioning.

Gebeschus and Walther were by no means the only individuals making life interesting for corporals, sergeants and officers plugged into their private lives. Men of the U-595 also gave forth with a healthy helping of raw sex from time to time. Others used a more blatant, screw-the-Yanks approach: shrieking, shouting, farting and, (those listening thought) occasionally masturbating as well, each of these activities conducted as close to microphones as possible.

Several thousand enemy prisoners were held at Fort Hunt (1942–1945). They were moved in and out in windowless buses and few Americans seem to have wondered what was going on. For instance, Joseph O. Baylen, a young lieutenant busy with intelligence work at Fort George Meade, saw those strange-looking vehicles fill up, depart, return half full or empty. Thirty years later he was astounded to learn of the existence of Fort Hunt. "So that's where those buses went! No one ever told us and we didn't ask any questions." In 1977 National Park Service staff responsible for Hunt still were unaware of that site's true World War II role.

Although no German prisoners escaped from Fort Hunt, at least one man was shot and killed there. Kapitänleutnant Werner Henke, a member of the same naval class as Guggenberger and holder of Oak Leaves, died in June 1944, ostensibly as he was climbing over high wire fences which surrounded that secret base. Presumably Henke was distraught because of threats that he might be turned over to the Canadians and feared what might happen to him, since his captors claimed that his *U-515* had machine-gunned survivors of a British ship, the *Ceramic*.

Although this intelligence-gathering operation on the banks of the Potomac may have been crude and inept, it can be viewed as a tribute to wartime secrecy, for no one—Baylen, the National Park Service, or thousands living and working in the Washington area—knew what was going on there. Like millions of Germans later maligned for not asking questions of a stern dictatorship, Americans, in the midst of war, reacted in much the same way.

By the end of 1943 a large group of former U-boat officers, individuals possessing considerable intellectual ability and diverse skills, had been screened at Fort Hunt and shipped inland to the hills of Tennessee. At the same time, scores of seamen, also submarine veterans, were gathering in numerous dreary compounds throughout America. Unwittingly, as these Hunt "alumni" talked about their experiences, the United States government was building up a coterie of substantial talent with only one thing on its mind: escape.

Chapter 3

CROSSVILLE, STRINGTOWN AND THE ENCHILADA EXPRESS

Once a man left Fort Hunt and arrived at a more permanent billet, he was no longer special; instead, he was just another captured German with a number, part of a faceless mass presenting the United States Army with unprecedented headaches. Every major conflict in American history—the Revolution, Civil War, World War I—produced its share of stockades, compounds, fences and guards. Yet only in the 1860s was the POW population on American soil substantial, and never before had those on the home front faced the unnerving prospect of having thousands, even hundreds of thousands of a foreign enemy in their midst.

At the end of 1942 there were only 1,881 prisoners of war in the United States; twelve months later, 172,879; and on V-E Day, 425,871. This peak total comprised 371,683 Germans, 50,273 Italians, 3,915 Japanese, all of them former servicemen, not civilian internees. In April 1942 the British government asked if the United States would be willing to take a large number of POWs off its hands. Somewhat reluctantly—since according to the Geneva rules each captor is legally responsible for the prisoners it takes—the United States agreed to accept 150,000 men and began to build camps for them in the South and Southwest. Six months later a State Department functionary signed an agreement increasing this total to 175,000; however, because of the upturn in Allied fortunes, none of those British-held enemy ever came to America.

In theory at least, in North Africa and on the continent of Europe the two partners were supposed to divide captives 50–50, with the British permitted to shift an excess of 175,000 to Uncle Sam. By March 1945 this ratio was woefully out of balance. General Eisenhower wanted to evacuate 400,000 more Germans stateside, but the Pentagon said no. Still facing what might be a long war in the Pacific and not certain when fighting would end in Europe, Army generals said there simply was not enough manpower in America to handle such a massive migration. (A month later, as V-E Day approached, Eisenhower and his troops held 1 million prisoners; the British, 100,000.)

Yet two great waves of German POWs did cross the Atlantic. The first bumper crop came in the spring of 1943 with the fall of North Africa, the second during the first weeks of the Normandy landings. In each instance, pragmatic considerations dictated what happened. It was impossible to house and feed thousands of enemy soldiers in war-ravaged Algeria, Tunisia and Libya, and equally impractical to pen them up close to the front lines in France. Each day empty vessels were returning to America for supplies, so they brought along the crew of the U-595, Wolfgang Clarus, Wilhelm Günther and thousands of their countrymen as passengers, most of them entering the United States through ports such as Hampton Roads in Virginia and Boston.

In the beginning U.S. officials, fearing escape and sabotage, locked these men up deep within the interior of the nation, but seeing no evidence of rampant unrest, they concluded they could use this reservoir of labor to relieve an acute shortage of wartime workers. Soon prisoners were living in old CCC barracks, National Guard camps, surplus air bases, empty schoolhouses and various other facilities throughout the land. By the end of the war there were 155 large base installations and 511 smaller branch camps in forty-five states.

Spreading prisoners of war so widely in countless towns and cities often had unexpected results. Americans, their minds filled with horrifying tales of brutal Nazis and reinforced by memories of the cruel Hun of two decades earlier, found the enemy anything but threatening face to face. Natalie Lancaster, a vivacious teen-ager living in West Virginia, was stunned when a truck loaded with good-looking, carefree youths stopped briefly in Wardensville. "Why, they looked just like boys I was dating. No difference at all. What was this war all about? How could you possibly hate people who looked like that?"

By terms of the Geneva Convention and subsequent agreement among the major adversaries involved in the European theater, all men held by the United States received ten cents a day in canteen credits, funds to help them buy at least a few necessities and perhaps cigarettes. NCOs and officers got somewhat more, depending on rank. (Americans in German hands sometimes were granted similar compensation.) No prisoner was supposed to possess currency of his captors, although this regulation did not deter any POW, regardless of where he was held and by whom, from accumulating bills and coins whenever he could.

An enlisted man thought to be relatively trustworthy who volunteered for work could earn another eighty cents a day in credit to be used to purchase an occasional beer, tobacco, candy and toilet articles, or to be held in reserve until peace came. This might mean working on an Army base in mess halls, laundries, motor pools and general construction. Men also were hired out to private contractors to cut pulpwood, pick fruit and vegetables, and work in various factories; however, prisoners could not participate in any activity related directly to the war effort. Also, they had to maintain their own quarters without additional compensation.

Numerous wartime boards and agencies carefully regulated contract work. Those wishing to use POWs first had to make sure no Americans were available for jobs they had in mind, and if none could be found, pay the prevailing wage to the U.S. government for each prisoner hired. Federal authorities then granted the man eighty cents credit for his day's work, the rest of his salary going for general upkeep of the camps themselves. Needless to point out, organized labor never was very happy with these arrangements, and one reason for a hasty POW exodus early in 1946 was to make certain that returning heroes and defeated warriors did not compete for jobs.

Any labor other than normal housekeeping chores within compounds technically was "volunteer" duty, but American camp commanders made it quite clear that their policy was "no work, no eat," and Swiss representatives who visited U.S. compounds backed them up. (Article 27 of the Geneva Convention says belligerents "may utilize the labor of able prisoners of war.") NCOs and officers did not face such pressures, although NCOs were required to perform supervisory tasks; nothing prevented any POW, regardless of rank, from "volunteering" his services at any time.

POWs leaving their compounds to work were supposed to wear clothing plainly marked "PW," a rule which, like many others, often was ignored. According to the Army's *Reference Manual on Prisoner of War Administration*, the ratio of guards to Germans on contract work should be 1:8, on other details 1:10. If prisoners were Italians, regardless of employment, the ratio was only 1:15. For the most part, POWs were eager to join work crews, since such activity made boring hours pass more quickly, gave them a chance to meet American civilians (including women) and also presented the best opportunities for escape.

A base camp usually was part of a large military installation. It had a guard company, composed of American GIs and their officers, which was responsible for maintenance of the prisoner-of-war stockade. The stockade was subdivided into compounds, and each base camp often had smaller branch facilities under its command, groups of two or three hundred men detailed closer to specific jobs such as picking cotton, cutting wood or working in a cannery. Efforts were made to weed out dedicated Nazis, SS and Gestapo stalwarts, and confirmed troublemakers, most of them being consigned to Camp Alva in Oklahoma. In time, enemy officers, NCOs and enlisted men, members of various services (army, navy, merchant marine, air force) and POWs of different nationalities were kept in separate compounds and sometimes in separate camps as well. At the outset, however, segregation of this sort was less evident.

Each camp and sometimes each compound had a spokesman (as a rule the highest-ranking individual) who conferred regularly with the American commandant, but the power of these representatives was extremely limited. POWs, like good soldiers everywhere, had to do as they were told. If they were dissatisfied, their only legal recourse was a written complaint through proper channels to the Swiss government. This did not prevent heated words, disagreements and strikes, and in retaliation U.S. commanders often locked up ring leaders, transferred them to other camps or put entire compounds on bread and water for a few days.

The Army's *Reference Manual*, essentially a how-to-do-it booklet for young officers in charge of POWs, came down hard on fraternization between prisoners and guards, conceding that the caliber of U.S. personnel assigned to POW camps was "often far from ideal." GIs were to be told to "shoot to kill" any escapee who did not halt after *three* orders to do so. This manual discussed how guards should handle escapes detected in progress and stockade riots. The word "tunnel" was not mentioned.

This placard was to be displayed prominently near each guard post:

TREATMENT

Firm and Fair.
Be a Strict Disciplinarian.
No Coddling.
Insist on Obedience.

REMEMBER YOUR POSITION

You are a Soldier—He is a Soldier.
You issue Orders—He Obeys.
You are the Captor—He is the Captive.

WORK

Require an Honest Day's Labor.
No Loafing.

Thirty years later, men who were at Crossville, Tennessee, in 1942–1943 remember it as a relatively happy place. This installation, a 194-acre site with barracks built to house 1,000 officers in four areas and 416 enlisted men in two additional compounds, was completed in December 1942, an outgrowth of a conscious desire on the part of local citizens to have POWs in their midst. Unlike many of their fellow countrymen, they pressured various state and national politicians to set up a "concentration camp" at Crossville to aid that region's economy. (Americans never could make up their minds just what to call a place housing a group of war prisoners: concentration/detention/internment camps, detainment centers, service command units, each somehow seemed out of place in a democracy and thus made them a bit uncomfortable.)

To keep up their spirits the men living in the Tennessee highlands applied constant pressure on their guardians. Mirbach remembers gleefully one occasion when a group of officers, by design, shipped off conflicting complaints to the Swiss. Some said their quarters were too hot, others found them much too cold. Food was too highly seasoned, too bland, contained too much starch, too little starch, was monotonous, skimpy, and so on. The "great mail strike" was another ploy.

Unhappy with an American decision of some sort, all officers and enlisted men refused to write home. Within a few weeks Swiss representatives began making inquiries and soon the Americans were asking the Germans to *please* write to their families.

The "typhus tempest" was more serious. Trouble developed when the Americans decided to vaccinate all POWs against typhus. Some Germans, having read in the New York *Times* of proposals to sterilize all of their countrymen, feared vaccination for typhus might be the first step in such a program and adamantly refused to cooperate. Eventually German doctors agreed to administer the vaccine and the impasse was resolved.

A U.S. officer who became experienced in the ways of these prisoners of war says they were much like boys in prep school, always experimenting to see just how far they could go, what they might be able to get away with. If counter-pressure was applied, then they usually retreated and re-grouped, only to push forward with some new scheme a few days later.

A fragmentary diary kept by a German officer held at Crossville in December 1942 describes some of these maneuverings during the Christmas season of that year. On the fifteenth the Germans and their guards became embroiled in a hot dispute: must POWs salute Old Glory as it was being lowered at the close of the day? When the Americans forced prisoners to attend retreat, they gave out with a resounding triple "*Sieg heil!*" A few days later, without permission, a group of officers knocked down several interior walls in one of their barracks to create a spacious lounge room, only to be told to put things back the way they had been.

"The situation is growing more tense," the officer wrote on the twenty-third. Eight associates of Wattenberg were trans-ferred to another part of the camp, precipitating a mild at-tack of "passive resistance." Both Christmas and New Year's, however, turned out to be more pleasant than expected. The Americans permitted officers and enlisted men to celebrate together, recanted and allowed the larger day room to remain, after all, and presented some of the prisoners with new clothing. For unexplained reasons, buttons had been removed from everything except shirts. On January 1 Wattenberg uttered a few appropriate words as the prisoners burned their Christmas trees in the traditional manner.

By March 1943 Crossville, under the command of Colonel Harry E. Dudley, apparently a very able man, had 266 Germans, 219 of them enlisted men, and 197 Italians, 122 of them enlisted men. Each officer compound contained thirteen twenty-man barracks. Six months later there were 726 Germans, all of the Italians having departed for Monticello, Arkansas. This total was comprised of 428 general officers, 15 medical officers, 17 NCOs and 266 enlisted men.

Chief spokesman for this group was Colonel Hans-Georg von Werder, member of an armistice commission captured near Casablanca in the fall of 1942. However, the colonel was an easygoing individual and allowed Wattenberg to become, in effect, camp leader. Dudley soon had his fill of this tall, lanky gentleman from Lübeck who seemed determined to cause as much trouble as possible. Not only did Wattenberg view any cooperation with his captors as tantamount to treason, he reportedly threatened a fellow officer who dared to disagree with him, warning him he would be hanged if he did not shape up. On July 5 and again on August 2, Crossville's intelligence officer requested that the Fregattenkapitän be transferred elsewhere.

On August 10, G-2 decided that Wattenberg, Helmut Rathke, Otto Behringer and Hermann F. Kottmann were the chief agitators in the camp: "These four are Gestapo agents." (One must, of course, weigh such assertions with care. Any POW causing difficulty usually was classified as a rank Nazi, regardless of his political beliefs, if any.) Six weeks later Dudley recommended that Wattenberg, Rathke, Kottmann and seven other men be shipped to Alva, Oklahoma. On October 10 he insisted that Wattenberg be sent to that camp, but to no avail. This man, he reported, was a very disturbing influence and believed to be head of a secret police organization within the camp, "Gelapo" (Geheime Lagerpolizei).

Although much of what Dudley said may have been true, it is quite possible that Wattenberg was given credit for the deeds of others. He seems to have been, by nature, sort of a lightning-rod personality. The Americans expected him to cause trouble, he looked as if he were capable of causing trouble, so they concluded, when trouble erupted, that Wattenberg had caused it. This "lightning rod" stance, consciously or unconsciously diverting suspicion from others, would prove extremely useful to Quaet-Faslem, Guggenberger, Maus and Kraus when they got to Papago Park.

Crossville now had 660 officers and 724 enlisted men. A Swiss representative who toured the camp late in 1943 noted that an officers' mess was "filthy." Wattenberg, Colonel Dudley replied, would not cooperate in maintaining the building properly. Wattenberg and Werder countered that men taking correspondence courses needed more books and additional mailing privileges. They also asked that forty-two NCOs be transferred to the officers' compounds, woolen shirts be provided for all POWs (it turned out that fewer than a dozen actually needed them), and that white shirts recently confiscated from naval officers be returned at once.

Another provocation for complaint was a public highway that split the camp into two parts, officers on one side, enlisted men on the other. That road, with civilians driving along it each day, intrigued Wattenberg. At a meeting of officers he suggested that placards be made up to appeal to these Americans: "Help Us"; "Come and Get us." There must be, he added, plenty of good Americans with German blood eager to heed such pleas.

Mirbach, some twenty years younger than Wattenberg and only a mere Oberleutnant, could not believe his ears. When no one else spoke up he finally exploded: "That is the silliest proposal I ever heard! In these Tennessee hills! Ridiculous. The guards would quickly dispose of the signs anyway." Wattenberg never forgot this outburst, but Mirbach obviously expressed the general sentiments of the group. No placards appeared and the subject was not discussed again.

Men like Wattenberg and tensions among enemy officers were by no means the most serious problems at Crossville. Over and over, when prisoners got an opportunity to speak directly and confidentially to American intelligence, they stressed the danger posed by stalwart, die-hard NCOs. This is how one observer analyzed the Crossville scene in May 1943:

> You see, those old German non-commissioned officers are 100 percent Nazis and they surround themselves with the same kind of soldiers. It is just too bad for those boys who are trying to get away from Nazi rule. They will never give those boys a chance. I sincerely believe those German non-coms should be separated from the men and put in a special camp. The men should have a chance to express their opinions without fear or without being called traitors. With those non-coms around, the boys never have a chance to say things the American way. There are not more than 30 percent Nazis in that camp. The rest are all free-thinking men and would gain a lot if they weren't suppressed by 100 percent Nazi non-coms.
>
> I believe they would kill a man if they caught him talking against the Nazis.

For many POWs at Crossville the most important event of 1943 was the escape of Captain Wolfgang Hermann Hellfritsch, who, according to camp authorities, disappeared sometime before five o'clock in the afternoon on October 23. Mirbach says Hellfritsch had left several weeks earlier, carefully hidden in a trash can. The escape was discovered only when someone else tried to sign his monthly pay voucher. Hellfritsch, born in Japan and able to speak fluent English, was found seven months later working as a farm hand near Lexington, Kentucky. It was the departure of Hellfritsch that prompted Colonel Dudley to gather up all white shirts, suspecting they could be used as part of a civilian disguise by potential escapees.

In a letter to the *American Magazine* (May 1944), J.

Edgar Hoover noted that Hellfritsch was back behind barbed wire but gave no details as to how he got there. The previous month the *American* had published Hoover's article on POWs, "Enemies at Large: Here's How Uncle Sam Tracks Down These Dangerous and Desperate Foes When They Escape," which became quite famous. Many Germans are convinced that Hellfritsch was victim of an incredible coincidence. After escaping, they say, he found a wallet complete with draft card, identification papers, social security card, everything. Hellfritsch took on the man's identity, got a job and settled down, only to be arrested months later because his benefactor had failed to pay federal income taxes. Faced with such a serious charge, he quickly admitted his true identity.

There were other escapes from Crossville, one with a tragic conclusion. Three enlisted men, one of them from the *U-162*, got away from a work detail and fled into the Tennessee woods. Several days later the trio came to a mountain cabin and started to get water from a pump. An irascible granny appeared in the doorway, aimed a gun in their direction and told them to "git." Unschooled in the ways of mountain folk, they scoffed and paid no attention. A few moments later she drew a bead and fired, killing one of the seamen almost instantly. When a deputy sheriff informed the old lady that she had killed an escaped German prisoner of war, she was horror-stricken, burst into tears and sobbed that she would never have fired if she had known the men were Germans.

"Well, m'a'm," he asked, puzzled, "what in thunder did you think you were aiming at?"

"Why," she replied, "I thought they wuz Yankees!"

Escape tales and pressures and counterpressures by POWs and guards should not obscure a constructive side of Crossville. Within a brief time, with American aid and encouragement, a real functioning university sprang up, nurtured by correspondence courses. "Before long," Emmerich von Mirbach recalls, "I was studying Spanish every day. We had an Austrian arrested somewhere in the Himalayas who taught math. Others were learning bookkeeping and accounting, and so on. It was wonderful."

Wolfgang Clarus also has high praise for "Crossville University." "It is hard, very hard for young men to be held in 'prisonship.' The trouble we caused there was a joke, just fun to keep our spirits up. If guards reacted, then we backed down. We had no choice. They had guns.

"What helped even more was to study and to learn. We had all kinds of men there, army, navy, merchant marine, air force, men who had been professors, teachers, doctors, businessmen, people from all walks of life. I was there about eight months, and strangely enough, actually enjoyed myself, at least compared to Papago Park. There was so much to do."

"Crossville," Fritz Guggenberger notes with considerable emphasis, "was a prison camp, yes, but it was somewhat European in character, attitude and atmosphere. It was much like my Bavaria with hills, forests, rural spaces. Papago Park possessed a weird, compelling beauty. I liked the vastness of the desert; it reminds one of the sea. But it was an alien land inhabited by alien people, very different from the American East."

Soon after he arrived in the Tennessee hills in the fall of 1943, Guggenberger too was studying. English, not Spanish or mathematics, interested him most. Each day he went for a long walk with Maus, Kraus and Quaet-Faslem. Maus, the most proficient linguist, was teacher: "Now, for one hour we talk nothing but English. Nothing but English, understand?" Already the four captains were planning their escape. Learning to speak like a native was the first step.

One day, as their first barbed-wire Christmas approached, Maus and Guggenberger thumbed through the pages of a Sears, Roebuck catalogue. What to order for the holidays? What did they want for Christmas? "Well," Maus said, ever the optimist, "the Americans owe us one hundred and seventy dollars, so by December, let's see, they will owe us two hundred and twenty."

"But," Guggenberger objected, "as far as we know they have not really credited our accounts with anything yet."

"Oh, they will. Don't you worry. You can trust the Americans."

So they ordered a smoked turkey, rings, watches, a set of dishes, and several items perhaps of use to a potential escapee. "We got practically nothing," Guggenberger says, laughing as he remembers Christmas in Crossville. The dishes, however, did arrive. They had a colorful floral pattern, and according to Maus, were used nearly every day for two years, the two friends eventually dividing up the set when they returned to Germany in 1946.

In retrospect a disturbance which had erupted in February 1943 acquired considerable significance, much more than "Crossville U.," escape attempts and holiday shopping with the aid of Sears, Roebuck. (Two years later U.S. sources would call it a "mutiny.") When German officers resisted an American plan to search their personal belongings, guards equipped with riot gear were summoned, but eventually a compromise evolved: Werder, Wattenberg and one or two other officers would remain in the barracks to see that nothing was stolen, all other men going to an adjoining compound during the search. A guard, overzealous and irritated, hit an officer named Graf in the stomach as he was leaving—why is not entirely clear. Graf died of internal injuries a few days later.

As a result of this incident the U.S. Navy became convinced that it could exert more control over naval POWs if enemy sailors and their officers were isolated in separate compounds, and preferably in separate camps. Never completely happy with Army supervision of naval POWs and fearful that military censors were inadvertently letting nautical secrets get back to Germany, admirals and captains in Washington launched a successful campaign to set up special enclosures throughout the nation. So, by the end of 1943, plans were afoot to consolidate 6,286 German navy men in four camps:

Blanding (Florida), McCain (Mississippi), Beale (California) and Papago Park (Arizona). Blanding already had an anti-Nazi compound, but reclassification of the other camps earmarked for seamen thought to be pro-Nazi meant considerable shifting around of 7,000 individuals, about 2 percent of 304,000 Germans then on U.S. soil.

On January 27, 1944, Clarus, Gebeschus, Drescher, Günther, Mirbach, Walther, Guggenberger, Maus, Kraus, Quaet-Faslem, Wattenberg, seventy-nine additional officer comrades and twenty-seven enlisted men left Crossville for Papago Park. One memento they left behind in Tennessee was a large cheesecake photo of a near-naked American starlet, under her well-endowed charms these words: *"Ein guter Soldat muss verzichten lernen"* (A good soldier must learn to do without).

Meanwhile in Stringtown, Oklahoma, 508 enlisted men, all German navy except four merchant marine seamen, were packing to join them. Not much is known about the facility in Stringtown. During the first months of the war this one-time penitentiary was an alien detention center, housing an exotic assortment of Samoans who held German citizenship (most of whom had never seen Germany) and a group of enemy nationals rounded up in Central America. A Swiss representative who visited there in July 1943 said Stringtown was "a most difficult camp to administer." POWs held there told him one man was bayoneted when he refused to work and complained that they were not allowed to render the "open hand" (Nazi) salute. (Throughout the war, by the way, as long as Adolf Hitler headed a functioning state, technically his government and its customs and practices had to be respected, even in POW compounds in America. Thus small pictures of der Führer, small flags, war decorations and the "open hand" salute were usually permitted.)

Nevertheless, men formerly at Roswell, New Mexico, much preferred Stringtown. The brick structures were clean. The inmates could buy one bottle of beer each day at their canteen, and occasionally they swam in a large lake not far from the camp. Those working on farms in the area were billeted from time to time in unfenced quarters, and Oklahoma farmers, delighted with their assistance, also took them swimming, or on rare occasions, to the movies.

For several hundred relatively contented prisoners of war to be uprooted and dumped in a new stockade amid new surroundings with a new commandant, new guards, new rules, new regulations was a very disruptive experience. Men who had been at Crossville, Stringtown, Meade, Ruston and numerous other camps throughout the South and Southeast had to forge new relationships and create a new internal organization, a new "pecking order." However, Papago Park possessed one very attractive feature: it was only 130 miles from Mexico.

In two world wars Germans held in U.S. compounds have looked south of the border longingly and with good reason. In 1917–1918 Mexicans and gringos had just stopped shooting at one another. During those years only a handful of enemy servicemen (1,346), nearly all of them German sailors, ended up on American soil. Some escaped from time to time, and fragmentary records at the National Archives indicate that a few, perhaps half a dozen, successfully crossed the waters of the Rio Grande and bade the United States of America a fond farewell. This story remains somewhat vague because those who got away rarely sought or got publicity. They were delighted to be free and kept quiet about it. The U.S. Department of Justice was not eager to acknowledge their success and joined in this curtain of silence.

Hidden within this drama of captured German seamen and interned enemy aliens who were more numerous than sailor POWs is one of those intriguing twists that makes history fascinating. On April 9, 1917, a few days after the United States declared war on the Central Powers, registration of all German and Austrian citizens living in America got under way. Disturbed by the dire threat these individuals presented to our way of life, a chunky, bright-eyed Department of Justice employee fresh out of law school began compiling a detailed list of 257,446 German male aliens residing in communities of 5,000 or more. Evidently the *first* of many lists produced by J. Edgar Hoover, it revealed, not surprisingly, that the greatest concentrations of potential saboteurs were to be found in New York State (50,467) and Wisconsin (32,899), with substantial numbers also in Illinois, New Jersey, California, Michigan and Pennsylvania. This tabulation, although of questionable value, was not in vain. It brought young J. Edgar to the attention of the War Department's military intelligence chiefs, and he was on his way to more lists and greater heights, beating the same drum and shouting the same message in the decades to follow.

With the outbreak of World War II, Hoover published numerous articles warning Americans of what POWs might do if they got free. He was especially distressed by the threat of sabotage and by fears that escapees might get across the border into Mexico. That country was an enemy of the Axis, having declared war on May 13, 1942. Yet this was a pragmatic, "official" hostility. The average citizen, stung by generations of high-handed Yankee superciliousness and blatant interference with his nation's affairs, displayed a shoulder-shrug enthusiasm for this new alliance. Any German with funds who got across the border probably could find individuals willing to lend him a helping hand—for a price, of course.

Even if this had not been the case, during World War II south was the only direction a POW could turn for escape, the only route presenting even the slightest hope of return to the Fatherland. Canada was no refuge. There were Germans in still more prison camps north of the border. Once a man was free from barbed wire and guards he had but two choices: get lost in the ethnic patchwork of a large city such as Chicago or New York or go to Mexico and hope to find a friendly ship captain who might take him to Chile or Argentina. From there he might be able to get back to Europe.

About a thousand German POWs escaped from U.S. compounds during World War II. Some achieved momentary freedom by means of intricate and ingenious schemes which Houdini would have applauded, others simply walked away from work details. A POW in Clyde, New York, bet a fellow prisoner a case of beer that he could get out of their compound. When he easily scaled the fence, so did his buddy. Both returned to camp a few hours later and gave themselves up. Several men working in Delaware became free unintentionally. Frantic when their GI driver drove off by mistake and left them stranded, they appeared at a gas station trying through gestures and broken phrases to explain their predicament.

Most escapees were back behind barbed wire within a day or so, usually apprehended by local authorities, *not* by the FBI or the Army, somewhat to the chagrin of both. According to the FBI, none of them committed acts of sabotage and the only harm they did was occasionally stealing a car or clothing to aid in their getaway. Key problems faced by these men were gross misconceptions concerning the true size of the United States and their heavy, telltale accent.

A POW from New Hampshire's Camp Stark enjoyed four months in Manhattan. He was picked up in Central Park, where he was painting pictures and selling them to the public. Fred Kammerdiner, an Austrian who fled from Fort Devens in Massachusetts shortly after V-E Day, took a different (and more pleasant) tack. He teamed up with a woman he met at Devens when she was a civilian employee there. They lived together on Nantucket Island for six months before he was caught.

The most baffling of these wartime escapades was engineered by an American, Dale H. Maple (Harvard '41, magna cum laude, Phi Beta Kappa), now a California insurance man. This attempt to spring a group of German POWs from Colorado's Camp Hale in February 1944 was engagingly recounted by E. J. Kahn, Jr., in a four-part *New Yorker* profile (March–April 1950). Maple, a brilliant student with no German blood in his veins but great admiration for Hitler's regime, gained some notoriety at Cambridge by singing forbidden Nazi songs at Verein Turmwächter meetings. On December 8, 1941 (telephone lines were clogged the day before), he contacted the German embassy staff in Washington and asked permission to accompany the homeward-bound staff back across the Atlantic. Rebuffed, a few weeks later Maple abandoned graduate study at Harvard and enlisted in the United States Army.

In time he ended up in one of three general service companies the Pentagon organized for "poor security risks" during World War II. When his camp in remote South Dakota closed down, Maple and his buddies (who were never issued guns) went to Camp Hale, an installation with 10,000 Americans and 300 German prisoners of war. Through some oversight this general service group was quartered only a short distance from the POW stockade. Inspired by the heady presence of *real* Nazis, three dozen pseudo-Nazis staged a glorious German-style Christmas in December 1943. Early the next month Maple, dressed in Afrika Korps clothing, spent a three-day pass inside the compound, where he convinced several of the Germans that he could get them out of the camp and on their way home. Six weeks later Maple and two POWs, Erhard Schwitchenberg and Heinrich Kirklius, were apprehended by an American border inspector on the Mexican side of the line sixty miles east of El Paso.

The trio claimed they were Jewish refugees looking for work, but ham found in Maple's knapsack (he said his name was "Miller") puzzled those interrogating him. Even more puzzling was the revelation that he was a private first class (U.S. Army) traveling with two escaped prisoners of war. Charged with desertion (not treason, which is a civil crime) and corresponding with and aiding the enemy, Maple quickly was found guilty and sentenced to be hanged. President Roosevelt commuted this decree to life, and in 1946 it was further reduced to ten years. As he got into deeper and deeper water Maple implicated four fellow privates and three WACs. All pleaded guilty and received sentences of four to six months for their part in this strange affair.

Obviously the Mexican connection, the "Enchilada Express," did not work for PFC Maple and his two friends from Camp Hale's stockade or for any other German POWs who climbed aboard, but this did not keep them from trying. At the same time that Dale Maple was walking on Mexican soil, so was Kapitänleutnant Jürgen Quaet-Faslem, former commander of the *U-595*, the scourge of Fort Hunt, and one of the new residents (very briefly) of Service Command Unit # 84 at Papago Park, Arizona.

The officers' club at Papago Park was quiet. Colonel A. H. Means, commandant, slowly nursed a large tumbler of Scotch. February really was a lousy month, rainy, depressing, dreary. To make matters worse, the camp had barely opened when he was greeted by a rash of escapes. This led to a predictable flurry of inquests, phone calls, telegrams, letters and reports.

As one of his staff had commented, the escape of five U-boat captains in a single day might not be a record, but it should stand up for a few months at least. Means knew almost by heart where they had originally been taken prisoner and when. Quaet-Faslem, *U-595*, North Africa, November 1942, the same month as the Allied invasion—and by a tank crew, of all things! Kottmann, *U-203*, Johannsen, *U-569*, both in May 1943 somewhere off Newfoundland with the help of the British and Canadians. Guggenberger, *U-513*, off the coast of Brazil two months later, and Maus, *U-185*, near the Azores in August.

Hermann F. Kottmann, a boyish-looking six-footer and one of the "agitators" Colonel Dudley thought should be shipped from Crossville to Alva, was born in Hanover in 1915. In his twenty-eight years, he had led a rather exciting life. Entering the navy in 1936, Kottmann trained at the academy at Mürwik and became a gunnery officer on the *Graf Spee*. Interned in Argentina along with Wattenberg and others, he escaped to Chile and made his way home across the Pacific on a Japanese vessel. This young man also served in the SS for a year or so, selecting that elite corps because, as he freely admitted, "They wore black uniforms and they looked better and neater."

After joining the U-boat service, he was on Guggenberger's submarine briefly, then became executive officer of the *U-203*. He eventually assumed command during that ship's last three patrols. On April 3, 1943, the 500-ton craft sailed out of Lorient on its eleventh and final cruise. Five days later Kottmann sighted the *Queen Elizabeth*, but seas were rough, visibility poor. On April 23 he fired two torpedoes at a destroyer or corvette. No damage; both missed. Forty-eight hours later, as the *U-203* was maneuvering to attack an aircraft carrier, H.M.S. *Biter*, it was hit by bombs dropped from a British plane.

H.M.S. *Pathfinder* picked up six officers and thirty-three seamen and took them to St. John's, Newfoundland. Early in May this group arrived in Boston. Fourteen of the crew went to Byron Hot Springs, and within ten days Hermann Kottmann was at Fort Hunt, where he proved to be singularly uncooperative. Some months later the "Post Mortem" on his submarine had this to say concerning its skipper:

> Kottmann was one of the most unpleasant U-boat captains so far encountered. He was arrogant, over-bearing, and demanding. It was impossible to conduct a civil conversation with him, and he took advantage of every opportunity to be insulting to his questioners. He is a fanatic Nazi and best described as a military robot. Any cultural or humanitarian impulse which may exist in his make-up has been completely sublimated by the political and military indoctrination to which he has been subjected. When it was suggested to him that Germany might lose the war, he replied that if such

should come to pass, Germany would immediately set about plotting for the day of revenge.

Kottmann's fanaticism and repulsive personality affected the other officers who tried their best to imitate him. They were all extremely security conscious and refused to talk on even the most inconsequential matters.

Again, as with Jürgen Quaet-Faslem, raw interview files at the National Archives do not support such a stern picture, although Kottmann, displaying a strange mixture of social decorum and arrogance, often simply refused to tell interrogators what they wanted to know. On May 14 he began a session by saying "No, thank you" when offered a cigarette. His standard reply to most questions was "I have my orders and if I do not obey them I will be a poor soldier." Within minutes he and his adversaries tangled when Kottmann refused to discuss Hanover.

—I am only talking about your home town. I know Hanover well.

—You asked about air raid damage.

—Well, certainly, everybody is interested after all the bombings. If I want to know some military information about the damage, I only have to get the photographs which are already made.

—I can't tell you.

—Did you have a camera with you when you last visited there?

—I can't tell you that.

—What can we talk about?

—I have already mentioned to you that I can't say anything and that's all.

—Will you see your friend Wattenberg if you go to camp?

—Yes, if it is possible.

—Do you know him well?

—Yes, I have seen him often.

—You were with him on the *Graf Spee.*

—We won't talk about that.

Kottmann then proceeded to brag about German culture: One German was as good as ten Americans . . . U.S. morale

was fine now, but wait until battle casualties commenced . . .
America can produce, true . . . "but I will never believe
that this mixture of races and peoples can fight together.
There is no unity and no common will to fight. Everything
in America is done only in order to achieve a more comfortable, soft life. America has no reason to fight the Third
Reich, no reason at all. Germans who live here are nothing
but *Schweine*."

"*Schweine! Schweine!*" Enraged, one of his questioners flew
into an angry tirade. If Kottmann could not conduct himself
as a human being, then *he* would be treated like an animal,
especially as long as he called people "*Schweine*" and treated
them like animals. "Guard! Guard! Return this man to his
cell until he can learn some manners."

Two days later two other Americans met with the Kapitänleutnant and discussed the word "*Schweine*" in much more
subdued tones. Kottmann explained he meant by that term
citizens of Germany living in America who fought against
the Fatherland, a view which these men agreed had some
rational basis, at least from where he sat at the other side of
the table. Strangely, although asserting civil conversation with
Hermann Kottmann was utterly impossible, his interrogators
managed to log in some fifteen typed pages of just that.

Hans Ferdinand Johannsen, another February escapee who
caused much trouble for Colonel Means, was quite a different
individual. Fort Hunt personnel thought him "extremely po-
lite and correct"; yet, in the end, they learned no more from
him than they did from Kottmann. He refused to talk politics,
emphasizing that he feared any reply would be twisted. Most
of the time he answered simply "*ja*" and "*nein*."

Johannsen, thirty-two years of age, went to sea when only
fourteen and eventually worked for the Hamburg-Amerika
Line, often visiting New York City. His wife, Hedi, and their
two children lived in his native Hamburg. Johannsen's *U-569*
seems to have been a jinxed craft. Sister ship of the *U-570*
captured intact by the British on August 28, 1941, it sank only
three vessels on nine patrols. Americans thought the crew

"unusually listless . . . morale extremely low . . . they were thoroughly disinterested in the war in general and in the U-boat arm in particular." Most of them answered questions readily, chattering endlessly about the bars of La Pallice near La Rochelle on the French coast, other waterfront hangouts and official brothels set up for their pleasure.

Johannsen, an Oberleutnant in the reserve, took command of the *U-569* in December 1942, adopting a "fatherly" attitude which most members of the forty-six-man crew appreciated. On the fourth cruise out of La Pallice he painted a new slogan on the conning tower: *"Los Geht's"* (Let's Go). But nothing seemed to help. Early in May 1943 the 500-ton vessel, known as *"Der alte Hase"* (the old hare) because of its age, left on what was to be its final outing even if disaster had not struck. Flotilla chiefs planned to withdraw the submarine from active service when it returned.

Late on the afternoon of May 22 two planes from the American aircraft carrier *Bogue* spotted the *U-569* within twenty-five miles of a large North Atlantic convoy. Swooping in from behind cloud cover, they released several bombs, which may have caused some damage. The undersea raider disappeared, only to come up five miles away about forty minutes later. Four more bombs were dropped from a height of six hundred feet. "The submarine," according to an official U.S. report, "submerged at once, resurfaced on a steep angle, bow high out of the water, sank again, stern first, finally came up again and surrendered at 1852."

As machine-gun fire raked the deck the crew tied first a small white flag to the periscope, then a much larger one. By the time the Canadian warship *St. Laurent* arrived on the scene, the *U-569* had been scuttled. The *St. Laurent* picked up twenty-five survivors and took them to St. John's, Newfoundland. A seriously wounded seaman remained there; the rest flew on to Fort Hunt, arriving at that interrogation center on May 31. A month later a United States Navy bulletin hailed this action as the first major engagement in the North Atlantic between carrier planes and enemy submarines beyond the reach of land-based aircraft.

The plan to escape to Mexico began to take shape soon after the officers from Crossville arrived at Papago Park. It was inspired by the confusion evident there and a small newspaper story that caught Quaet-Faslem's attention. A British officer held in Germany had exchanged places with an enlisted POW who looked much like him, joined a work detail, eluded his guards, made his way to Sweden and from there back to England. Less than a week after the U-boat officers got to Arizona, Quaet-Faslem told Guggenberger they should try to emulate that man's exploits. Since Colonel Means surprisingly had agreed to Wattenberg's request that officers be permitted to visit with their crews from time to time, such a scheme seemed feasible.

Within a few days five officers selected substitutes from the mass of enlisted men and began to collect money, papers, maps, anything that might help them get south of the border. Maus and Guggenberger, the first team, had some North African invasion currency issued by the U.S. government which looked surprisingly like stateside money. Between them, Quaet-Faslem, Kottmann and Johannsen, the second group, had enough American bills and coins to get them well on their way to Mexico.

Maus decided to be a South African seaman; Guggenberger (who still did not speak English very well), a Greek sailor. If questioned, they would say that their ship had been sunk in the Atlantic and they were on their way to San Diego to join a new crew. The other three men decided to be sailors from a Dutch ship berthed several hundred miles to the south in Mexico. If accosted, they would pretend to be traveling around the countryside for a few days. By Monday, February 7, they had food, clothing, various papers, maps carefully lifted from a jeep at a nearby airfield by a helpful POW ... and their plans were pretty much in order.

The following day the ten men exchanged roles. Five enlisted men entered Compound 5 for various routine duties at seven-thirty in the morning and melted into the general setting, and an hour later Maus, Guggenberger, Quaet-Faslem, Kottmann and Johannsen, dressed in dungarees, departed for the enlisted men's area, leaving behind them five very happy youngsters. During the remainder of the week the five officers joined work details and perfected plans for their escape.

Shortly after noon on Saturday, February 12, two POWs whom the Americans employed as drivers hid the officers on a truck loaded with plywood. A few moments later the vehicle was out of the compound and then somehow managed to get out of the camp as well. What the drivers told the guards, if they encountered any, is not known. Johannsen, for one, recalls that they were enclosed in a very small space under the wood; and all he knows is that after half an hour of bouncing around the two men left them on a lonely stretch of road several miles north of Papago Park and headed back toward camp.

The five U-boat captains lay in a ditch until after sunset, when they set out for Mexico. Maus and Guggenberger headed south to either Tempe or Mesa, where they caught an evening train bound for Tucson. They arrived there at about eleven o'clock, in a station filled with servicemen, their girls, war workers and itinerant Mexican laborers, much of this mass slightly inebriated. The two men studied the scene carefully, trying to decide what to do next. Guggenberger, not fully recovered from his injuries, leaned heavily on a cane and watched as Maus made his way through the mob to an information window.

He quickly returned, angry and flushed. There was no train to Nogales until Monday morning and there were no buses for another four hours. Here they were, stranded less than seventy miles from Mexican soil.

The crowded railway depot seemed to present at least a form of temporary security. Military police circled the waiting room from time to time, waking sleeping servicemen, checking papers and identification cards, but left them alone. A well-meaning middle-aged man tried to strike up a conversation with Guggenberger, who immediately fled to the men's room, unable to think of a suitable Greek phrase or anything that might sound like Greek. Maus explained that, sorry, his friend was not feeling well, too much wine. After that scare Guggenberger insisted they leave at once. The terminal was too risky. Maus got directions to the bus station and they started off down side streets and alleys.

"Hey, you there, you two guys, where are you going? Where do you live?" Officer William F. Ross, a veteran of ten years on the city police force, studied their faces above the headlights of his patrol car. Good-looking guys who said they were foreign seamen making their way to San Diego. Their ship had been sunk and both of them had spent some time at Bethesda Naval Hospital near Washington. Well, the war was now two years old and all sorts of folks passed through town, but this beat all. It was the first time he had met up with any foreign sailors this far from the ocean.

Are Greeks blond? These families who ran restaurants in Tucson sure weren't. They were dark, almost like Mexicans. As for the color of South Africans, he wasn't sure. Those packs on their backs? Why didn't they carry valises or hand luggage like normal people? Going down an alley to get to the bus station? Why? It just didn't make sense. Ross drew his gun and motioned Guggenberger and Maus into the car.

At police headquarters Ross and a lieutenant began to search through the bags these characters were carrying with them. They found two bottles of catsup, chewing gum from Mexico, tins of sardines, canned milk, beans, rolled oats, toilet articles, clothing. While the two lawmen puzzled over these items (many of them purchased at the compound canteen, and commodities often in short supply in civilian stores), Maus quietly dropped his wire cutters into a nearby trash basket.

Ross whistled quietly as he unfolded a military map of southern Arizona complete with airfields, military installations, highways, bridges and troop-maneuver plans. (It was something produced the previous year for the 92nd Division.) "What do you make of this, Lieutenant? Mexican gum, now this map. Have we got ourselves a couple of saboteurs here or what?"

Guggenberger and Maus tried to look composed, stoutly maintaining they were only merchant seamen. Their ship had been sunk five weeks before and they had just been released from the hospital. The map? Given to them by a friendly American soldier when they asked how to get west to California.

The lieutenant dug deeper into Guggenberger's rucksack and came up with several pieces of paper. A card belonging to Georgias Ohaki, a resident of Crete. Charles S. Rock's army identification tag, his Bank of America deposit book, a receipt for a $20 war savings bond, papers stating that Rock had been honorably discharged from the United States Army in March 1943. A letter written by Kathryn Holman of Mocksville, North Carolina, to a soldier stationed at Fort Huachua. Three sets of auto keys.

Suddenly the lieutenant burst out laughing. "Okay, so you boys are from up at Papago Park. Here's a compound pass for one Werner Boehm. Are you Boehm?" Guggenberger grinned broadly and admitted, yes, he was. And Maus was Eric Shoenfeld.

The police then separated the escapees, putting Maus in a cell with a Jehovah's Witnesses adherent who refused to register for the draft. A short time later another member of the city force asked Maus if he would be willing to talk with his, the police officer's, German-born mother; it would mean so much to her. Yes, if Guggenberger could join them. For half an hour or so the two U-boat officers chatted animatedly with the old lady, a native of Wuppertal, who still spoke fair German. As this conversation was ending it became obvious that city and state authorities were at odds over who was to have custody of "Boehm" and "Schoenfeld." The Arizona State Police wanted to move them to their quarters a few blocks away, in handcuffs. Maus and Guggenberger protested: no handcuffs, that was against the Geneva Convention.

"But, Lieutenant Schoenfeld, these cuffs once were used by John Dillinger. Think what you can tell the boys at camp and the folks back in Germany when you get there. Real handcuffs used by that great American gangster, Dillinger." They finally relented, submitted to manacles, and walked the four blocks to the state police headquarters, where Herman Tickel, local FBI agent, questioned them for an hour.

By late Sunday evening Guggenberger and Maus were back in Compound 5 at Papago Park, having been away for thirty-six hours. As astonishing as it may sound, until informed by the Tucson police that they had apprehended two German officers, the Papago Park authorities were unaware that anyone was missing. Now they were not certain who actually had returned. Identification records were in such a sorry state that no one knew who Guggenberger/Boehm and Maus/Schoenfeld really were. Eventually the two U-boat captains offered to give their true names and clear up the mess *if* no one was punished. The Americans readily agreed; Guggenberger and Maus resumed their true identities, and their stand-ins were demoted back to their proper compounds.

By Tuesday the Americans had established that three other officers were gone. News of their flight was fed to the local press in driblets. The *Arizona Republic* in Phoenix revealed the disappearance of Johannsen and Kottmann on Wednesday, Quaet-Faslem on Thursday. Forty-eight hours later Papago Park reported that two petty officers were also missing. At the same time the command released pictures of the three submarine captains, along with a stern warning from FBI agent H. R. Duffy in Phoenix:

> The men are known saboteurs and a menace to the community and to the individual while at large, as well as being valuable agents of the German war machine. It should be remembered that they probably have changed from the faded denim clothes they were wearing in camp and that they are now clean shaven. Any stranger whose actions are suspicious

should be reported to the FBI office. It would be unwise to attempt to detain them, but an immediate report of anything unusual to the FBI or any officer of the law will be of vital help.

This was a message heard with increasing frequency throughout Arizona during the months that followed.

The only lead that authorities got during the next few days turned out to be a false alarm. On Wednesday, the sixteenth, two men entered Steinfeld's Clothing Store in Tucson and tried to buy some civilian clothing from Dennis Weaver, a salesman. Weaver said both of them wore RAF insignias but had on khaki trousers and dirty jackets. They said they were returning to England soon and wanted to purchase several white shirts. Suspicious of their motives ("most of those British boys out at the base are snappy dressers"), Weaver told them he was unable to sell them what they wanted because of government regulations and rationing. "Then," he reported, "they became nervous and left. Only later did I read about those birds escaping from Phoenix. I am sure it was two of them." But Dennis Weaver was wrong; his strange-looking customers were not escaped German POWs.

After crawling out of that ditch outside the compound, Johannsen, Kottmann and Quaet-Faslem had headed south through the darkness—always, Johannsen says, keeping the North Star at their backs. Unlike their two friends, they planned to walk all the way to freedom, not ride. Determined to avoid highways in the Phoenix area, they first followed an abandoned railway line which took them over the Salt River by means of a rickety bridge. Only as they clambered down on the other side did they realize how foolhardy they had been. Two nights later they crossed another river, the Gila, and just at daybreak arrived at Maricopa, where they hid out in a railway car until it was dark once more.

In this fashion, walking as far as they could each night and curling up in bushes by day, the trio moved swiftly southward. Maintaining a steady course and occasionally consulting a frayed map, they climbed over fences, waded through irrigation canals (sometimes four or five feet deep), gave wide berth to barking dogs, villages and isolated farm houses, and pressed on. Their food consisted mostly of bread and canned goods carried in rudely constructed rucksacks. Sometimes they heated these cans of meat, corn and beans over small fires. One disadvantage, they quickly agreed, was that their tins of food were extremely heavy and burdensome. Water for drinking came from ponds, canals, wherever they could find it.

"Some nights the weather was very cold," Johannsen says, "and at higher elevations the ground often was frozen. After about ten days we were quite sure we were in Mexico. The border was not marked, but as soon as a high peak, Baboquivari (7,730 feet), was on our left and some distance behind us, we were certain of it. One of my biggest problems during the escape was to make Kottmann and Quaet-Faslem forget German and speak English. Neither one was very proficient, frankly, at least they did not know English as well as I did, thanks to the time I had spent in America."

For several more days the three officers continued south, hiding by day and walking at night; however, since they mistakenly supposed that Mexico was neutral soil, they gradually became somewhat less cautious. One evening, thirty or forty miles into Mexico, they decided it might be safe to contact someone. In fact, due to two pressing problems this was a step they had to take: the wading through ditches and occasional downpours kept their clothing damp, so they needed to stop and dry out their gear before they became ill; more important, they had to get advice concerning what roads to take southward toward their imaginary vessel.

The three men carefully approached a substantial group of ranch buildings with a high windmill turning briskly in the winter breeze. The large family, seated around a table eating tortillas, was quite friendly, apparently delighted to have unexpected guests. Johannsen, Kottmann and Quaet-Faslem introduced themselves as Dutch seamen from the S.S. *Bloem*

·

Fontein berthed in the harbor of Manzanillo. Each of them—Jan Koopman, Peter Van Brock and Willem Schippers—carried a pass from their captain, V. D. Velde, permitting them to take a ten-day "tramp trip" through northern Mexico. "According to regulations," these documents stated, "their personal papers are on board the S.S. *Bloem Fontein.*"

The family invited the three sailors to join them at the table, and although the Germans did not speak Spanish and none of the Mexicans could fully understand their mixture of English, German and Dutch, the group managed to communicate in a good-natured fashion. After dinner was over, their host escorted them to a small outbuilding where they built a fire, dried out their clothing and slept soundly.

The following morning, February 25, the visitors ate breakfast, got some basic directions, bade their cordial host and his family farewell, and once more began walking south down a rough country road. About five or six hours later, sometime early in the afternoon, two jeeps bearing their Mexican friend and a group of Mexican and American soldiers suddenly charged down the highway toward them.

"There was no time to hide or even think about doing so," says Johannsen. "An American officer said, 'Hands up, boys. Do you have any firearms?' When we assured him we did not, he smiled and offered us cigarettes."

The escapees then got into the jeeps and the group drove north to the little border community of Sasabe, where the Germans were held in the guardroom of the Mexican customs building. They were given coffee and searched in a perfunctory manner, but as the hours slipped by, it became obvious that their exploit was turning into an international incident. The Mexicans, it appears, were not happy with this Yankee incursion into their sovereign territory and refused to surrender the three escapees, at least not yet.

The following day Mexican authorities took the trio through a surly crowd of townspeople, who threatened them with fists and angry words, to two waiting automobiles, and in order to stay on Mexican soil, drove them by a circuitous route through

Altar and Santa Ana (175 miles in all) to Nogales, a larger border crossing only forty miles east of Sasabe by U.S. highway. En route Johannsen, riding with several guards in the rear vehicle, had a very unnerving experience. When they stopped for a rest, he walked a few feet from the car, and suddenly feeling uneasy, turned to face a pistol leveled at his head. To this day Johannsen thinks one of the Mexican guards may have intended to shoot him on the pretext that he was attempting to escape; however, an officer said something in Spanish, the gun was returned to its holster and the party resumed its journey.

In Nogales they were put in the local jail, "a stinking place," says Johannsen. The Mexicans questioned them from time to time and frequently urged them to sign a document written in Spanish. Unable to read what it said, they refused and demanded to talk with a Swiss diplomat or someone familiar with the Geneva Convention and the rights of prisoners of war.

"The three or four days spent there would have been extremely uncomfortable," Johannsen stresses, "if we had not had some American money. The authorities failed to find it when they searched us, and with those bills we were able to buy food and live quite well. One of the Mexican prisoners, it turned out, had a little restaurant operation right there inside the jail. His wife cooked the meals in her home, brought them in and he sold the food—much better than prison fare, of course—to those who could afford to pay his prices."

On March 1 Captain Cecil Parshall appeared and took custody of the three U-boat officers. On the long ride back to camp they discussed their travels and discovered that one of the many strange noises they had heard from time to time as they made their way across lonely stretches of desert was the warning rattle of deadly snakes.

Once back at Papago Park, they received no punishment for their two-week outing and were asked only one question: "Did you commit any acts of sabotage during your escape attempt?" Johannsen, Kottmann and Quaet-Faslem said they did not. Satisfied with their replies, the officer who had posed the question turned to a guard and said, "Okay, take these boys back to their compound." To the consternation of the guard, the three POWs were still dressed in civilian clothes. He pointed this out to the American officer, who reacted rather sharply. You have your orders, he told the GI; how prisoners are dressed is none of your business. So, clad in their escape gear, they marched back into their compound. Johannsen remembers rolling up his clothes and hiding them, but he never used them again. That was his first and last break for freedom, although several fellow officers, eager to make use of his knowledge of the United States, proposed that he accompany them on a similar venture.

This affair had the effect of increasing tensions between J. Edgar Hoover's agents and the United States Army, two forces existing in an uneasy, behind-the-scenes truce at best, each suspecting the other would get banner headlines for recapturing any Nazis who got away. The 9th Service Command proposed sending its own undercover men into Mexico to scout out potential escape routes, but the FBI said no. Runaway POWs were its business, not the Army's. Agents emphasized that the Army was "out of line" when its personnel went into a foreign country to track down Quaet-Faslem, Kottmann and Johannsen. This, they insisted, seriously interfered with and jeopardized the bureau's secret liaisons south of the border.

These escapes also alarmed E. H. Braatelien, superintendent of the Arizona Highway Department. On February 21, shortly after the entire region had learned that several officers were missing, he wrote Governor Sidney P. Osburn concerning his fears. The Germans held at Papago Park, he said, appeared to be very dangerous, highly intelligent, schooled in both the English language and escape techniques.

> These escaped prisoners are not the type that might be found skulking on the desert but rather seem to be well coached as to manners and customs of this country and also they seem familiar with the surrounding territory, streets, and building locations.

From evidence gathered it is apparent that the officers in charge of the camp are lax in their method of handling the prisoners. When asked to furnish a description of the escaped men it was found they had no recent photographs of the prisoners, they allow the officers to have civilian clothes, prisoners seem to have a generous supply of money, many men are entrusted outside of the camp with too few guards, and the manner of checking prisoners in and out is lax. The imprisoned officers are restricted to confinement but privates are allowed to work on detail outside of the camp. In nearly every escape an English-speaking officer has changed places with a private going out on work detail, and this has passed unnoticed by the guards or officers in charge.

During the establishment of Papago Park as a prisoner of war station, officers in charge requested suggestions from this office and we ennumerated a number of things that we felt should be put into effect such as fingerprinting, recent photography, "V" heels on shoes, direct communication with civilian enforcement officers, etc., none of which apparently have been adopted.

While I am not in a position to make any recommendations, I felt sure that you would want to be informed of the situation as we see it.

On Saturday, February 26, the day after Quaet-Faslem and his friends were recaptured in Mexico, Peter Doerell and Ferdinand Fuge, petty officers from the *U-664*, crawled under the body of a large truck just before it left their compound. According to a crisp FBI report, "They then walked out of the camp after dark on a road on which there is not a guard stationed."

This pair had only thirty cents between them and no true escape plan in mind. They hung around the Tempe railroad yards for several hours in a vain attempt to hop a freight. Finally a railway detective became suspicious and called police, and the two men were back behind barbed wire once more. Strangely, despite events of recent days Papago Park authorities were still not holding Sunday roll calls and did not know Doerell and Fuge were absent until brought back. Like Braatelien, FBI agents were highly critical of the camp administration: there were no Sunday head counts, no guards at main gates, no search of personnel as they arrived from Crossville and other camps, and officers were permitted to visit with their crews and issue orders to them.

Now only two petty officers were unaccounted for, the pair who had disappeared on or about the sixteenth. On March 1, the same day that the three U-boat captains returned from Mexico, an American GI discovered Friedrich Sternberg and Kurt Mohrdieck under a load of trash he dumped from a truck seven miles outside Papago Park. The two men had evidently spent nearly two weeks in hiding within the camp, waiting for the opportune moment to escape, only to be immediately apprehended.

With the return of the three officers from south of the border and the two POWs from the garbage dump, the epidemic of escapes ceased momentarily, although Fuge and Mohrdieck turned up missing again on April 24, Sternberg on September 14 and November 6. Fuge and Mohrdieck fled the second time with Vincent Lehmann, a forty-year-old engineer who had been conducting Spanish classes. They were two of his students. All of them were recaptured within a few days.

Yet the February outing and these subsequent escapes, although unsuccessful, were not in vain—far from it. As Quaet-Faslem told Guggenberger and others, these were merely "trial runs." It was like picking up a new U-boat at Kiel and going out into the Baltic to see how it worked. They had learned much since February 12. Getting across the border into Mexico was no problem. They might, with caution, even use trains and buses in the future. Most important, the next time they must know the country better and stow away more food, much more. They had to have enough to get each man deep into Mexico, fifty or sixty miles south of the border.

In addition to gaining valuable experience, Quaet-Faslem and company had accomplished something else. Their exploits made a quick removal of Colonel A. H. Means from Papago Park inevitable.

Chapter 5
MURDER, THREE COLONELS AND 1A COMPOUND

General William H. Shedd, commander of the U.S. Army's 9th Service Command, which encompassed Arizona and much of the western United States, leafed through the six-page report for a second time. The Pentagon clearly was very unhappy with conditions down at Papago Park. He stared out across the Fort Douglas parade ground and into the bleak Utah landscape. Should he pick up the phone and blast this man Means or call Washington and try to explain what was going on?

For a moment Shedd did neither. How in hell could a place be so screwed up! And why did it have to be in his area? The first German had arrived there on January 5. Two months elapsed and during that time nothing went right. Three weeks ago either seven or nine POWs were out loose somewhere. Means obviously didn't even know how many bodies he had in his compounds. They caught two officers in Tucson and didn't know their names for several days. Then they got three more down in Mexico. Several POWs apparently never really left the camp, just hid out some place for a week or ten days.

Once more, with considerable care, Shedd began to review this devastating document. Papago Park, home at various times to national guardsmen, CCC boys and black infantry units, now had 102 officers and 1,348 enlisted men, all German navy or merchant marine, although five compounds could hold up to 180 officers and 3,160 EMs. Officer hutments apparently were poorly constructed. No insulation; roofs leaked. Enlisted men's quarters came in various sizes, many of their barracks converted from old stables and supply sheds. Tan gypsum board covered about half of these structures, poor-grade jute paper the rest. Officers had steel beds with mattresses; enlisted men slept on cots.

Sanitary facilities, guard towers and fences seemed adequate, although rough and uneven terrain presented drainage problems and also made it impossible for guards to survey the entire camp. Kitchens, rations and the hospital were in order, but only 379 EMs, less than a third of them, actually were working. And, as this report noted, there certainly was much they could be doing in a new installation.

> It appears very little effort is being made by the camp officers to facilitate the maximum use of prisoners of war. The prisoners perform approximately 6 hours of work each day on whatever projects they are engaged. There is a large amount of work which could be done within the stockade and recreation area such as building roads and walkways, removing debris, and making necessary improvements to the recreation area. It was suggested to the camp commander that a large group of prisoners be put to work on these projects.

This survey said the recreation facilities were "primitive." That was to be expected in a new camp. It takes time to develop such things. But, by God, if those men didn't get off their asses, they would *never* see any sports equipment of any kind. He would see to that personally! The canteens were poorly stocked, didn't even have toilet articles. That was poor policy. Men won't work if they have nothing to work for.

Captain Wattenberg and Petty Officer Hox, spokesmen for

the POWs, had put together a predictable list of gripes. Some were trivial and repetitious. Shedd checked off each item with a red pencil as he scanned the list.

No recreation rooms.
No recreation equipment.
No educational program.
Not permitted use of recreational areas.
Insufficient food being served to prisoners.
No work shop.
No hand tools provided for making chairs, tables, and other furniture and equipment for recreation rooms.
Inadequate stock in the POW canteens.
Inadequate housing facilities for the POW canteens.
American officers assigned to duty within the stockade will not listen to suggestions or complaints of spokesmen.
American officers fail to take heed of the necessary maintenance work required on stockade buildings.
POW canteen officer will not place orders with mail order houses for items requested by prisoners of war.
Lights are not provided in some of the officer hutments.

What irritated the general most of all was the comment that Means had "no suggestions or recommendations to make" and the remarks by the man who compiled this report:

No locked boxes were provided for prisoner of war mail, and the mail was being handled by prisoners of war. Very inadequate records of outgoing prisoner mail are being kept. These records are kept by prisoners of war and could easily be falsified.
Many prisoners of war succeeded in escaping from this camp during the past month, but all had been apprehended and returned at the time of this visit.
The undersigned officer was very surprised at the extreme laxity of all American personnel at this camp. The main gates to the stockade were not in use, but were lying on the ground partially buried in mud. The sentry at the main gate casually glanced at trucks as they passed in and out of the stockade and made no attempt to stop vehicles for inspection.
This officer was permitted to walk thru the main gate and the gate to compound no. 4 with no identification required.

The sentry merely passed the time of the day with this officer. The undersigned officer witnessed an alleged count of prisoners within the stockade at or about six fifteen A.M. on 3 March, and it was obvious that a very ineffective count was made. Only one American officer was present, and very few American noncommissioned officers.

The American noncommissioned officers finally obtained the information from the American duty officer as to where he wished the count to take place. The German prisoners milled around and finally were marched to a lighted area and segregated by companies. The count of prisoners was made by American noncommissioned officers who apparently were not familiar with their own officers since two of them reported to the undersigned officer that their respective companies were present and accounted for. No attempt seemed to be made to ascertain how many prisoners from each company were on duty in the mess halls or still making use of the various latrines.

The men didn't even know who their own officers were and reported to the man from Washington. It could be funny, Shedd sighed, but it actually was pathetic.

An inspection of the five compounds at this camp indicated that even the American officers were not familiar with the physical layout of the camp. The keys to the gates of compounds no. 1 and no. 2 could not be found although officers and enlisted personnel were of the opinion that they might be found either at the guardhouse, fire station, or at headquarters. Upon inspection of the compounds (unused), it was found that the gates were open.

Upon inspection of compound no. 4 on Saturday morning, 4 March 1944, only two American officers were found to be with the four prisoner of war companies within that compound, and neither one of these was familiar with his duties. One of these officers was badly in need of a shave, presented a very poor appearance, but stated he was going to make an inspection of his prisoner of war company at ten that morning.

The undersigned officer thoroughly discussed with the commanding officer all the many and more important deficiencies noted and left with the impression that very little effort would be made by the commanding officer to correct the situations as they existed.

Shedd laid the papers on his desk. There really was no point in talking with either Colonel Means or Washington. Means had to go, and the sooner the better.

Within seventy-two hours any doubts Shedd may have had concerning the departure of Colonel Means vanished completely. It was shortly before noon on Monday, March 13, 1944, that the general first heard the name of Werner Dreschler. The colonel in charge of internal security for the 9th Service Command suddenly appeared at his office door and told him that POW Dreschler was dead. That was not a particularly startling bit of news, but the fact that some of Dreschler's fellow countrymen down at Papago Park had murdered him was.

Details were sketchy. Apparently 350 German seamen had arrived at the train station in Tempe about twenty-four hours earlier, sometime Sunday morning. By four o'clock in the afternoon they were processed and distributed to various compounds. At about six o'clock Monday morning a guard found the battered body of Werner Dreschler hanging in a shower room of Compound 4. He had been dead perhaps six to eight hours. So far, there were no leads.

Before the day ended, Captain Parshall was able to supply Fort Douglas with a few more details, and in time the whole gruesome story unfolded.

Dreschler was from the *U-118*, which had left Bordeaux on its fourth and last patrol on May 22, 1943. On June 12, six hundred miles west of the Azores, nine U.S. planes caught the craft on the surface. It dove quickly, but had to come up within eight minutes. Seventeen men were rescued, one of whom later died. Two men, seriously hurt, were operated on at sea en route to Norfolk. Dreschler, shot in the leg but able to hobble about, and thirteen others arrived at Fort Hunt on June 30.

By this time most men remained at P.O. Box 1142 for only a few days, perhaps a week. But Dreschler was at Hunt for more than six months, not leaving until January 8, 1944. Early in October he had spent a few days in the hospital at Fort

George Meade but soon returned, for the Americans at Hunt found Dreschler extremely cooperative. Why this young man talked so freely is not clear, but talk he most certainly did. At first he was written off as rather stupid, yet within a short time his intellect seems to have improved markedly in U.S. eyes. An interrogator commented in December 1943 that Dreschler was intelligent, an individual "of immense conceit and vanity . . . very cooperative if flattered enough."

Dreschler provided those questioning him with nearly eighty pages of information: what type of mines the *U-118* carried, how they were laid in the Gibraltar Straits in February 1943, a description of the submarine base at Bordeaux (even pinpointing the location of official brothels two blocks from Place Gambetta), and numerous technical details soon circulated to all those waging antisubmarine warfare. In addition, Werner Dreschler (a Mechanikerobergefreiter, or seaman first class) became one of Fort Hunt's most successful stool pigeons, certainly the best-known, anyway. Given the name "Limmer," he was placed in cells with men from various boats. Assured he never would be sent to a camp where he might be recognized, "Limmer" posed as an Obermaat (petty officer) from the *U-118* and proceeded to ask questions and encourage conversation.

A postwar report on Fort Hunt had this to say concerning stool pigeons (SPs) and their activities:

> A stool pigeon, along with listening devices, became an essential aid in the obtaining of military intelligence through prisoner of war interrogations. The more security-minded the prisoners, the greater the need for stool pigeons in "breaking" them. Thus, during the earlier part of the war with Germany, stool pigeons were considered as essential to an interrogation center.

By 1944–1945, however, with defeat looming, POWs were more cooperative, yet occasionally a stool pigeon was still used. Such a man, this report noted, had to be chosen with "utmost care." "He must be thoroughly reliable, a quality normally not to be expected of men who are willing to perform this degrading function."

Degrading or not, Dreschler "performed" admirably. During the months he was at Hunt scores of men met with him, then moved on to camps such as Stringtown and Papago Park. Before long, "Limmer" was a prime source of speculation. And, in time, aware that "Limmer" was a phony name, *U-118*'s survivors concluded that he must be Werner Dreschler.

In January 1944 this youth was sent to Meade once more and from there to Fort Leonard Wood, Missouri. Several weeks later, for reasons never explained, he was shipped to Papago Park, where he should have been put in the base hospital. As Parshall described it, by four o'clock on the afternoon of March 12, fifty-eight new men, including Dreschler, were in Compound 4 getting to know other POWs and renewing old friendships.

Within a very short time a small group of seamen decided that "Obermaat Limmer" had to die, although many more must have known something was afoot. Finding out who those men were was a grisly, drawn-out affair, ably described by Richard Whittingham in *Martial Justice: The Last Mass Execution in the United States*. The United States Navy, furious because of what had happened, refused to cooperate in this investigation. Eventually twenty POWs from Compound 4 were singled out as prime suspects, and in May nine of them were parceled out to various California camps where they were grilled mercilessly, denied food, water and sleep, and apparently suffered some physical abuse as well.

In August 1944, at a trial held in Florence, a little community seventy miles southeast of Phoenix, seven of these men were found guilty of the murder of Werner Dreschler and sentenced to death. Under extreme pressure all had confessed but were unable to understand why killing a man who turned against his homeland in time of war was such a serious crime. General Shedd, who reviewed their cases, recommended that the death penalties be set aside and commuted to life imprisonment. One year later President Harry Truman, reacting to the wave of revulsion which swept the United States as the full horror of German concentration camps was revealed, did not agree, and in August 1945, still puzzled, all seven were hanged at Fort Leavenworth. (In the final weeks before V-E Day, American authorities had made some effort to exchange fifteen German POWs—all involved in the murders of fellow countrymen on U.S. soil—for American POWs under death sentences in Germany, but fighting ceased before anything was accomplished and the Leavenworth Germans lost any leverage they may have had. Truman eventually commuted one man's sentence to twenty years; the others died on the morning of August 25, 1945.)

It is impossible to say how widespread stool-pigeon operations were at Fort Hunt and other POW installations. There are indications that American officers scattered cooperative prisoners among various camps from time to time. These men were provided with aliases and told to write directly to a "Captain Peters" whose address actually was the central censorship bureau in New York City. Officials in Manhattan were ordered to forward all letters (unopened) directly to P.O. Box 1142 in Alexandria.

By far the most extensive and most successful of these "SP" experiments occurred at Byron Hot Springs in California. Five German enlisted men, one of them a U-boat veteran, were formed into "a special interrogation unit" and granted unique privileges. Unlike Dreschler, these individuals seem to have had sound reasons for doing what they did. Two were not German citizens and had Communist ties, another had spent some months in a concentration camp for political activity. They arrived at Byron early in 1943 and soon the commandant was speaking of them as "my pets." In interrogation summaries they were identified simply as "PWs X, Y, Z," etc.

This quintet, described casually as "all more or less loyal to the U.S.," was provided with bogus names, paid the usual eighty cents per day granted all POWs who worked, allowed to wear civilian clothes and GI uniforms, permitted use of the post swimming pool and post exchange, and occasionally attended movies off the base in the company of an officer and a guard. In return for their intelligence efforts they were assured that the United States would give them full protection at all times and look with favor upon any requests to remain in this country after the war ended.

Everything went smoothly for about seven months, but slowly all five became disenchanted with the attitude of a captain who, they later claimed, was using them to gain higher rank and threatened to ship them to a POW camp if they failed to do as he wished. They also began to wonder if the U.S. government would keep its word and look out for their future welfare. Several had gone so far as to sever all correspondence with their families in order to protect all concerned.

In July 1943 this group was transferred to Fort Lewis, in Washington State, for ten days, apparently on a special assignment of some sort, but soon they were back on the job at Byron Hot Springs. In September the commandant pressed G-2 in the capital without success for a letter which might assuage the fears of these men. Several weeks later two of them, with the knowledge of their comrades, escaped and went directly to the police station at Pittsburg, twenty-five miles away. They asked to talk to the FBI, and when that request was granted, told of the clash with the captain, noting that this seemed the only way to inform the base commander of his actions.

Following an inquiry, American officers at Byron concluded that the usefulness of these five POWs was at an end and shipped all of them (under bogus names) to a camp being formed in Nebraska. The colonel in charge of Byron followed up this decision with a letter to their new commanding officer indicating that these men were "treacherous" and "untrustworthy." When the Pentagon learned what had happened, a blistering rebuke was dispatched westward. How could anyone, the Director of Military Intelligence asked, treat men who had been so cooperative so shabbily? Also, he demanded to know how those five POWs knew the true names of American personnel and the actual location of P.O. Box 651. The director, by the way, believed what these young men said about the captain, who, they alleged, had "used" them for his own ends. "Only confirms what I have always thought of him," he wrote.

Alarmed by this turn of events and fearing for their lives, the five "SPs" appealed directly to their new commanding officer. Their very detailed, carefully phrased letter emphasized: "We might truthfully claim that all PWs who passed through the camp between January and November 1943 were interrogated exclusively by us." American authorities took no action, although these young men documented this assertion with a complete list of individuals they had interviewed, plus an item-by-item account of what they had extracted from them on behalf of the Allied cause. Late in 1944 when the Nebraska camp was deactivated, aware of what had happened to Werner Dreschler, the Army transferred the men to a POW compound in Canada.

In addition to recruiting stool pigeons at Hunt, G-2 and ONI also toyed with the idea of enlisting POWs to become spies in their homeland as well. In November 1943 the Joint Chiefs of Staff discussed the possibility of prisoners volunteering for duty with the OSS. What they had in mind was secreting anti-Nazis into Europe via England or Yugoslavia; however, several officials noted that any cloak-and-dagger operation of this sort would have to recruit men *before* their capture had been reported to the enemy. This scheme obviously was fraught with pitfalls and got nowhere, for turning a fresh captive loose on his native soil on the premise he would aid his former captors was risky business indeed.

Walter Kozur and Johann Kremer watched as the two American officers shook hands, then Colonel A. H. Means got into his car, a GI driver quickly shut the door, and they were gone. Lieutenant Colonel George Barber, a World War I veteran who came to America from his native Serbia shortly before that holocaust began, now was commandant of Papago Park. Shedd had told him this was a temporary assignment for perhaps ninety days or so and ordered him to straighten out the camp as quickly as he could. What this change of command would mean to the Germans was far from clear. Guards had warned them that Barber was "damned hard . . . the bloodhound of the 9th Service Command"; "He'll fix your kraut asses, you just wait and see!"

Kozur, Kremer and their comrades quickly discovered that Barber was an unpredictable, aloof man who occasionally roamed the compounds within their stockade area by himself, but he did little to strike terror into their hearts. During his months as Papago Park's commander, roughly mid-March to August 1, Barber made some superficial improvements, and the stockade gates were dug up, dusted off and locked each night. Yet some American officers stationed there were convinced that Barber's "reforms" did not go far enough. All too often, they felt, he consulted the prisoners, not them, before issuing orders.

William M. E. Rachal, a young captain who was in charge of Compound 4 for several weeks in the summer of 1944, says the staff rarely saw Barber. "He spent an inordinate amount of time closeted with Wattenberg and loved to entertain groups of Phoenix ladies for drinks and tea. The camp pretty much ran itself and not very well either. Going there from a spit-and-polish base, I was appalled, even shocked. It was the dirtiest, sloppiest place I have ever seen.

"I made my men police up the headquarters in Compound 4 and act like soldiers. I know I didn't make myself popular.

"I guess Barber consulted with men like Parshall and his boss, Major Eugene Tays, the director of security. He must have. Parshall was an experienced, regular Army type. He was a conscientious officer, an up-from-the-ranks sort, inclined to the iron fist without any velvet glove."

Thirty years later, Parshall, now in his eighties, once the trim, mustachioed provost marshal begrudgingly admired by Rachal, still boils at the mention of Barber's name. "He was a foreigner who, despite his years in America, simply didn't understand Americans. He got some work under way at the camp, I concede that, but damn little."

Nevertheless, representatives of the U.S. State Department and the Swiss government who visited Papago Park for two days early in June 1944 generally were pleased with what they saw. Barber now ruled 2,493 POWs, 639 of them enlisted men living in an agricultural camp near Mesa. Wattenberg was no longer spokesman, having been replaced, at least temporarily, by another officer. The guard contingent at Papago Park consisted of 367 men and four officers. Twenty-seven administrative officers also were attached to the base. Sanitary conditions were good. The 150-bed hospital had about ninety patients each day and there was a dispensary in each compound. Six U.S. surgeons, nine German doctors, two American dentists and two POW dental technicians staffed these facilities.

Recreational life and educational programs had improved markedly. Officers were permitted to go horseback riding at times, and all of the men occasionally could swim in the irrigation canal flowing by the camp. Each week EMs saw one movie, officers two, and during any seven-day period they could send a letter and a postcard to relatives in Germany. To some extent, horseback riding and other special privileges were part of a subtle American scheme to foster animosity between officers and NCOs, a ploy which bore some fruit. Guggenberger recalls that he, Maus and others studied stolid groups of Indians huddled silently along the canal banks as they swam. Could they use these dark, quiet people? Might they help them escape? They finally decided the answer was no.

Study courses in French, English, Italian, history, commerce and law were "fairly well" organized. Actually they were much better "organized" than either these State Department visitors or the camp command realized until months later. Lecturers frequently digressed to discuss interrogation techniques at Fort Hunt (just in case any student still might end up there) and to talk about how to stay free once one managed to escape.

"We were able," Wolfgang Clarus notes with some pride, "to increase substantially the amount of time individuals eluded capture. After all, if a prisoner was going to the trouble of breaking out it was our duty as officers to give him any assistance we could. The Geneva Convention, you know, recognizes escape as a legitimate sport. Three articles or more, at least by inference, establish the right of every POW to try if he gets the chance."

Escape *per se* was no great feat. Enlisted men sometimes worked outside the stockade without guards, and as many as twenty of them might be transported by an unarmed driver (no guards) to work projects twenty-five miles away. Basic problems any restless POW faced were two in number: where to go in Arizona's desert country if one did escape, and how to stay free. These were the very matters Clarus and other officers addressed themselves to in their classroom seminars.

Despite improvements, certain features of Papago Park continued to trouble both American and Swiss observers. Only seven hundred POWs were employed and earning eighty cents a day. This meant the great majority of officers and enlisted men did nothing much each day except eat, sleep, gossip, attend "interesting" lectures, go to the movies, swim and perhaps plot ways to spend their time much differently as far away from Papago Park as possible.

"There is a strong undercurrent of opposition to all forms of work on the part of the prisoners," a State Department functionary commented. "One of the greatest problems of the camp administration is to create a spirit of cooperation among the prisoners. This certainly is one of the most difficult prisoner-of-war camps in the entire United States. Its personnel is made up primarily of naval officers and submarine crews. In addition, there are a number of officers and crews from merchant marine vessels as well."

When this observer talked of cooperation "among" prisoners, what he really meant was cooperation *between* the prisoners and those guarding them. The cooperative spirit among POW ranks was excellent—much too good, in fact. At the time of this visit Wattenberg and several other trouble-makers were already lodged temporarily in separate enclosures, two other prisoners were confined for insubordination, and an officer was being held in protective custody.

In spite of these measures, or perhaps because of them, the Germans tended to give Barber a much higher rating than his American associates. They sensed his European background, thought his aloofness, which Parshall, Rachal and others found repugnant, was in fact a very correct, "Prussian-like" bearing, and naturally enough, delighted in canal swimming, horse-back riding and similar recreational innovations.

Lieutenant Colonel Barber clearly was making some progress, but on August 1, 1944, as prisoners, guards and soldiers watched and sweltered in the summer heat, he formally handed over Papago Park to William A. Holden, a full colonel and a new man sent down from Fort Douglas by General Shedd. He now was commandant, with Barber as his executive officer.

As Holden, a distinguished-looking, heavyset man with gray hair, walked past their compound fence, Kozur giggled and nudged Kremer. "Tito, Marshal Tito. He looks like him, doesn't he?" Kremer agreed, and within hours, as far as his German charges were concerned, Colonel Holden was "Tito."

While Means, a geologist in civilian life, apparently was not interested in running a POW camp and Barber adopted a simple "don't bother me with your troubles" approach and more or less let the place run itself as best it could, Holden was a professional. He had served in World War I with Parshall and later gained substantial experience with prisons and prisoners as an administrator in the Wisconsin state penal system.

Early in 1942 Holden had helped set up an alien detention center near Florence, somewhat to the chagrin of both U.S. senators from Arizona and local Rotarians who feared trouble if relatives of those held there congregated locally. A year later, defeat in North Africa transformed Camp Florence into an Italian POW facility, evidently a very contented, happy installation. Guards rarely were seen, one visitor noted. "The camp looks more like a town than a prisoner-of-war camp from the outside." In fact, Camp Florence was almost *too* contented. Some American officers wondered if they might not have a considerable number of homosexuals on their hands. Normal men just didn't sing opera as they picked cotton, nor did they walk about hand in hand.

At that base Holden pioneered in the development of work camps independent of the main installation, and one of his first decisions at Papago Park, in an attempt to increase labor output, was to move all troublemakers, escapees, repeaters and noncooperatives to Compound 1. If the Army refused to ship Wattenberg and his buddies to Alva, Oklahoma, where they belonged, then he would create his own "Little Alva" right there in Arizona. Holden then divided that compound into two parts, one housing officers and seamen who seemed bent upon following their leadership, and the other containing assorted NCOs who refused to perform even supervisory duties, as required by the Geneva Convention.

Only one American voice was raised in protest against this proposed use of Compound 1, that of Captain Cecil Parshall. As soon as the camp opened he warned Means, then Barber and in turn Holden that a "blind spot" existed in Compound 1 between guard towers 2 and 3. "The men simply could not see several square yards of the stockade at that point. I told Means. He just grunted and did nothing. I wrote a memo to Barber. He threw it into a wastebasket, so I wrote another. I had several people, including my secretary, initial it and then filed it away for future reference.

"Those Germans were a fine bunch of men, smart as hell. And it made no sense to put the smartest of them in Compound 1. I knew they would discover that 'blind spot' and they sure did. But by that time I had a new boss, Major Eugene Tays. He was responsible for camp security and intelligence, not me. Tays had no personality. He was sort of a nice old woman and there was no point in trying to get through to him. He was smart but very slow."

Rachal notes, in defense of Tays, that everyone was "slow" during Colonel Barber's regime. No one knew what was going on. No one felt capable of making decisions. It paid to be cautious. This same careful mood, he says, tended to permeate Holden's administration, although both Rachal and Parshall agree he was by far the best of the lot, a man who meant well and was heading in the right direction. As they see it, Holden simply didn't sweep clean enough as fast as he should have. And, of course, Barber remained as executive officer into November, long after the escape plans of the men in Compound 1 A were well under way.

Yet Lieutenant Commander V. R. Taylor, USNR, who made a thorough inspection of Papago Park about a month after Holden took over, heaped praise upon what had been accomplished. Taylor, perhaps overwhelmed by camp hospitality, saw the installation in a far different light than Rachal, Parshall and their fellow officers. Holden, he told his superiors, possessed "a world of experience in handling men . . . Barber's ability and driving power is well known. The Intelligence Officer is Major Eugene Tays, an engineer by profession, and a very competent person. The other officer personnel is above average. The finesse of the commanding officer, coupled with Colonel Barber's drive, makes, in my opinion, an outstanding team."

Taylor then proceeded to analyze the "Nazi-ness" of the men at Papago Park, dividing the officers into four groups: Super-Nazis, Cooperative Nazis, Opportunists and Anti-Nazis. To a large extent these groupings were based not upon any subtle understanding of politics, but solely on how cooperative, from their captors' point of view, these men appeared to be. That these prisoners of war might simply be bored, filled with love of country or imbued with prankster spirits and juices that activate young minds and young bodies everywhere does not seem to have occurred to this naval officer.

There are among the officer PWs four distinct types.

1. The Super-Nazi, represented by Wattenberg and his ilk. There are about 30 officers in this category. In order to prevent real trouble, this group has wisely been separated from the others. This group has, so I am reliably informed, even prepared a list of their fellow officers who are to be disposed of. It appears that anyone who in any way cooperates with the American officials is immediately dubbed a traitor. For example: Wattenberg issued orders that any person who is not required to work under the terms of the Geneva Convention who does any kind of work is a traitor. The reason being that any work performed is of assistance to America. Wattenberg refuses to speak English with any of the Americans, refuses to accept the privileges which are granted, i.e., attending movies, going for walks, etc., and has intimidated the other officers to such an extent that they dare not. There are many instances showing how he attempts through the medium of messages concealed in books transferred from one compound to another, plus underlining words in books, to keep the boys in line. Wattenberg told me that there would be a writing strike. That is, they would try to imply through the mails the idea that they are being ill treated by simply writing "we are well" and nothing more. He is complaining bitterly to the Swiss legation of his treatment. The whole performance revolves itself around one idea: Cause the Americans all the trouble possible.

2. This group is represented by Rathke and Neumann who are Nazi but believe in cooperating with the Americans: (a) for their own personal comfort, and (b) because the more they work and otherwise cooperate will, in the long run, make them better officers physically and mentally, thus of greater service to the Fatherland after the war.

3. Then the group I call Opportunists. The fortunes of war having turned decidedly in favor of the Allies, this group is now ingratiating itself with the winner. They are the group who will revert to type if the heat is put on them by the Nazis. This group is represented by Captain Keller, the compound leader.

4. Then finally the group by conviction anti-Nazi and who have more or less had the courage to express their opinions. They have been held in line by fear, primarily fear of retaliation against their families in Germany and secondly of their own personal safety. This group is represented by von Hopff-garten, Bewersdorff, Weber, etc.

In attempting to ascertain the feelings of the enlisted men, it has been a most difficult job in that to walk in a compound to speak to anyone but the Spokesman arouses a suspicion and puts the person to whom one speaks on the "suspicion list." However, it has been possible, through various means, to interview a cross-section of this group. It can be safely said that 65% of the group believes Germany will lose the war. They know there is no danger at this time and, it may well be said, less danger as time goes on, of any man expressing his feelings. This freedom of speech is more obvious as the results of the changes in the situation on the battle fronts favors the Allies. It is believed that about 20% always were anti-Nazi, but this group fears to assert itself.

Among the petty officers about 50% are anti-Nazi, some of my informants claim less. One maintained 70% Nazi. It is an interesting fact that one PW, a petty officer, formerly a member of the Hitler movement, now believes that Germany should be occupied by the Americans and British; that all Nazis should be disposed of; that the occupation should last long enough to educate the German people so that they can govern themselves under a truly democratic government.

The Merchant Marine is about 90% anti-Nazi. As a matter of fact a petition was signed by 96 volunteering to serve on a United States vessel or vessels.

Taylor added to this rather simplistic analysis a list of nine officers and ten enlisted men to be transferred to Blanding, Florida, an anti-Nazi camp, individuals who he suggested "will be of invaluable assistance to the United States and Britain during the occupation of Germany." Among them was Berndt von Walther und Croneck, late of the *U-162.* Thirty years later he was still wondering why the Americans singled him out. Taylor indicates that mail sent and received by these nineteen men revealed anti-Nazi leanings, or at least American censors thought this was true.

Walther says he and four fellow officers traveled to Florida dressed in U.S. uniforms, resplendent with small Nazi lapel pins. En route they gave their word of honor not to escape and were pretty much on their own most of the time. Two incidents occurred on the train which both intrigued and amused them. At El Paso all black Americans were herded into a single rear car, and two girls who chatted excitedly with these handsome young officers fled in terror when they learned they were consorting with the enemy, Nazi POWs!

After five days this group reached Blanding, located about forty miles west of Jacksonville amid pine trees and sand hills. This was a substantial installation housing 4,600 POWs in a base camp and eleven nearby branches. At the main facility there were 850 army prisoners, and in a separate compound, 250 navy men. As Walther and his friends approached the navy group they were stunned by their reception. This camp, anti-Nazi all right, was overflowing with Communists. "I had a terrible time there," he recalls. "The camp was full of Reds, criminals and traitors. I slept each night with a large stick by my bed, fearing for my life. We adamantly refused to go into the main compound and eventually persuaded the commanding officer to erect a 'dead line' separating us from the 'anti-Nazis' so-called." A U.S. inspection report of April 1945 concedes that a division of some sort existed within the naval area at Blanding but fails to explain how or why it came about. "Fifteen officers refuse to associate with the other men whom they consider virulently anti-Nazi and voluntarily live apart from them. They feel they are permanently branded, fear for their relatives at home and for themselves after the war." On the other hand, this report adds, one officer spurned these comrades and lived with the enlisted men instead.*

In addition to praising Holden's work at Papago Park and recommending transfer of a handful of men to Florida, Lieutenant Commander Taylor suggested that the colonel also become commandant of Camp Beale in California, "since the PWs there are all navy men and your knowledge and ability to handle them is superior to that of strangers." Oddly enough,

---

* Soon after V-E Day, Walther was transferred to Fort Eustis, Virginia, where he and 130 of his fellow countrymen worked for nearly a year translating Werner von Braun's rocket notes and other vital materials, work which won them special commendations from the U.S. government. Walther returned to Germany in July 1946.

Colonel Holden was not entirely pleased. On October 3 he wrote General Shedd that a regrouping of naval POWs probably was desirable, but all concerned should realize that those segregated as super-Nazis would have to be written off as a labor source. Whatever camp or compound became "Alcatraz" should be staffed, he emphasized, by superior U.S. personnel:

> It must be borne in mind that the professional German naval officer and non-commissioned officer, who intends to continue his profession after the war, will cooperate fully in all of the subversive policies and activities of the Senior Super-Nazi officer. The explanation is that these officers and non-commissioned officers must come through this period of captivity with a good conduct certificate signed by the Senior German officer. Continuation after the war of the only profession they know is involved and, therefore, we may assume that no cooperation with the American army beyond that permitted by the Senior German officer can be expected. In fact, we may safely assume that these officers and non-commissioned officers will successfully sabotage any employment program for prisoners of war if any contact with other enlisted prisoners is permitted.

Except as part of a general regrouping scheme, Holden didn't think shipping nineteen POWs to Blanding made much sense. "These men represent a class and *all* should be transferred if any of them are." As the colonel viewed the situation, 31 officers and 265 out of 472 NCOs at Papago Park were Super-Nazis and most definitely under the sway of Fregattenkapitän Jürgen Wattenberg, "the no. 1 Super-Nazi of this camp." Again, unless the War Department envisioned a complete reshuffling of all Super-Nazis, Opportunists, Cooperatives, and Anti-Nazis, there was no reason, in his opinion, to shift men from one part of the country to another.

Holden went on to remind the general that he already had submitted plans for a separate camp a few hundred yards from Papago Park "to be called Camp Apache, Pima, Yavapai, or something like that." Four days later Holden wrote Shedd once more concerning this matter, which was, he noted, "imperative." "The group now segregated in part of Compound 1 and which it is proposed to house in this converted stockade have threatened other prisoners and are persistently attempting to sabotage the entire work program at this camp." He noted with considerable pride that 1,063 POWs now were working in the 9th Service Command Repair Shop, at the Quartermaster Laundry in Phoenix, and on various agricultural projects. (Holden might have added that some prisoners employed in the laundry came down with venereal disease, but didn't.)

What he had in mind was expanding Papago Park's guardhouse stockade into a small, independent facility capable of housing perhaps fifty or sixty incorrigibles, a "Little Alva" where they could stew in their own juice. This would effectively isolate Wattenberg and his troublemaking comrades from the rest of the men, end sabotage of the camp work program, and in complete conformity with Geneva Convention rules, permit him to appoint a "reliable" senior officer as spokesman, someone who would cooperate.

On October 16 General Shedd asked Washington for permission to spend $11,447.84 to transform Holden's dream into reality. Eleven days later the War Department said go ahead, build. On December 7, 1944, the Pentagon issued ASF Circular no. 399 establishing Pima Camp—but nothing happened. Because of wartime shortages neither Shedd nor Holden could get construction materials.

Meanwhile Holden and others took solace in how well the men were adjusting to life in Compound 1 A. The entire guard company marveled at the change. Their spirits were better, flower beds were larger and well tended, the compound was much, much neater, its surface carefully raked several times each day. Once a very messy enclosure inhabited by thirty or so truculent Germans, Compound 1 A had become a veritable show place—well, relatively so.

William Rachal says he and his fellow officers attributed this dramatic change to typical German efficiency and organization. What they failed to realize was that all of this activity was part of a much bigger plan, for in addition to tending the flower beds, raking the gravel, and so on, these men were digging a tunnel.

When the four U-boat captains and their comrades decided to construct a tunnel they had plenty of precedent, for prisoners in every war have come to similar conclusions. As Wolfgang Clarus observed wryly, "You stare at that fence for hours on end, try to think of everything and anything that can be done, and finally realize there are only three possibilities: go through it, fly over it or dig under it."

The British seem to have excelled in this tunneling business, at least they have written the most compelling stories about such efforts, notably *The Wooden Horse* by Eric Williams and Paul Brickhill's *Great Escape*. The *Horse* tells of an ingenious scheme by Williams and two friends to cover up subterranean subterfuge. A rudimentary vaulting horse similar to those used in high school gym classes, constructed boxlike out of timber and Red Cross packing cases, became part of a daily exercise routine at Germany's Stalag-Luft III during World War II. What their captors failed to realize was that each day as some prisoners cavorted, jumped and vaulted, others who were carried out inside the horse to a site close to the fence were digging a 120-foot tunnel. This was a complex undertaking, but a successful one. The trio who conceived the plan escaped and returned to England.

The *Great Escape* tunnel, widely known because of the subsequent movie with Steve McQueen and his roaring motorcycle, was an extremely intricate excavation at Sagan, sixty miles southeast of Berlin. This tunnel, completed in March 1944, had no ruse such as a "horse," although the overall scheme consisted of at least three tunnels: "Tom," "Dick" and "Harry." If their captors found one of them, then the prisoners concentrated their efforts on the others.

"Harry," the winner, forty feet underground, had relatively spacious rooms and ventilating equipment, and was nearly four hundred feet long. Yet at the time of the breakout the men discovered that they had surfaced fifteen or twenty feet short of the woods they were aiming for. Seventy-six POWs managed to flee before German guards discovered what was up. Only three of them got back to England. The Gestapo, with Hitler's approval, murdered fifty of those retaken so as to teach other prisoners of war "a lesson." After the war ended the British went to considerable trouble to bring the men responsible for those deaths to justice, a search fascinatingly recounted by Brickhill.

Two escape tunnels through American soil are of more than passing interest. One is a relatively well known Civil War exploit, the other an obscure World War I adventure. In February 1864, 109 Union officers burrowed their way out of Richmond's Libby Prison. Since these men did not face language barriers, other than regional accents perhaps, and were only thirty miles from friendly territory, a substantial number made good their getaway. Fifty-nine reached Federal lines southeast of the city along the James River, forty-eight were recaptured, two drowned. Those who escaped were granted thirty days' leave before returning to active duty with their commands.

The other tunnel also was constructed in the South, at Atlanta's Fort McPherson, an enclosure reserved for enemy servicemen, most of them German sailors interned as soon as the United States entered World War I. On the evening of October 23, 1917, the weather was cool and fair, perfect autumn weather with both a memory of summer and a hint of winter. Over two hundred local households were holding evening prayer meetings to drum up interest in a forthcoming Billy Sunday crusade, and flags and bunting decorated Atlanta's streets in preparation for a huge war-bond rally to be held the next day.

At eight o'clock, just as those praying warmed up with opening hymns, the first of ten Germans (who undoubtedly also were invoking the Almighty with considerable fervor, if less noise) broke upward through the soil in a wooded area just outside of a fence surrounding Fort McPherson. He had made his way through a 143-foot shaft dug in an incredible fourteen days. Camp authorities were reasonably certain of the time required, since most of those involved had been at McPherson only two weeks. The entrance, hidden under a mess hall, led to a tunnel about three feet in diameter and eight feet deep.

Within forty-eight hours two Germans, one of whom attended the war-bond rally and took in a vaudeville show, were recaptured when they tried to obtain jobs in a local cotton mill. Yet near-panic reigned throughout the region and interest in two of the escapees was especially keen: Lieutenant Hans Berg, reputed to be a Don Juan with a world-wide retinue of female admirers, and Arnold Henkel, a thirty-eight-year-old Neumünster native, who had just made his fourth (or perhaps fifth) break for freedom in almost as many months.

According to the Atlanta *Journal* of October 26, its readers saw Huns everywhere:

> Five tramps had been seen shivering around a small fire in the woods near Griffin. They were Germans! A soldier had dragged a civilian out of a soda stand near Five Points. He was a German! A man with a red nose had asked a housewife in Decatur for a slice of pie. He was a German! A stranger on a Forrest Avenue car had stared suspiciously at a soap advertisement. The police were notified.

So it went. But as rumor after rumor was run down by the secret service operatives from the Department of Justice, only to fizzle out, it became more and more certain that Lieutenant Hans Berg, reputed to be the hero of a hundred Gretchens' hearts, Arnold Henkel, the modern Monte Cristo, and their companions had either put many a mile between them and the city or were tucked away in some secret place which the police had not yet been able to locate.

However, luck was not with Henkel, at least not yet, and on October 27 a group of south Georgia farmers captured him, together with four fellow prisoners of war in a swamp near Surrency in Appling County. When the group arrived in Atlanta twenty-four hours later, a *Journal* reporter found Henkel engagingly frank. Why did he escape? "To be free." Would he try again? "Yes, I will try again," he said, nodding, and added with a smile, "How . . . I don't know. Underground was the best way; right now I don't see any other. No, I don't know yet. But I will try again. I think I need an aeroplane, yes?"

Two weeks later Hans Berg and a fellow officer were apprehended near Laredo, Texas, as they waved to Mexican citizens in a frantic effort to get across the Rio Grande. A cowboy who was riding by, actually a customs man in casual dress, promptly arrested the pair. The tenth man was found after several weeks working as a doorman on New York's Fifth Avenue.

Six months later another group of POWs almost duplicated this feat. On Friday, May 3, 1918, an American officer discovered a tunnel seventy-five feet long, four feet in diameter, under the German officers' quarters at McPherson. Equipment at the site (planks, tin cups, clothes, even an electrical warning system) indicated considerable outside assistance. The immediate reaction was more guards, more searchlights, closer surveillance of visitors, elimination of gardens, and plans to raise all structures at least four feet aboveground so as to discourage future tunneling. Several individuals thought to be pro-German, among them an American lieutenant and the local YMCA secretary, were transferred elsewhere.

These men dug with tools brought from their own ships which, incredibly, they were allowed to keep. Also, it appears that officials at McPherson had substantial warning from many quarters. Pro-German groups in Atlanta reportedly boasted that "something big was about to be pulled off," several officers noted "various flower beds around the compound appeared to be increasing in height and size," and Social Democrats among the POWs told the commandant a tunnel was being dug. Less incredible was the retirement of that gentleman a short time later.

News of tunnels complete and incomplete and burial of several deceased prisoners in a national cemetery in nearby Marietta created a wave of local concern. A Fulton County grand jury protested that enemy personnel held at McPherson enjoyed "guest-like treatment . . . they are well fed, well housed, well clothed, and are permitted to lead a lazy, indolent life." More widespread were fears that escaped prisoners and pro-German factions might stir up unrest among blacks or that the social virus evident among some of them might take root on American soil. (In some reports of POW life, U.S. spokesmen equated socialism with anarchism, often using the terms interchangeably.) However, Germans were so few in number and American involvement in World War I so brief that no general outcry developed, nothing compared to what would happen a quarter of a century later.

Although Arnold Henkel did not participate in the second McPherson tunnel, his American career demands further comment. According to rumor this stocky, well-built man was an engineering officer tossed out of the Germany army for some indiscretion committed in the Far East. As his exploits in the United States increased, reports circulated that he had escaped from a British POW camp during the opening months of World War I. On one occasion Henkel alluded to a much more prosaic background, noting that he had worked in Aurora, New York, as a hardwood-floor layer before being arrested in Richmond, Virginia, as an enemy alien in June 1917.

Lodged briefly in a Norfolk jail, Henkel soon was free, leaving behind a note of thanks for courtesies extended to him by his guards. After being caught in Danville, Virginia, he was transferred to an enemy alien compound at Fort Oglethorpe, Georgia, near Chattanooga. Henkel escaped twice in August 1917, the second time from the so-called guardhouse where he had been placed following his previous outing. Army authorities tried to put him in a federal penitentiary but the Department of Justice said no. Henkel, they noted, had committed no crime.

Rebuffed, local officials quietly moved this determined prisoner to McPherson. On October 24, 1917, Washington officialdom realized what had happened and dispatched a letter seeking an explanation: Why was Arnold Henkel, a civilian, at McPherson? Of course, by the time this inquiry arrived, Henkel was somewhere in the south Georgia swamps.

Transferred back to Oglethorpe following the tunnel exploit, Henkel lay low for several months. Then, shortly after noon on May 20, 1918, he and three friends made a break for freedom. His companions were recaptured, but this time Arnold Henkel prevailed, making his way to Mexico and from there presumably home to Germany. This odyssey assures this man of a unique niche in POW annals. He is apparently one of a mere handful of German prisoners in two world wars who managed to escape from a compound within the United States and get out of the country.

One anonymous World War II escapee, like Henkel, deserves mention as well. According to the New York *Times* of August 9, 1946, this man broke out of an Oklahoma camp (just when is not known) and made his way to the coast where he stowed away on a boat bound for Lisbon. He then hitchhiked across Portugal, Spain and France, only to be seized by French police at Forbach on the German frontier. This is, of course, one of those fascinating tales of an almost unbelievable feat almost pulled off. Arnold Henkel, on the other hand, did prevail. Even if he had not, he certainly would have earned high marks for persistence. Five escapes from American hands in eleven months is an impressive record.

German prisoners of war dug numerous tunnels through American soil during World War II. On October 15, 1943, U.S. Army officers found a 150-foot shaft at a camp near Trinidad, Colorado. Twelve Germans escaped briefly through a sixty-foot excavation discovered at Camp Barkeley, Texas, on March 31, 1944. At least two tunnels were found at California's Fort Ord several months later, and undoubtedly there were others which the Provost Marshal General's Office preferred not to mention.

Gerd Kelbling, a U-boat captain held in Canada for several years, boasts that men north of the border did their share of digging too. "The only difference was guards found our tunnels before we got out." At times captors let their charges dig, knowing it would keep them busy and happy, then "discovered" their work on the eve of escape; at least that seems to have been established policy in some camps in Germany.

What makes the Papago Park enterprise unique is that the tunnel was completed and twenty-five German prisoners of war escaped. For several days the Americans were unaware that a tunnel even existed. In short, this was a highly successful undertaking, the most astonishing breakout from U.S. compounds during World War II.

Three decades later no one is quite sure who started the tunnel. At an extensive inquiry held at Papago Park after the mass escape, U.S. authorities concluded that three petty officers, Kurt Mohrdieck, Ferdinand Fuge and Kurt Strehle, began the work, discovered it was a much bigger job than they had anticipated and enlisted the assistance of others.

Gerhard Ender, a "mystery" man from the *Burgenland,* took substantial credit for the affair. Ender, who claimed he was virtually Adolf Hitler's right-hand man throughout the tumultuous 1920s, vowed that he and Fregattenkapitän Jürgen Wattenberg were the ringleaders. Emmerich von Mirbach thinks Martin Peter Reese, a young Leutnant zur See from the *U-606,* and Jürgen Schröder, a merchant marine officer, may have initiated the digging, but he is not entirely certain. "Whoever started—in the beginning they did it very secretly even within our Compound 1 A. Only a very few were taken into confidence, but as you can imagine, it was not long before everyone in 1 A knew about the digging.

"There was one man . . . also transferred in the beginning to our compound by the U.S. officials . . . I forget his name. He was transferred in as a cleaner, and as far as I can remember, he worked before as a cleaner in the officers' compound, where most of us came from.

"He once had confessed, I don't know to whom, that he was a Communist. Though his mental capacity was quite according to a cleaner's, we mistrusted him because of this. And especially to him we kept secret the whole tunnel-digging business. But finally he approached the Kapitänleutnant in charge of enlisted men's affairs within 1 A, saying he felt injured that we mistrusted him and volunteered to help dig, although he did not want to escape. We were very much impressed and in the future he was most eagerly helping us."

When digging began is more easily established. Colonel Holden took command of Papago Park on August 1, 1944. Within a month or so, certainly by mid-September, he had transferred many of the so-called troublemakers to part of Compound 1, subsequently designated as 1 A. In time the remainder (1 B) contained NCOs who refused to perform supervisory duties as stipulated by the Geneva Convention, although it stood empty throughout much of September. The other four compounds housed men considered generally cooperative, officers and enlisted men of course being segregated.

Otto Reuter, now a bookseller in the Hamburg suburb of Barsbuttel, learned of the tunnel in a bizarre fashion. Reuter, a navy man captured in North Africa and a gregarious busybody with a nose for news, was first sent to Alva, then to Papago Park. At both camps he ran a surreptitious newspaper, what he laughingly calls "Reuter's News Service." Within a couple of weeks of his arrival in Arizona, officials at Papago Park learned what was up and decided to let Reuter go legitimate. So for over a year, from March 1944 to April 1945, he produced, with official blessing, a small daily news sheet, all items clipped and condensed from American sources. He especially liked Hanson Baldwin's columns and frequently reproduced them.

In September 1944 Reuter got into trouble and was sentenced to ten days in an isolated compound a short distance outside Papago Park, the area later designated as Pima Camp. His sin was referring to Dwight David Eisenhower as "a bandit general." "It was a perfectly reasonable statement," Reuter says with a smile and a shrug. "He urged bandits—resistance forces, the underground, rebels and traitors—to aid his cause . . . so, a general who uses bandits is of course 'a bandit general.' "

Within forty-eight hours the powers at Papago Park conceded that Otto Reuter had not knowingly or intentionally insulted the supreme commander of Allied forces in Europe and told him all was forgiven: he could return to Compound 3 and resume his journalistic career. But having learned of the tunnel being dug in 1 A, Reuter chose to serve out his sentence.

"Had I gone back into my compound before my sentence was over, my comrades would have been suspicious. 'What did Reuter tell the Americans? Why was he let out of the guardhouse early? Has he perhaps become a spy?' I know how prisons work. I was held by the French for several months in 1940, captured at Dakar. Then, later, I got into trouble for listening to English radio broadcasts. I learned about the flight of Hess to Scotland and the sinking of the *Bismarck* in May 1941. For this I end up in jail once more. However, I told no one about the tunnel, no one at all. Yet on the eve of the escape most of my friends knew something big was about to happen. Prisons are very close, tight communities. It is very hard for long to keep secret anything."

The tunnel entrance was three and a half feet from the eastern end of Building T-508, a bathhouse and the structure closest to the fence surrounding Papago Park. About ten feet from the bathhouse was a large coal box, perhaps eight by ten feet and four or five feet high, easily moved about to hide any activity from guard towers, especially if the top of the box was left upright. In addition, this work was occurring in the midst of Captain Parshall's "blind spot," and the guards admittedly were not too effective, a fact Colonel Holden alluded to during the subsequent inquiry: "It must be borne in mind that we have some guard personnel at this station with faulty hearing and faulty eyesight and other physical deficiencies." One of these deficiencies seems to have been an inability to stay awake while on duty. Early in 1945 a Cheyenne youth died of a broken neck after falling from his post in a Papago Park tower. A routine patrol found his body several hours later.

By loosening boards in the side of T-508 adjacent to the coal box, the men of 1 A created an easy passageway to their excavation site. A POW could walk from his barracks, enter as if going to take a shower or wash clothes, then step through the end of T-508 and slip down into the tunnel. The entrance was covered with several feet of dirt by day, and as a double precaution, clothing was hung out to dry on lines stretched from the coal box to the bathhouse.

The entrance shaft, six feet deep, connected with a horizontal tunnel about two and a half feet in diameter. Those digging used a coal shovel (provided for the purpose of lifting coal into buckets so it could be carried to the bathhouse heating system and to stoves in the barracks when needed), a small pick with a shortened handle, and various tools given them for handicrafts.

According to Emmerich von Mirbach, work progressed in this fashion. "All those who volunteered to dig were divided into groups of three. Three groups worked each night—one from about eight to nine-thirty, the second from nine-thirty to eleven, and the third from eleven to twelve-thirty. A fourth group carefully distributed some of the soil the next day, in the afternoon, always showing the American personnel that we were working on improving our compound.

"Each group of three was divided as follows: one man was working in the head of the tunnel, the second was down in the entrance of the tunnel lifting the soil in a bucket to the third man, who also paid attention and was, in effect, 'the lookout.'"

In time, as the tunnel grew longer, the men built a small cart out of a shower-stall base with ropes attached to each end. The worker sitting at the bottom of the entrance pulled the dirt-filled vehicle toward him and then handed the dirt to the lookout. When the little four-wheeled cart was empty, the man at the end of the tunnel pulled it back down the shaft for another load.

Also, as work progressed, an electric wire connected to a bathhouse socket provided light for those underground. The wire, something Mirbach picked up at Crossville "because it looked as if it might come in handy someday," was not entirely satisfactory. Its insulated covering was badly worn and every man experienced numerous shocks. Frau Quaet-Faslem recalls with a laugh that her husband had a very healthy respect for electricity for the remainder of his life. "Many times he told me of the horror of being six feet underground, stretched out in mud and water, and getting a solid blast of electricity. It must have been a frightening experience."

The Americans thought the ground was extremely hard. In fact, according to the post engineer, he and his men often used jackhammers and compressors when digging through what was technically called "caliche," a form of decomposed granite. If they had to go deep, they used dynamite. It was, in his words, "just like knocking through tile." But according to the diggers themselves, the soil under Papago Park was not nearly as hard as the Americans thought, or as hard as they perhaps wanted those questioning them after the escape to think it was. Hans Werner Kraus says on good nights they sometimes cleared up to three feet of dirt. However, about ten feet along the way they ran into an extremely rocky section. "Some evenings we excavated only a few buckets of soil," he says. "Other times, even less. It was very disheartening. Everybody got discouraged."

At that moment this former skipper of the *U-199* became ill and spent two weeks in the base hospital. When he returned his comrades somehow had broken through the barrier and once more were moving several feet of dirt each night. To his amusement, when the Americans checked the tunnel after the breakout, those present said they took soil samples only from the "rough" section, thus substantiating what they already believed or wanted others to believe.

With work under way, several serious questions had to be answered. Precisely in what direction were they going? How far did they want to go? Was the tunnel level . . . or should it, in fact, be level? Must they go deeper in some areas than others? Would they have to build supports for any part of the tunnel? So those with engineering skills—Kraus, Mirbach and Wolfgang Spehr (a merchant marine officer from the *Weserland*)—went to work. Choosing the proposed exit and measuring the length of the tunnel were the least troublesome aspects of this dilemma. About fifty feet outside the second fence, just past a drainage ditch and a patrol road encircling the camp, stood an electric-light pole in a clump of bushes. This undergrowth was perhaps fifteen feet from the edge of the Arizona Crosscut Canal.

It was a simple matter to create a right-angle triangle centered on the tunnel entrance with the pole as a second point, the third lying somewhere out in the compound at 45 degrees to the pole and on a line parallel to the bathhouse. By measuring the leg of the triangle within the camp they knew it was 178 feet from the bathhouse to the pole.

As weeks went by, less scientific minds became concerned and wanted to measure the distance with a string. Late one night a line with a small weight attached sailed high into the air, out over the fences, over the ditch and road, landing in the bushes close by the pole. A few moments later Kraus froze as he saw a jeep and two GIs come patrolling along the highway.

"That string caught one of them right across the neck. Fortunately they were moving very slowly. He simply brushed it aside, said nothing, and the vehicle disappeared into the night. But the line broke and was still hanging on the far fence weeks later. Several times the Americans walked by, stared at the string, wondered how it got there and why. After the escape they knew."

Keeping the tunnel level, at least for much of its length, was quite difficult. Kraus rigged up a rudimentary device which helped somewhat: two candles on a plate. By placing water in the plate to be sure it was held level and sighting through two flames at a third lighted candle in the distance, one could get some idea of how things were going. Nevertheless, he concedes the tunnel actually went up and down, curving this way and that. "The drawing made by the Americans is much too neat, too complimentary to our efforts. Nobody had the slightest idea how to dig a tunnel. It was our first, you understand."

The biggest problem the diggers faced was how to get rid of the dirt. A few days after excavation began in earnest Quaet-Faslem and Guggenberger stood in the shade of a barracks and pondered the difficulties confronting them. For a week or more they had been laying out new flower beds, flushing dirt down toilets and even storing it in attics, but it was becoming apparent to all that some other means of disposal soon would be needed.

The two men stared out across the hot dusty ground toward the canal. Most of their companions were inside, away from the heat, sleeping, sweating, playing cards, chatting, dreaming of being anywhere except Papago Park. It was that pleasant, listless lull after a Sunday-midday meal when not much was happening, the major occupation being undisturbed digestion of food, nothing more.

Quaet-Faslem turned and looked through the maze of wire fences dividing the camp into numerous enclosures. To the north, Camelback Mountain glistened in the heat; to the south, the Papago Buttes loomed large. Everyone had disappeared. No one was moving anywhere.

This reverie was snapped by loud shouts as a group of GIs in shorts came piling out of the American enlisted men's area and started toward their athletic field several hundred yards away. As they went by 1 A a tall blond youngster dribbled a basketball in the dust. Another youth carried a baseball bat over his shoulder, a leather catcher's mitt hanging from it like some prize being brought home from a hunt. Were they going to play basketball or baseball? It was hard to tell.

Suddenly Quaet-Faslem posed a question: "Fritz, shouldn't we have a sports area in this compound? We are not really being disciplined. We are not in the guardhouse or anything like that. Does the Geneva Convention say anything on this point?"

"I think they are supposed to 'encourage' sports. Does tunnel digging qualify as an outdoor sport even though it is underground?"

"I'm serious. We at least had a level spot back in Compound 5 where we could play faustball occasionally. The guards called it 'volleyball,' I think. Here we have nothing. The ground is too rough. It needs to be leveled out over there by the canal."

"Needs to be leveled out. That's it, Jürgen! If we go to work creating a sports area, dirt gets moved about. Tunnel dirt can be brought up here. Wonderful! Besides, who knows, it just might work."

An hour later the four captains gathered for a strategy session on the site of the proposed athletic field. Maus was ecstatic, jumping up and down as if already playing faustball. Kraus watched in amused silence, smiling broadly, but he remained skeptical. He didn't think the Americans were foolish enough to allow it. "It is almost too obvious. They will be suspicious of loose dirt lying around—or they should be. But I think all of us should talk with Lieutenant Watson as soon as possible."

Guggenberger, grinning broadly, quickly agreed. "However," he added, "while we're at it we should consider the whole scope of this undertaking. We dig the tunnel. We get rid of the dirt at the sports field, at least most of it. It will probably take us about ten or twelve weeks at the rate we're moving. During that time we must think about food, supplies, clothing, identity papers, how to keep our departure a secret as long as possible, who shall go out . . ."

"Wait a minute. What do you mean, who shall go out?" exclaimed Maus. "Anyone who digs can leave. That should be made clear from the beginning. Those who do not dig cannot go. And another thing—before long we'll be forced to tell everyone what's going on. How do you explain groups of three wandering off to the bathhouse every few hours throughout the evening? The guards may not notice; the men will. I had to tell Clarus and Günther today. They are eager to help out. They said they would recruit a third man and set up another digging crew.

"Actually, Fritz, you are raising several key issues here. How do we prepare for our departure? How do we conceal it? We can't use substitutes this time. How do we plan to make our way to Mexico? What I propose is that we try to see Watson tomorrow morning and meet in the afternoon for a round of bridge to talk over these matters. That should give us time to reflect, think over what is actually involved."

Quaet-Faslem, silent so far, nodded vigorously in agreement. "Food is the most important thing. That is what caused Kottmann, Johannsen and me much trouble. We must have something light, easy to carry, and enough to last three weeks. Thirty or more men may get out, so I don't think any of us can use buses and trains this time. We'll have to walk in order to contact as few Americans as possible."

The next morning, as soon as the head count was over, the four young officers, together with Wattenberg, chatted briefly with the American lieutenant. By this date the Fregatt-enkapitän had become what one might call "chairman of the board." Technically he was leader and spokesman for 1 A,

permitted to revel in whatever prestige that position bestowed upon him, but throughout the compound, little doubt
existed as to who was really calling the shots: Guggenberger,
Maus, Kraus and Quaet-Faslem.

William S. Watson, an affable, gregarious man, was also in
charge of their old area, Compound 5. He quickly agreed
that they could build a faustball field, with Colonel Holden's
permission, of course. The Americans would provide them
with shovels and rakes which, Watson emphasized, would
have to be turned in to the guards at the end of each day.
He even offered to get Lieutenant Thomas V. Jackson, the
post engineer, to bring in a few truck loads of dirt to speed up
the work.

Holden was as pleased as Watson when he learned of the
plans for a sports field in 1 A. He quickly gave his approval,
and later that day two shovels and two rakes appeared. Wattenberg lifted the first bit of soil in mock ceremony as thirty
men cheered and applauded. About half of them knew the
true purpose of the faustball field; soon all would share in the
great secret.

Late that afternoon Guggenberger, Quaet-Faslem, Maus and
Kraus sat around a small table in the shade of Barracks 6.
Mirbach looked down on them from an open window, on
guard to be certain no one overheard their discussion. They
both were and were not playing cards. It was a desultory
game interspersed with much talk and considerable laughter.

Quaet-Faslem was back to food again, his favorite topic.
They could get chocolate, Red Cross black bread and coffee,
and perhaps pick some fruit along the way, at least near
Phoenix, but they needed some basic item, he stressed, around
which to build their diet.

Kraus raised his hand slightly as if seeking attention in class.
"Let's consider something we can get by on for up to three
weeks. I think we could toast American bread, pulverize it
into crumbs, and package it tightly so it will not spoil. Then
for a meal we could mix a package with milk or water. It

would make sort of a mush that might be monotonous but it would be nourishing and easy to carry."

Guggenberger agreed with a smile. "You know those little breakfast-food boxes we get, the individual size? How about saving the waxed-paper envelopes, filling them with the crumbs, then resealing them?"

Even Quaet-Faslem was satisfied. Bread crumbs it would be. After further discussion they reiterated that those planning to use the tunnel must help dig and men would escape by twos and threes, no more than three in a group. It would be up to each group to assemble food, clothing and other necessary items; however, the four captains would review planning as it took shape.

How to conceal their departure? "Well," Guggenberger said, "if we all go out, then it's impossible. It should be a weekend and preferably a holiday. I'm aiming for Christmas. This place will fall apart then, I'm sure of it. Remember what Crossville was like?"

"But we are not all going out," Maus said. "It is just not feasible. You recall, Fritz, the last time we thought we had a five percent chance of success. I'm sure it's even less now." He looked up at Mirbach and grinned. "I'm for the tunnel and will work hard, but both Emmerich and I have our doubts. We are not sure we want to go out. My point is, even if we told every man in 1 A about the tunnel this evening, I am sure ten or fifteen of them would feel the same way. Remember, this is not such a bad life. No work, good food, leisure time, soon a sports field even.

"Besides, someone has to be here to seal up the tunnel. If twenty men go, that leaves eleven of us. We can't possibly cover up so many absences for very long. They take head counts twice a day during the week and now once on Sunday, too. Of course, that is the reason Fritz is aiming for a weekend and he's right. If the escape takes place on Saturday night, we might hide it until late Sunday afternoon, perhaps sixteen to twenty hours, no longer."

"Unless," interjected Wattenberg, who had walked up quietly and was standing behind Maus, "we somehow confuse the count taken that Sunday evening. That would give us even more time."

"Yes, but how? How, Fregattenkapitän Wattenberg?" Mirbach asked from the barracks window. "What truly marvelous scheme do you have in mind?"

Wattenberg ignored this impertinence, continuing to concentrate his attention on the four cardplayers. "We must insist that these counts be taken only by officers, not sergeants. It is only proper that as German officers, we have respect and equal treatment."

"So, you think an American major or lieutenant colonel will come out twice a day to count you, Günther and Spehr?" Mirbach asked, laughing.

"No, Mirbach. I'm sure that will never happen. But creating confusion concerning the count could work to our advantage."

"Wait a minute, Emmerich," Guggenberger said. "Fregattenkapitän Wattenberg may be on to something. Screwing up the counting process is about all we can do. It's our only hope. However, first we should build some more flower beds, get the faustball field under way, and start hoarding food. We are on good terms with the Americans at the moment. Let's not rock the boat for a few weeks, anyway. I agree that insisting on a high-ranking officer at roll calls is much to ask. But if we ask for much, we may be able to compromise and settle for something less."

Ten days went by and hopes for speedy progress on the tunnel soon evaporated. A hard vein of rock resisted all efforts to push it aside, Kraus was in the hospital, and Lieutenant Watson produced no dirt, although each morning he promised a truckload would appear shortly. To make matters worse, Wattenberg was insisting that the head-count battle commence at once. Somehow this had become their elder statesman's sole contribution to the tunnel affair. He did not dig. Only that morning at breakfast he had pointedly reminded Maus and Guggenberger that he was, after all, compound spokesman.

The four captains finally decided that everyone had to be told about the entire plan—tunnel, sports field, head count. Maus also proposed that they leave a pile of dirt out by the athletic area and see what happened. He agreed it was very risky but pointed to two possible advantages. "I've noticed," he said, "that Watson and Jackson, the post engineer, do not know each other very well. It is possible that our little compound commander might *think* the engineering officer brought in some dirt even if he didn't. And if the head-count fracas causes fireworks—and I believe it will—they might not notice the dirt at all. If so, we are in business again, providing we can blast through that rock wall down there. In any case it is worth a try. Of course to be correct we should inform W."

An hour later they told Wattenberg of their decision, suggesting he tell the men what actually was going on. Just after evening roll call the Fregattenkapitän met the enlisted men in their barracks, Maus and Mirbach standing guard at each end. The result was electrifying. The tunnel naturally interested them most, but they also found the head-count ploy provocative and amusing. Supper was the noisiest in days; even the guards commented that something must be happening in 1 A. The Krauts, they concluded, must be dipping into their raisins-and-fruit-juice mixture again.

The following morning Corporal Eugene Hoya, acting sergeant for Compound 1 A, tried unsuccessfully to conduct roll call. The enlisted men formed in two ranks, but the officers refused to leave their barracks. Kozur, detailed by Wattenberg, politely informed the American of their new policy: officers must be counted by officers of at least equal rank, not by enlisted men.

Hoya eventually gave up and left, but twenty minutes later was back, accompanied by Lieutenant Watson. Watson conferred briefly with Wattenberg, Günther and Spehr, told them they were courting disaster, and then he, too, departed. Shortly before noon Colonel Holden appeared and warned the prisoners that unless every man stood evening head count, the entire compound would be put on a restricted diet. "And," Holden added emphatically as he turned to leave, "this compound will remain on short rations until it conforms to the accepted rules of the Geneva Convention."

The roll-call strike lasted sixteen days. Actually the diet was not as limited as the Americans thought. The nonworking NCOs in 1 B managed to get some food through the fence to them from time to time. Red Cross packages stored away for snacks also helped ease hunger pangs. Eventually a compromise of sorts was worked out which the Germans accepted because they had to begin accumulating food for their Christmas vacation.

As a matter of fact, many of them noted wryly, the American colonel was doing them a favor. They would not have to dig such a big hole for slim bodies. The compromise stipulated that all men, irrespective of rank, would be present for roll call every morning except Sunday at 0900, every afternoon at 1615. Senior officers were responsible for assembling all personnel so that a physical count could be taken each weekday morning, a cross-over roll call in the afternoons. By tacit agreement, however, those above the rank of Kapitän-leutnant—that is, all senior officers—merely had to appear at the doorway of their barracks to be counted.

Wattenberg had won a small victory, the tunnelers a much bigger one. While the Americans fretted and stewed over the head-count strike, a pile of dirt appeared near the sports area, as Maus had suggested. No one said anything about it. It simply set there, attracting no comment, no questions, no attention, nothing. Meanwhile the tunnel crews broke through into softer soil, and a new routine developed. Each night's production came to the bathhouse and then was taken out to the pile site, most of the dirt there having been spread by another crew shortly after dark. American guards and officers soon became accustomed to the mound, roughly the same size and shape from day to day, not realizing that each morning when the sun came up its rays illuminated a fresh supply of dirt.

Yet Wattenberg's strike had other, more subtle effects which should not be ignored. It made of 1 A a relatively cohesive unit. Men and officers hungered together, dug together, sweated and swore together as they moved tons of dirt about, all sharing the same great secret. Whether such was Wattenberg's intent is not clear, but the common ordeal spawned by his head-count skirmish was a key ingredient in making the tunnel enterprise a success. Of course, breaking through the rough area at the same time was of substantial importance, too. It seemed to the men that somehow their sacrifice was being rewarded, their prayers answered . . . and it was all worthwhile.

A high point of this adventure, just short of the moment of escape itself, was the visit in mid-November of a group of high-ranking officers from the 9th Service Command headquarters. These gentlemen, sent down from Fort Douglas to see how a really efficient POW operation worked, toured all of the compounds, including 1 A. While there, a colonel planted both feet firmly on top of the tunnel entrance and proclaimed in a confident voice that Papago Park need never be concerned with tunnels. It simply was impossible to dig in this soil; it was hard as a rock. Everyone smiled, including some of the prisoners themselves. Fortunately, none of them laughed—that is, not until the American officers left.

The last month of digging went well enough. Crews reported for duty with new zeal as the end grew nearer and the men became almost professional, skilled as diggers and equally adept at camouflaging what they were doing. The last fifty feet were by far the hardest. In this section the prisoners had to allow for a six-foot drainage ditch and the adjoining roadway used by jeeps that patrolled around the entire camp. This meant they had to go deeper so as to leave sufficient support for both, although, as it turned out, no shoring was needed—the soil was firm enough to form sides and a roof as they cut through it. But having dug deep under the roadway, the tunnelers had to come up quickly to exit near the electric-light pole and not, by mistake, break into the canal and flood months of extremely hard labor. The result was a stair step, a double elbow (not shown on the U.S. Army drawing of the tunnel). Also, problems posed by the ditch and road created a cul-de-sac where breathing was extremely difficult. To that point the men were able to breathe fairly well, since the tunnel was reasonably level, but from there on, the diggers could remain underground for only a few minutes, ten or fifteen at the most.

On December 20 the four captains decided they had gone far enough. The tunnel was exactly 178 feet long, but did it end where they thought it did? Guggenberger concluded there was only one way to find out. "Quaet-Faslem and I took a long poker from the bathhouse and crawled the full length of the tunnel. We also had a very thin stick with a small rag tied to one end. With the poker we drove a hole upward into the open air. It smelled fresh and good rushing in from the outside. Then, up went the little flag. For a few moments —it seemed an eternity—nothing happened. Had we failed? What had gone wrong? Had we done all of this work for nothing? Then we heard cheers. Men on the roof of one of the barracks had seen the flag, after all. And it came up right where we hoped it would. All we had to do now was finish off the exit, 'pack-all-our-stuff,' as the American guards frequently ordered us to do when we got shifted from camp to camp or compound to compound, and be on our way. Merry Christmas! Merry Christmas!"

In these exciting months the men of 1 A were given immeasurable assistance by Colonel Holden. He had collected the most experienced breakout artists in the camp and put them together in a single compound which, as hindsight revealed (and foresight might have, too) was ideal for tunneling. He would not let them join work details outside their compound, allowed them to sleep late each morning and constantly added to their numbers, thus only increasing the supply of tunnel diggers. In September there were thirty "troublemakers"; by Christmas Eve their ranks had swelled to sixty-two.

Just how one earned a place on Colonel Holden's "bad boy" list was not always clear. Escapees such as Guggenberger, Maus, Quaet-Faslem, Kottmann, Mohrdieck, Sternberg (three outings to his credit) and Fuge (two) knew why they were in Compound 1 A. So did Artur Karstens, a seaman from the U-575 sunk in the North Atlantic in March 1944. This twenty-two-year-old Barskamp native had jumped to momentary freedom from a speeding train near Tucson on May 6, 1944.

Karl Heinz Frenzel and Herbert Fuchs, two enlisted men who fled from a work camp in Safford, Arizona, on August 30, 1944, realized why they qualified for membership. So did Kurt Strehle, a six-foot petty officer captured in North Africa. In June, Dieter Elbert and Strehle escaped from a work detail the latter was supposed to be supervising. They got as far as an Indian-reservation store at Sells, where Elbert, who had once worked briefly in Detroit, encountered difficulty when he tried to make a purchase without ration stamps.

Johann Kremer, Walter Kozur's friend from the U-162, also knew why he was in 1 A. He and another man had escaped from Stringtown. His companion was shot dead during that break for freedom. Kremer's record alone probably would have gained him admission, but when he and Kozur adamantly refused to pick Arizona cotton, they, too, ended up in 1 A. All told, these men had accounted for at least seventeen escapes and thus had a very valuable cache of experience to be shared with comrades eager to emulate their exploits.

Fritz Kaiser was classified as a troublemaker because he conducted fraudulent head counts when the five U-boat captains escaped in February of 1944, Fregattenkapitän Wattenberg because he obviously and constantly did cause trouble for one camp commander after another, always complaining about innumerable minor issues. Wolfgang Clarus got to 1 A because he taught enlisted men to escape "better" and how to stay out longer.

But three decades later some men are still unsure just how

and why they provoked Holden's ire. Hans Werner Kraus thinks an Iron Cross must have equaled "troublemaker" in American eyes. Emmerich von Mirbach says only a few men knew precisely why the colonel transferred them to his special compound. But all agreed on one thing once they got there: if the Americans thought they were "troublemakers," then, like good soldiers, they must live up to their reputation.

Yet there was no point in following Wattenberg's example and causing trouble merely to cause trouble. Mirbach, Kaiser, the four captains and their comrades agreed that whatever they did must have a purpose, a reason. Once they began to dig underground, much of what they did aboveground was designed to throw sand in American eyes, keep their guards and officers confused and unaware of what was actually going on in Compound 1 A on the banks of the Arizona Crosscut Canal.

Chapter 7

GETTING READY FOR CHRISTMAS

By the last week in November, thirty-one of the sixty POWs in Compound 1 A had formed twelve escape teams composed of two or three men. Several petty officers in 1 B, although unable to dig, expressed keen interest in joining them. At first Maus and Guggenberger were opposed. Activity from the adjoining compound could wreck the entire operation. Maus insisted that only those who dug should go out, but Wattenberg's stern announcement that he was leaving and taking two men from the *U-162* with him, Kozur and Kremer, undercut this argument somewhat.

Prime candidates from among their neighbors were Reinhard Mark and Heinrich Palmer, the young petty officers from the *Weserland*. Instrumental in passing food to 1 A during the hunger strike, they said they would go out together, collect their own provisions, clothing, everything. On the twenty-fourth Guggenberger told Kremer to pass the word: Mark and Palmer could go.

That same day the two men began a rigorous training program, jogging around their compound, first for only fifteen minutes, slowly building up to forty-five minutes, then an hour. Each day, hot, cold, rain, wind, Mark and Palmer made their rounds. Some 1 B men, not aware of the tunnel, thought they were nuts, "the two crazy runners." Guards wrote them off as a couple of health freaks, taunting them as they splashed through puddles of water or passed by a tower, sweat streaming down their faces.

Since contact with 1 A was somewhat limited, these two men were on their own. They had to prepare for Christmas as best they could. To get American money Palmer, with Mark's assistance, speeded up his production of Nazi paraphernalia. Using shoe polish and sand for molds and melted toothpaste tubes as metal, he turned out Iron Crosses, Eagles, shoulder clasps, and so on, all eagerly snapped up by GIs as soon as these souvenirs were properly painted and scuffed a bit to show wear. Occasionally, instead of demanding money, they traded some knickknack for a shirt, socks, any piece of clothing that might come in handy.

By December 20 these petty officers were packed and ready to go. Each of them had fourteen bags of bread crumbs, canned milk, a canteen of water, some German Red Cross food packets, extra socks, a sweater, a jar of brewed coffee, six bars of chocolate, several packs of cigarettes, matches and toilet articles. Each man also carried a prize item, a personal contribution to the success of their venture. Mark had a Conoco highway map of Arizona and northern Mexico given to him by a *Weserland* seaman from Compound 3 who found it one day while on a work detail near Mesa. Well, he didn't actually "find" it; the man lifted it from the seat of a parked car near a field where he was picking cotton.

Palmer's treasure was a tube of shaving cream into which, by carefully opening one end and then with equal care and skill resealing it, he had inserted two $10 bills wrapped securely in cigarette paper. Palmer also had a very valuable going-away gift from a friend in Compound 2: a compass appropriated from a U.S. Army truck.

Holiday preparations in 1 A were similar, although more coordinated. Walter Kozur, who, it turned out, would be one of the last men to go out through the tunnel, eagerly took on the task of creating the cover to be placed over the exit. Early in December he spent several minutes with Mirbach and Guggenberger, found out precisely what size the opening would be, and then built two shallow boxes out of scrap lumber. Each was about a foot wide and a foot and a half long. Placed side by side, they would fit neatly over the opening.

One afternoon Kozur and Kremer worked on the faustball field for several hours while actually analyzing the ground outside the fence. The cover must blend in well with nearby soil and bushes. That evening they filled the boxes with dirt, sand and tufts of grass. Twigs and leaves could be added later. Within ten days, carefully watered and placed under an empty barracks, the crop was doing nicely.

Karl Heinz Frenzel and Kremer became the tailors for the escapees. Anyone with clothing to be repaired or transformed into civilian garb saw them. Frenzel, a twenty-one-year-old youth with wavy blond hair, spoke English quite well. Captured by the British near Bengazi, he and another youngster, Herbert Fuchs, were promoted to 1 A after they escaped from a branch camp in August 1944. Fuchs, a year older than Frenzel, was a U-boat veteran from Dresden. Their six-day vacation puzzled the Americans. The pair obviously made no attempt to go far or head for Mexico. "These mountains," Frenzel said with a grin when captured, "remind us much of home. We only wished to hike and go on holiday."

Kraus and Clarus handled passports and identification papers. Getting recent photographs was an easy matter. Although no one in the compound had a camera or any way to obtain or develop film, their captors proved to be surprisingly obliging. Eager to show how well the troublemakers were being treated, an almost steady stream of photographers snapped portraits to be shipped home to relatives in Germany. Some, of course, stayed in Papago Park, and with the aid of official-looking stamps cut from leather and rubber scraps, soon looked somewhat like passport photos. For example, a document carried by Wolfgang Clarus during the escape, purported to be of Guatemalan origin, was copied from an illustration found in *Life* magazine.

"If I ever run a prisoner-of-war camp," Hans Werner Kraus declared three decades later, "the very first thing I would do is ban photographers. Every last one of them." This ex-captain noted it might be well to outlaw radios, too. Given the expertise in their midst and the fact that enlisted men who worked in and around U.S. Army installations easily could pick up all sorts of equipment (and did), almost every POW compound in America soon was listening to stations broadcasting from the Third Reich. Needless to add, 1 A in Papago Park was no exception. Each day the troublemakers had two versions of the news: Otto Reuter's little sheet, which Colonel Holden permitted him to produce, and their own handwritten edition compiled from sources at home.

Since all of these POWs were navy men, their disguises, in one way or another, whatever tales they chose to weave, began with that fact. Like Guggenberger and Maus before them, most planned to pose as foreign sailors of Allied or neutral persuasion somehow cast adrift in Arizona's desert country. If accosted by local authorities, each group would say it was trying to get from the Gulf Coast to California or vice versa.

Perhaps this was not a very believable tale, but given the circumstances, what other story was possible? The object of the game was, of course, to get into Mexico so quickly that they would meet no one. With luck they might not have to produce phony documents or tell stories of any kind.

To some extent, food was a personal matter. Each man had to hoard his own and provide a bag or rucksack for his gear. Yet, since everyone had to get by with less in order to pile up these stores, food was a compound problem as well. Nearly all of the supplies for the escape were placed on shelves in the compound kitchen, where they attracted no special attention. Since the prisoners ran their own mess hall, where and how they stowed things away was pretty much their own business. As long as the compound was neat and reasonably clean, few questions were asked.

Each group was free to chart its own course once it got outside the camp. All would travel by night, hide and rest during daylight hours. Whether they would use trains and buses provoked some debate. Quaet-Faslem did not think it would work. "More than thirty men dressed in strange clothing and speaking with foreign accents showing up in Phoenix and Tucson at about the same time? No, it's much too risky. Also, I don't believe we are familiar enough with the idiosyncrasies of everyday American life. The slightest misstep could be disastrous, you know. It will take longer but it will be much safer to strike out across the open country. Move only in the dark. Speak to no one."

For all of these reasons, Guggenberger and Kraus agreed. And there was another very compelling fact: they would need every cent they had when and if they got south of the border. Money, it was rumored, was one language almost any Mexican understood.

Wolfgang Clarus listened intently to whatever the four captains had to say concerning escape techniques. They had experience. This would be his first attempt. Yet every time he looked at a map of Arizona he already felt tired. He was a naval officer, not a foot soldier. The border was at least 130 miles from Phoenix. By the time he and the men in his group went up and down mountains, around towns and villages, backtracked to find just the right spot to hide during the day, lost and found their way, they probably would trudge another forty or fifty miles, perhaps even more. That was nearly two hundred miles . . . 320 kilometers!

Clarus studied the map closely. Sasabe, Lukeville, Ajo, Gila Bend. These were strange names. Gila Bend. His eyes narrowed as his right index finger traced a river, the Gila, winding its way from a juncture with the Salt just west of Phoenix to Liberty, Buckeye, then south to Gila Bend. After making a large U turn, as the name of the town suggested, the Gila flowed southwest to join the Colorado, almost at the international boundary. The Colorado was huge, and according to the map, the waters of the Gila increased substantially about forty miles west of Phoenix.

Excited, his mind filled with a wild scheme that just might work, Clarus measured the distance from Gila Bend to Yuma on the Colorado. It was perhaps 120 miles. Why not float down the mighty Gila? They could walk forty or fifty miles westward from Papago Park, then ride that river's waters the rest of the way to freedom.

Günther stared at Clarus, his mouth hanging open in disbelief. This young man had taken a train from Tunis to Bizerte when it couldn't be done. Now he wanted to build a boat and cruise down some river instead of hiking to Mexico. Günther burst out laughing. It was so outrageous that it was worth considering. The coast artillery captain turned toward Friedrich Utzolino, the third member of their escape unit. "What do you say, Fritz? Do you want to go to sea again in the middle of the great American state of Arizona?"

Utzolino, slightly shorter than both Clarus and Günther and a year or so older than the captain, also coast artillery and like them captured in North Africa, rubbed the two-day growth of red-blond stubble on his chin. He neither smiled nor laughed. By nature Leutnant Utzolino was a serious man. "Clarus," he asked in an even, matter-of-fact tone, "how do we get our boat out through the tunnel?" The word "our" indicated that Utzolino was ready to go into the boat-building business at once. As far as he was concerned, the matter was settled. He assumed, as did Clarus, that they could find scrap material easily enough.

"It seems to me that we can make a canvas skin which can be rolled up, and a wooden frame—struts, if you will—that could go into a second bag." As Clarus talked his hands cut through the air outlining what he had in mind. "Each part will have to be no more than eighteen inches wide when folded up. One problem is, in contrast to the other men we will be carrying the boat, and food and clothing, too. But I think it can be done. It will not be heavy, just awkward. Once

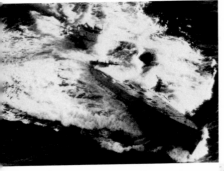

LEFT: The *U-185*, caught off the Azores in August 1943, nearly completed a hair-raising cruise marred by French sabotage and numerous air attacks which also included the rescue of two other U-boat crews from doomed craft.

RIGHT: Sailors on a Canadian destroyer pick up survivors of the *U-569*, the first sub sunk by American carrier-based planes in the North Atlantic in May 1943. About half of the forty-six-man crew of this over-age 500-ton craft, destined to be retired from service when it returned to France, were rescued.

LEFT: Men from the *Weserland*, a German blockade runner en route from Japan to Europe, wait to board a U.S. warship. The *Weserland* and two other large ships laden with war supplies from the Far East were sunk in the South Atlantic, January 3-5, 1944.

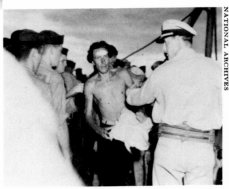

RIGHT: Moment of capture. August Maus, age twenty-eight, dazed commander of the *U-185*, is helped aboard the *Core*, the American carrier whose planes have just sunk his submarine.

Emmerich von Mirbach (*standing*) chats with Jürgen Quaet-Faslem on board a U.S. transport bound for America. Quaet-Faslem was captain and Mirbach engineering officer of the *U-595*, scuttled off Algeria in November 1942. In an ironic twist, this sub crew was captured by a U.S. tank unit.

Weserland crewmen enter a temporary enclosure in Recife, Brazil, the first of many barbed-wire compounds they would call home.

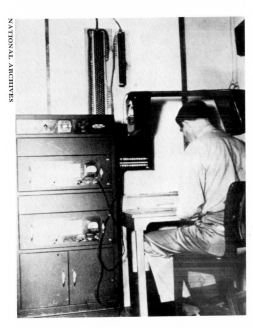

A GI at Fort Hunt, a secret POW interrogation center near Washington, D.C., monitors cell conversations which included politics, gossip, sex, jokes, songs, and even parodies of American interrogation techniques.

The nerve center at Fort Hunt. Blackboard gives roster of POW "guests" and lists American experts responsible for interrogating them.

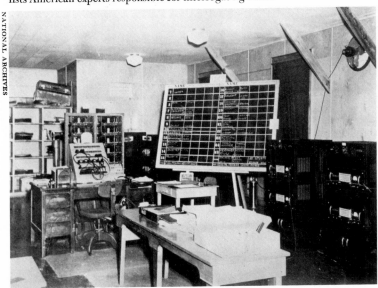

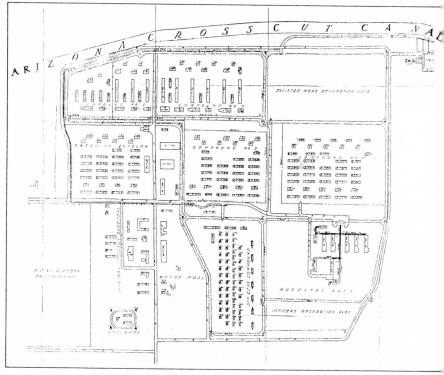

Camp Papago Park near Phoenix, Arizona. Compound 1 (in upper left-hand corner close by the Arizona Crosscut Canal) was divided so as to provide special quarters for "uncooperative" POWs.

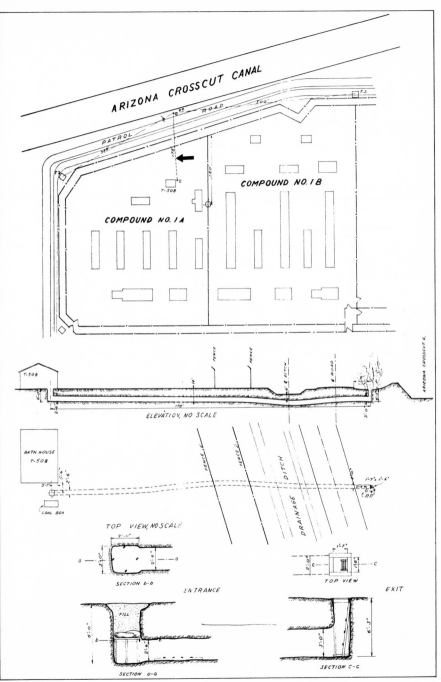

Compounds 1 A and 1 B and the 178-foot tunnel. According to the tunnelers, this U.S. Army diagram of their work is much too complimentary. It actually zigged, zagged and went up and down. "Nobody had the slightest idea how to dig a tunnel," says Hans Werner Kraus. "It was our first, you understand."

The tunnel entrance was strategically placed between a bathhouse and a coal box shown in the foreground. Note sand bags which filled the opening and for several hours thwarted all efforts to locate the entrance.

The carefully constructed exit. Dirt-filled boxes covering this opening held grass and weeds cultivated to blend with the surrounding area.

PHOENIX GAZETTE
Phoenix, Arizona
Thursday, December 28, 1944

Wily Germans Elude Chase

The greatest man hunt in Arizona's history continued to baffle authorities Thursday as they pressed the search for the 19 escaped German prisoners of war.

Each tip received by authorities is being checked, but so far all have been without results.

Twenty - five Germans, many of them officers, escaped from the Papago Park camp last

Capt. Jurgen Wattenberg

Sunday evening. Within a short time six had been captured or had surrendered. The remaining 19 have since remained at large.

The search is being concentrated in the desert area between Phoenix and the Mexican border, 191 miles to the south and extending to points near the Gulf of California.

Military personnel, agents of the Federal Bureau of Investigation, sheriff's deputies and other police officers, in addition to interested citizens, are taking part in the search.

Officials are authorized to pay up to $25 to the person or persons capturing a prisoner of war. They will pay $25 if the man is captured and returned to the camp. If the army is called to return a captured man, $15 will be paid.

Pictures of the 19 escaped Germans have been released to newspapers by the FBI in a hope that their publication will help lead to apprehension.

$25 REWARD FOR EACH OF THESE MEN

Kurt Mohrdieck	Capt. Jurgen Quaet Faslem	Reinhard Mark	Second Lt. Martin P. Reese	Johann Kremer	Heinrich Palmer
Walter Kozur	First Lt. F. Utzolino	Capt. Hans Werner Kraus	Capt. Wilhelm Gunther	First Officer Jurgen Schroder	Second Lt. Helmut Drescher
Capt. Fritz Guggenberger	Second Lt. Hans Zundorf	First Lt. Wolf Clarus	Friederich Sternberg	First Lt. Otto Hoferichter	Artur Karstens

Countless Arizona ranchers and Indian scouts carried this clipping from the Phoenix *Gazette* (December 28, 1944) in their pockets, and several put it to good use.

LEFT: The masterminds. These four U-boat captains coordinated and carried out this daring exploit. *Left to right:* Hans Werner Kraus, Friedrich Guggenberger, August Maus and Jürgen Quaet-Faslem. All except Kraus had escaped from Papago Park once before.

RIGHT: The troublemakers in Pima Camp. All of these men played some role in the escape plot. *Left to right, standing:* Fuge, Hoffman, Guggenberger, Kraus, Schröder, Wattenberg, Maus, (unidentified), Clarus, Quaet-Faslem and Strehle. *Left to right, kneeling:* (unidentified), Mohrdieck, who escaped from Papago Park three times, and Ender, the "mystery man."

Three decades later. Margarete Kozur of Dortmund listens intently as her husband, Walter Kozur (*center*), tells the author about his tunnel adventure and weeks spent in the mountains of Arizona.

out of the tunnel, most of our troubles are over. And once at the Gila, we simply drift downstream to Mexico. Let the river do the work. Here is a sketch I've made."

Three heads bent intently over the small piece of paper Clarus spread out on his bed. Günther, a man of considerable practical experience who had come up through the ranks, studied the drawing carefully and with a short laugh pronounced the plan feasible. He suggested that the cross pieces be somewhat stronger and was about to propose another minor alteration when he saw Mirbach approaching their barracks. "Emmerich, do you have a moment? See what you think of this. After all, you are an engineering man and have served on U-boats."

Like Günther, Mirbach thought the scheme ridiculous, preposterous, wonderful. Taking a folding boat out through a 178-foot tunnel was insane, of course. But Mirbach agreed that it was just insane enough to be feasible. They probably would not be able to float all the way to Yuma. There would be dams and open stretches near towns and villages. Nevertheless, he agreed it could be a quick, easy, even comfortable way to cover many miles.

Within an hour the boat, still only a sketch, was the talk of 1 A. By suppertime Wattenberg had offered to christen the craft, and others already were proposing names: "Gila," "Freedom," "Faustball," "Oberst Holden," "Watson's Warship," "The Arizona," "The Troublemaker," "The Papago Park Packet Line," and so on. Clarus, Günther and Utzolino scoffed good-naturedly at all of these suggestions. "If you wish to help," Clarus announced in serious tones, "then give us not names, ceremony and advice, but wood. Pieces of wood, that is what we really need."

Some minor changes here and there to make up for the lack of materials, and within a few days the frame of a flatboat just large enough to carry three men and their gear began to take shape. The "three mad boatmen," as they were now called, did much of the work under the eyes of guards. But for all they knew, this was simply another silly handicrafts project. Pieces were fashioned during the day, then assembled and tested at night, only to be immediately broken down and stored in an empty barracks, the same building where Quaet-Faslem, Guggenberger and others now were training regularly with forty-pound rucksacks.

The skin or covering presented a small but not insurmountable problem. Wattenberg easily convinced Lieutenant Watson that the roof of Barracks 5 needed repair, which was true. Being seamen, he added casually, they believed canvas and tar would work best and the men would gladly do the job themselves. Watson was delighted. The troublemakers were coming out of that silly roll-call strike quite nicely. They even were offering to fix up their own quarters for the winter.

"Sewing that canvas was a tremendous job. I broke needles, fingernails, thread. It must have taken me at least two weeks," Clarus recalls, shaking his head in mock sorrow. "Without the help of Frenzel and others it would have been impossible. About mid-December, perhaps ten days before we were to go out, the covering was finished."

At last they were able to put the boat together. All that remained to be done was tar the skin, test the boat in water, and then break it down for packing so it would go out through the tunnel. The assembled craft, tarred, stood in an empty barracks for nearly a week. Clarus still wonders how come the Americans didn't discover it.

"They were, I am certain, lulled into a sense of false security. Lock up sixty men behind double fences eight feet tall, have guards watch them around the clock . . . what could they possibly do? What difference did it make if some of the barracks in 1 A were empty? Actually, it made considerable difference. We put that space to good use. And, strangely, any shakedown or impromptu inspection always concentrated on the buildings we were living in. The Americans assumed the empty structures were locked tight. I suppose they were, I can't remember now, but it was a simple matter to go through a window or pry open a lock so it easily could be closed again if necessary.

"Testing the boat for leaks was a compound-wide affair, almost a celebration. One evening, as soon as it got dark, we simply dug a hole between two of the barracks, filled it with water and put our boat in it. The 'ship' floated beautifully. If it hadn't, I am sure I would have burst into tears. First I crawled in, then Günther and Utzolino. It was big enough, just big enough. Scores of faces loomed at the windows above us, all eager to see the 'three mad boatmen' and their crazy creation. Our combined weight forced the boat to the bottom of our shallow test tank, but the craft seemed waterproof. It did not leak, not a bit. We had done our work well. It was a proud moment. Later it turned out that we actually had made one very serious mistake. In fact, two."

Santa Claus, Bastogne, citrus-fruit schnaps, Field Marshal Karl Rudolf Gerd von Rundstedt, curtailment of beer-drinking privileges. At first it is rather difficult to see how these items are related. Yet on Saturday, December 23, 1944, they melded into a marvelous brew that almost blew the lid off Compound 1 B in Colonel Holden's Papago Park. Rundstedt, a brilliant, thin-lipped veteran of World War I, led the Christmas offensive of 1944, the so-called Battle of the Bulge. It proved to be a "last hurrah," but for a week or more, rolling westward into Belgium, killing and capturing thousands of Allied soldiers, German legions made one last grasp for the laurel leaves of victory. This Nazi onslaught cast a dark pall over the holiday season of their adversaries, increased rationing and war-bond sales in the United States, and delighted German comrades scattered throughout the world. POWs in Staffordshire, England, rioted in celebration, and every camp in Canada and the United States seethed with excitement and unrest. Perhaps, just perhaps there was a chance, after all.

This unexpected offensive by a supposedly beaten enemy even pushed Joan Barry, Charlie Chaplin and Lupe Velez off the front pages of American tabloids. Miss Barry claimed Chaplin was the father of her daughter. The fiery Lupe took an overdose of sleeping pills, killing herself and her unborn child, but not before fingering the man presumably responsible.

The trouble at Papago Park really started on the night of December 15. German successes on Europe's western front, celebration of a POW's birthday, and too much beer inspired a raucous party in Compound 1 B which guards finally broke up at two o'clock in the morning. From time to time prisoners were allowed bottles of beer; however, this was a special privilege and the beer was supposed to be consumed in the compound's canteen, not in the barracks. As a result of this outburst Holden ordered all beer removed from 1 B's canteen for a period of thirty days.

With the approach of the holiday weekend Papago Park's command prepared for still more unrest. The Americans were aware that even without Rundstedt's offensive and curtailment of drinking privileges in one of the compounds, the Germans would try to disrupt normal camp routine so as to spoil Christmas for their captors. What they failed to realize was the lengths to which the men in 1 A were willing to go . . . had, in fact, gone already.

At 1300 on the twenty-third, Colonel Holden called his officers together and issued a stern proclamation which, translated into German, was then posted in all compounds.

MEMORANDUM/MERKBLATT No. 48   23 DECEMBER 1944

1. Effective immediately, and until further orders, the following regulations will govern Stockade management:

   a. All inter-compound and button passes are suspended.
   b. All inter-compound athletics, entertainments, and visiting are suspended.
   c. The gates to all compounds will be closed at all times except for the passage of service vehicles and work parties.
   d. Scheduled attendance at the Post Theater will be by compounds only and for those compounds which go to and from the Theater in strict formation.
   e. The Post Chaplain will arrange religious services in compounds.

f. Communication of any kind between or among compounds by prisoners is forbidden.

2. As all button passes are suspended, temporary passes will
be issued only to medical personnel, the recognized compound spokesman of each compound and to individuals employed about the post. As there is no Camp Spokesman,
each compound spokesman is authorized to deal directly
with Stockade Headquarters on all matters.

After reading this statement, the colonel reiterated what
everyone knew. Rumors of trouble were rife throughout the
camp. A general strike, it was said, might commence on the
twenty-sixth. No one would report for work details until after
New Year's. Holden stated that he frankly feared, because
of this Rundstedt offensive, that the prisoners might try to
overpower all the guards at once and make a mass break for
freedom. Letting that sink in, he said nothing for about thirty
seconds, then ordered each compound commander to conduct
a very thorough search for home brew, illegal food and beer.
With a final reminder to be alert and see that their men
were, too, Holden dismissed the group with a hearty "Merry
Christmas."

The meeting over, Major Eugene Tays, director of security
and intelligence, hurried back to his office. He had just one
more small job to do and then he would be off for three days.
Tays shut the door, draped his coat over a chair and pulled a
large manila envelope from a desk drawer. He shook it. A
shower of ribbons, artificial walnuts, a miniature Santa Claus
or two, and bits of colored paper tumbled out in a heap. What
would those Germans think of next? Hiding messages in
Christmas-tree ornaments. He wondered if the Red Cross
knew these things were there when the parcels were shipped
to the prisoners.

Tays carefully pried open a gilded walnut shell. So this was
what counterespionage was all about. Several ribbon book-
marks fell out, each bright with drawings and little messages: "Weimar, the poet town—Goethe & Schiller"; "I remain
faithful"; "Wien—Stephansdom"; "By the lamplight we want

to stay as before, Lili Marlene"; "Your heart will be my anchor."

Turning to his typewriter, Tays began two-fingering a brief note to Fort Douglas.

> Complying with your request dated 20 December 1944, the decorations on Christmas trees received from the International Committee of the Red Cross were removed and examined. Inside of the artificial walnuts were found some printed slips, bookmarkers, and some little trinkets. Representative samples of these are forwarded, attached to the enclosed sheets of paper, with translations of same.
>
> For the commanding officer:
>
> > Eugene Tays
> > Major, CAC
> > Director, S & I

Tays quickly folded the papers, slipped them into a large envelope, scrawled the address, grabbed his coat and locked his office door. A few moments later he dropped the bulky package into a bag of outgoing mail destined for Fort Douglas and hurried toward his car. Near the entrance to Compound 5 he saw Lieutenant Watson and a corporal emerging from an inspection tour. Both men grinned broadly, indicating all was going well. Then Tays saluted the guard at the main gate and was waved out into the real world.

Ahead lay Phoenix, scattered across a flat plain. The city looked anything but festive. Heavy clouds, drooping with rain, glowered in the distance. Even the mountains, usually bathed in sunshine, looked ominous and foreboding. Although only midafternoon, it was already growing dark. Streetlights and a few swags of colored bulbs stretched between telephone poles along Van Buren Street tried valiantly to dispel the approaching gloom, but it was a losing battle.

While Tays was driving past last-minute Christmas shoppers toward the Westward Ho—that white tower which then dominated the Phoenix skyline and was his home until he and his wife could find an apartment—the first of two major outbursts erupted at Papago Park. Second Lieutenant George W. Boyer stirred up a hornet's nest when he tried to remove beer from the canteen in 1 B. A week later Boyer, a heavyset blond Georgia youth who could doze off at a moment's notice, told those questioning him concerning what had happened, "Sir, I had a compound full of trouble that afternoon!" He went on:

> After the officers' meeting, Sergeant Loy, PFC Straus, and I went to 1 B, which is my responsibility, to conduct a search. They found four gallons of alcohol in the latrine. In a refrigerator there were about thirty cases of beer. Now, beer has been restricted there since that party on the 15th, and we have been confiscating all we have found. I instructed PFC Straus to get a truck and remove it.
>
> Then one of the Germans ran out of the canteen and soon I was facing an angry mob, my back to the refrigerator. About a hundred or so men were in there yelling, shouting, calling me all kinds of vile names, and all of sudden two men came toward me, pushed me aside, and the prisoners grabbed all of the beer.
>
> I left and came to headquarters, at which time the officer of the day and a number of guards entered the compound, lined up the men against the fence, and checked their barracks. They found about fifty cases of beer, twenty-two gallons of fermenting alcohol, a lot of contraband such as an armature to a motor, another thing someone said was a wireless set, but I don't know for sure, I didn't look at it closely. Then there were bags of food, and in one trash can they found a case of evaporated milk. On orders of Colonel Holden we removed all citrus fruit from the compound since they use that to make alcohol and any food that should not have been in the barracks, such as bread and butter.

Second Lieutenant Frank A. Fice, officer of the day during this melee, corroborated Boyer's tale:

> After we got the call from 1 B, I armed seven men with carbines and Thompson sub-machine guns, placing them just

outside of the west gate of the compound. I put another ten men with riot clubs at the gate, then held a roll call and determined that everyone was present.

I informed the spokesman I intended to inspect for illegal possessions, especially alcoholic beverages. I allowed the spokesman to detail one man to each barracks to watch as we searched so later no one could be accused of stealing or souvenir hunting. This inspection was very thorough, lasting perhaps two hours, during which time the prisoners laughed, whistled, hooted, and guffawed. Several times I had to order them to be quiet.

Those who heard Boyer and Fice describe their ordeal were somewhat puzzled by so much beer in a compound where it was prohibited. How, they asked PFC Straus, could this happen? "Lieutenant Boyer and I," he replied, "removed all the beer from the canteen of 1 B on December 16, right after that party. About three days later the lieutenant found a few more bottles. Whenever we found a bottle or a case of beer after that time it was returned to the post exchange. I honestly don't know how they got more beer, perhaps from Compound 2."

Major Tays was quite certain the beer came from the adjoining area "because we found holes from time to time under the fence between the two compounds large enough for a man to crawl through. No, there is no doubt in my mind that it was passed through the fence there." Tays, informed by phone of this fracas, said he attributed no special significance to it at the time. "I thought they were just getting ready for Christmas. That's an unruly bunch. I simply chalked it up to their damn cussedness, trying to make a little trouble for us and spoil our holidays."

Shortly after supper another outburst occurred in Compounds 1 B and 2. Lieutenant Fice, the distraught officer of the day, later described what happened:

I had just finished eating when a sergeant rushed in and said the men in 1 B and 2 were at it again. We hurried over there and found most of them lined up in formation on each side of a single fence separating the two areas. They were singing Nazi marching songs, "Deutschland, Deutschland, über alles," and some stuff I didn't recognize.

A man standing in front of the Compound 2 group was waving a large German flag, I would say 5' by 7', and an accordionist was playing music. Of course, both groups were singing lustily, facing each other. The noise was attracting much attention from other compounds.

Fearing this could be the signal for a general disturbance, even the break-out Colonel Holden spoke of, I took steps to immediately end this disorder. I first called the guardhouse where fifteen men were standing by in anticipation of trouble and told the commander of the guard to hurry over with them and also to bring some tear gas grenades.

I then went into Compound 2 and told the spokesman, who actually seemed to be the leader, that the demonstration must cease at once. He and his interpreter refused to speak English. I knew some of those prisoners understood me, so during a lull in the singing I repeated my order, adding that I would take other measures if necessary.

Then I left Compound 2 and went into 1 B. There I told several men whom I knew understood English that the disturbance must end at once. I was greeted with hoots of derision, laughter, and clownish shrugs indicating no one knew what I was saying, which I knew to be untrue. The singing continued, even grew louder.

I went out of the compound area, picked up a grenade, and in plain view of everyone, took it from its case, pretended to pull the pin, and dropped my arm back as if to throw it. The singing stopped abruptly. There was almost complete silence.

Corporal Gebhardt, official interpreter of the post, arrived and told the spokesmen of both compounds that any further disturbance would be broken up by more stringent means without warning. That ended the trouble. I got off duty at midnight.

During these outbursts Compound 1 A remained calm and peaceful. Even Lieutenant Watson's search for illegal beer and homemade schnaps went off without a hitch . . . well, almost. For some reason Watson couldn't find Ferdinand Fuge, custodian of the canteen, and was unable to get the keys to that area. The lieutenant also admitted he and Corporal Gebhardt did not look in the attic of every barracks; nevertheless, they found three gallons of alcohol, which they confiscated.

> We had made a routine check of 1 A for cleanliness and general policing only that morning [Watson said later], looking in all of the barracks, kitchens, mess halls, latrines, and shower rooms. It was an ordinary Saturday inspection and, I would like to say, I never saw Compound 1 A looking better. The men even had some rather attractive hand-made Christmas decorations hung up in their mess halls.
>
> There are only seventeen structures there, some of them unoccupied, and Corporal Gebhardt and I had to do Compound 5, a much larger area which I also command. It has over seventy structures. After a thorough inspection of 5, we returned to 1 A, located Fuge, checked his canteen, and found it in good shape.

Why Compound 1 A was quiet, orderly and never looked better than it did on December 23, 1944, is obvious. It was not quite the night before Christmas, but as Clement Clarke Moore wrote, "not a creature was stirring, not even a mouse." After the painful, backbreaking labor of the past one hundred days no one was foolish enough to invite trouble. With visions of freedom, not sugar plums, dancing in their heads, twenty-five excited prisoners of war checked and rechecked their gear, dozed fitfully or glanced at their watches, nervously counting the hours.

But these men who were about to go out through the Papago Park tunnel were not waiting for St. Nicholas, nor could they wait. They had to leave as soon as possible after the Saturday-afternoon head count. They were merely waiting until it got dark.

Chapter 8

The three officers sat huddled around a small table in a dimly lit barracks. Guggenberger and Quaet-Faslem lay stretched out on their beds a short distance away. Supper was over. It was almost six o'clock, and thanks to a heavy overcast sky, already dark. Maus, Mirbach and Kaiser talked in low tones so as not to wake anyone. For various reasons this trio had scrapped plans to go out through the tunnel. Maus developed stomach pains while digging which later proved to be a hernia. Mirbach simply was not feeling well, a touch of the flu and an upset stomach. Kaiser cut his ankle working underground. It did not heal as fast as he had hoped.

From the enlisted men's quarters they could hear the opening salvo of KTAR's *Your FBI,* a radio show many of the prisoners found especially amusing and occasionally instructive, too. It would be followed, they knew, by *Spotlight Band,* then *Grand Ole Opry* at seven-thirty, and at nine, *Your Hit Parade,* which Guggenberger jokingly told Maus he must listen to. They had a small wager on "Don't Fence Me In," the favorite song in every POW compound across America, and when the FBI brought him back, Guggenberger said he planned to collect. He thought "Don't Fence Me In" would remain on the *Hit Parade* throughout January; Maus said it wouldn't.

Actually, the three officers were not downcast. It would be fun to go out for a few days, get away from the compound routine, but they agreed the chances of success were very slim indeed. The odds against them were too great. Even if one got away from the Americans, the route back to Germany was long and tortuous, and from the tenor of news broadcasts, what they could deduce from both U.S. and homeland sources, the Third Reich could not hang on much longer. Rundstedt's offensive was already grinding to a halt and the Russians were gathering momentum in the East. It was difficult to understand why the Führer had not switched sides and joined up with the Allies against the Communist threat.

Having decided to remain in camp, these three men now formed a coordinating committee deputized to see that the others departed in good order. "Our flight crew," as Quaet-Faslem dubbed them. He and Guggenberger, team # 1, would go out first at nine o'clock. The other groups would follow at twenty-minute intervals. With any luck, the last man, one of those 1 B petty officers, would be covering up the exit shortly after one o'clock in the morning. Perhaps then everyone inside 1 A could get some sleep.

Once more they rechecked the list:

1. Quaet-Faslem, Guggenberger
2. Karstens, Mohrdieck, Sternberg
3. Fuchs, Fuge, Strehle
4. Kraus, Drescher
5. Schröder, Reese
6. Günther, Clarus, Utzolino
7. Hoferichter, Zundorf
8. Gugger, Streng, Frenzel
9. Wattenberg, Kozur, Kremer
10. Palmer, Mark

The minutes dragged slowly by as the three men discussed what chances of success their friends might have once they got outside the camp. One thing in their favor, Maus noted, was that most of them had escaped before and had experience.

At eight forty-five Kaiser and Mirbach slipped out through the end of the bathhouse next to the coal box, the "revolving door" as they called it, carefully scraped away several inches of dirt and removed a heavy piece of plywood, disclosing the tunnel entrance. Then out came six potato sacks filled with sand, and there it was: a beautifully built ladder leading down to the bottom of the shaft. And 178 feet away, out by the edge of the canal, well beyond the second fence, was freedom.

Moments later—no dramatics, but with both of them giggling like two schoolboys about to put something over on their teacher—Quaet-Faslem and Guggenberger disappeared beneath the surface. Kaiser crawled down after them and relayed their packs as Mirbach handed them down to him. It soon became obvious that going out of the tunnel was a much more arduous task than supposed. Three days before, these young Kapitänleutnants had made it all the way to the end in less than eight minutes. Now, struggling along on elbows, belly and knees, alternately pushing and lifting a forty-pound pack where no room for leverage existed, and at the same time trying to keep rolled-up clothing relatively clean . . . well, it was virtually impossible to do.

Near the 150-foot mark Quaet-Faslem slipped, plunging face down flat into a puddle of soupy mud. Guggenberger, who was leading the way and could not turn to see what was happening behind him, heard spitting and a series of oaths. Both men rested for a few moments, whispering and gasping.

Ten minutes later Guggenberger uttered a soft "Hurrah, we've made it!" as he reached the foot of the exit ladder. Pushing his pack to one side, he climbed up and very cautiously lifted the cover Kozur had made. A guard-tower light was sweeping across the canal, but just as they had hoped, the exit was well within the shadows, hidden by bushes and undergrowth. A light rain was falling, drops dotting the surface of the waterway a few feet from the exit.

Guggenberger glanced at his watch. It was nine thirty-five. They had started out a bit early, too, and it still took them over forty minutes. He reached down and lifted out his pack, then Quaet-Faslem's. He quickly went up over the bank and down into the water. It was ice-cold at first, then not so bad. The water came only to his knees. Crouching, moving slowly and with great care so as to avoid searchlights, the two men made their way down the canal along the edge of the camp and out into the night.

Those who followed did much the same thing. Pushed, shoved, swore, tugged, prayed, almost gave up, beseeched the aid of the Almighty and various saints, and somehow wiggled their way to the exit. Once they started down the shaft there really was no way to turn back. One had to go on. By midnight, however, the groups were far behind schedule and several nonescapees turned to and helped transport gear through the tunnel. Only five groups (twelve men in all) had gotten out. Maus was disturbed but tried hard not to show it. These men were nervous enough without heated words or argument adding to the tension.

He glanced behind him. There were the three crazy boatmen with their folding bathtub. If this didn't jam up the traffic flow, nothing would. For a moment he considered letting Hoferichter, Zundorf and Frenzel and his two pals go ahead of them. He looked at Wolfgang Clarus and smiled. This youngster was poised like a sprinter at a race, on his mark ready to go. No, he couldn't do it. Maus motioned to Clarus, shook his hand and wished him well. The three boatmen and their incredible creation disappeared out through the end of the bathhouse and into the ground.

Actually, the boat presented no special problems. The time posted by Clarus, Günther and Utzolino differed little from that of the other groups, only a half-hour or so. At two-ten Palmer and Mark, having cut their way through from 1 B, entered the tunnel. Kaiser, who had volunteered for the job, followed them down the shaft, and shedding his clothes, slithered along in their wake. At the end he helped seal up the exit from the inside. Mark, down on his hands and knees, scattered leaves and twigs over what had been a hole a few seconds before. Now it was raining very hard.

A few minutes later Kaiser's head emerged near the bathhouse. He sagged heavily against the ladder, his tall frame streaked with mud and dirt, but there was a smile of triumph on his face. "It's done. The other end is tight as a drum. Where are those bags of sand?" he gasped in whispered tones. "Let's fill up this hole and get some sleep. I'm filthy, dead tired and ready for bed."

For the men now on the outside, what was left of the night was a mix of sudden exhilaration, bravado, extreme caution and drenching rain. Most of them carried a roll of clothes on their heads as they waded down the canal, then abandoned garments soiled in the tunnel and donned clean pants, shirts and sweaters. Once under way, they had two immediate goals: put as many miles as possible between themselves and Papago Park and find a dry place to hide during the day.

Even before they left the canal, several escapees were in deep trouble. Frenzel, in his haste to depart and also to avoid piercing searchlights, stumbled and fell into the water. Unfortunately he was carrying the food not only for his group but for Fuchs, Fuge and Strehle as well. For despite what their officers had said, six of the men had decided to stick together.

Guggenberger and Quaet-Faslem struck out along the railroad tracks leading east from Phoenix. Their refuge during the first day (and almost their last hiding place as well) was a large culvert. A hunter and his dog and then a roving jeep almost flushed them out. "We had two very close calls," Guggenberger says. "We were extremely lucky." Christmas Eve, on the other hand, was quite pleasant. Because of a drenching rain, these two officers holed up in a small stable amid comfortable bales of hay, celebrated the occasion with a meal of roasted bread crumbs and canned milk, and listened as a Mexican family living nearby sang Christmas carols. "It was most enjoyable. We were free. The weather was mild, even if wet. The stable, however, was dry and indeed appropriate."

At first the three boatmen proceeded with great care. Instead of crossing a highway, fearful of approaching autos, they squirmed and pulled themselves and their boat through a refuse-filled culvert which went under it. A mile or so farther on they encountered several Saturday-night drunks who wished them a "Merry Christmas" and then disappeared into the blackness.

Shortly before sunrise the rain began to come down hard. "It was a real downpour," Clarus recalls. "So we snuggled up in a patch of bushes on the outskirts of Phoenix, pulled the boat canvas over us and went to sleep. It fitted beautifully. However, the tar ran somewhat and we all got dirty. But more important, the damn thing shrank. Mistake number one: we should have washed the material before stitching it. Several days later we had to shorten all of the struts.

"During the day we heard children at play coming toward us. One of them even called to his mother, 'Look, come see what we have found.' I peeked out. They still were some distance away, so we grabbed everything and ran as fast as we could.

"Christmas Eve we walked right through the suburbs of Phoenix. No trouble whatsoever. Whenever people spoke to us we just nodded. I guess they assumed we were carrying holiday gifts in our bags. The windows of the homes were bright with Christmas trees and decorations. It was very nice, a Christmas time I shall never forget. We were happy, so very happy, trudging along in the rain. We even sang a bit at times."

Mark and Palmer spent their first day of freedom sleeping uneasily in a bunch of creosote bushes, raincoats drawn up over their heads. "I can hear that man even today," Mark says with a laugh. "That farmer and his cow. Her name was

Nellie. He kept saying, 'Come on, Nellie. Come on, Nellie.' They passed within three or four meters of where we were hiding, too, but didn't see us.

"That evening we got up, stretched, scratched, ate a little food and set out. It was still raining, very hard at times. Every so often we would check our compass and highway map to be certain we were heading in the right direction. About midnight a very strange thing happened. We heard voices in the distance, *German* voices!

"I stopped, listened carefully. There was no doubt about it. Germans. Palmer and I crouched down along the side of the road. Then we could see them, silhouetted against the sky, coming toward us. It was the three boatmen, their folding craft slung over their shoulders.

"We had a joyous reunion, although perhaps 'reunion' is not quite the correct word, since we hardly knew each other. Then we walked through some grapefruit groves until we arrived at Roosevelt High School. I believe it was in South Phoenix, but I am not sure. The school was closed for the holidays. We went in through a basement window and that was our home for about twenty hours."

These five POWs dried out their clothing, curled up in a furnace room where a boiler was being repaired, and spent a warm, rather enjoyable Christmas Day. In the evening they started out once more, the three boatmen heading west toward the Gila River, Mark and Palmer striking south for the Mexican border. Before they left the school, however, the boatmen gave the two petty officers the addresses of some presumed contacts in Mexico and South America, individuals who might help them if they got that far; and Heinrich Palmer, feeling refreshed and in an exuberant mood, opened a textbook and wrote in English: "This is a very nice house for a prisoner of war on his way back to Germany."

Sunday morning usually was a leisurely time in 1 A—in fact, throughout all of the compounds within the stockade at Papago Park. There were no head counts or roll calls, no work details other than routine duties. But on December 24, 1 A was unusually quiet. One reason was the absence of 40 percent of its personnel. Only fifteen of the thirty-nine men still there got up for a late breakfast between nine and ten o'clock. Rain continued to come down hard. The steady, resonant hum of water hitting the roof and sliding down windowpanes only added to the drowsy atmosphere as tired men turned in their beds and bunks, half asleep, half awake.

By noon, however, everyone was up. Before eating lunch, Maus made a quick trip to the bathhouse to check the tunnel entrance. Rain had erased scores of footprints. The area in and around the coal box looked much like the rest of the compound, except, of course, the unfinished sports field, where digging continued spasmodically from time to time.

Strangely, no one said much about the tunnel; the men simply smiled at one another in a knowing way. It had become their "great secret," a surprise Christmas gift for their captors. Lunch was marked by a special tribute to their absent comrades: a silent toast of citrus schnaps, one of three gallons that Watson and his gang had failed to find. It had been bubbling and brewing under a barracks, and only a turned-up radio and some impromptu singing concealed the containers from Corporal Gebhardt. This was, Kaiser had to admit, the best batch yet produced. The men were learning.

Although the noon meal represented a moment of triumph, all of the prisoners in 1 A were apprehensive. What would happen at afternoon roll call? Would an officer appear to count them, or only a corporal or sergeant? How much longer could they hide the fact that twenty-three of their comrades had mysteriously disappeared?

The meal over, Mirbach returned to his barracks and curled up with a copy of the *Arizona Republic* given to him by a guard. "NAZI DRIVE SLOWS DOWN 10 MILES FROM FRENCH FRONTIER." A map with sweeping arrows appeared alongside a front-page article describing last-minute shopping madness in Arizona's largest city. C. P. "Cash in Five Minutes" Stevens urged local citizens to be patriotic: "Sell your car and buy war bonds. Your car is depreciating every day. War bonds increase in value." Lupe Velez funeral held in Hollywood. A-14 gas coupons were now valid. Twenty-four gallons must last until March 22, the paper said. Gallons . . . that was how many liters? The horses were running this weekend at Sportsman's Park. Admission: $1.00, or free with the purchase of war bonds. War, war bonds. It was impossible to get away from it.

There was a lot of dancing going on, holiday gatherings at the Willow Breeze, Camelback Tavern, Riverside Ballroom. This evening Bob Stafford's ten-piece orchestra would play at a USO dance for American servicemen to be held in Adams Street. There would not be much dancing outdoors unless the rain stopped. Would any of those men be stupid enough to attend such a dance? God knows they were horny enough to try almost anything. Mirbach was uneasy about Wattenberg and his "aides" and wondered where they were. The others clearly were heading for Mexico. What Wattenberg had in mind was a secret. Whenever he was asked, "Fregattenkapitän Fuji" (short for Fujiyama) merely smiled mysteriously from his Olympian height and said nothing.

Mirbach shrugged and turned to the movie page. "Hey, Fritz," he said, glancing toward Kaiser, "listen to this. There is a double feature—that is, two shows for the price of one— *Fernando Valley*, Bruce Bennett and Erik Rolf in *U-Boat Prisoner*. We would get many laughs out of that one, I am sure."

The Western movie reminded Mirbach of Karl May, a prolific German writer who made the American West come alive for several generations of young readers. In scores of volumes he traced the adventures of Old Shatterhand and his noble Indian friend, Winnetou. Ironically, Mirbach thought, whatever the escapees had read in those books was about all most of them really knew about life in the desert.

But if the men on the outside had problems, so did those

who remained behind. The first hurdle was afternoon roll call. Somehow they had to confuse the Americans and cover up the escape for as long as possible.

Shortly after four o'clock Corporals Eugene Hoya and Frank Gebhardt entered Compound 1 A and tried without success to conduct a roll call. This is how Hoya later described the frustrating experience that followed:

> At that time it was raining, so we informed Ender, the German NCO, we would hold the count in a mess hall so the men would not have to stand out in the rain. They came in and it was obvious they were not all there. We had nineteen officers and twenty enlisted men. So Corporal Gebhardt and I decided to wait until 4:30 for the rest of the men to come into the hall. We were under the impression they were in their barracks and didn't want to come to roll call—they have done that before, they want an American officer present—and then we asked Ender where the rest of the men were and he said he did not know.
>
> So at 4:30 Corporal Gebhardt and I left and tried to locate Lieutenant Watson by phone, but we couldn't find him. I remembered that Captain Homer Davis, commander of all of the compounds in the POW stockade, was at the post theater, as I had been working there earlier. I sold him a ticket as a matter of fact.
>
> We paged him at the theater and told him the men in 1 A refused to stand roll call. He then called the officer of the day who armed some men with clubs and, as I recall, it was between 4:45 and 5 o'clock when we went back to the compound with them. At that time we lined the men up right east of the mess hall. We got the same figures as before.
>
> I remember Captain Davis went storming into the barracks. He was mad. We all were. It was raining hard, Christmas Eve. We thought they were just being ornery, trying to spoil our holidays. When he came out of the last barracks he didn't say anything, and those Germans, they didn't say anything either. But they were all smiling.
>
> Then he told the guards to keep the prisoners in formation. We went into 1 B and found that compound two men short. Meanwhile, some men conducted roll calls in other compounds and still more men made a thorough search of 1 A, under

buildings, in empty barracks, all over, any place they might be hiding.

PFC Straus, one of the men who helped take the head count in 1 B, said there should have been 266 POWs in that compound.

> We had a lot of trouble. Most of them suddenly had to go to the latrine, all of them at the same time. I speak German and followed each name as we called it out. When we got to Mark, no answer. They said he was sick. I went inside and found a man who said he was Mark, but I was suspicious. Yet we had the correct number, 266.
>
> Later, however, about six o'clock or so, we summoned the whole guard company. We again called each man's name, then he answered with his serial number. I went up and down the ranks with a flashlight, shining it in their faces to see if we recognized them. When we got to Mark some jokester said "furlough," and the same thing happened when we called Palmer's name. So we knew they were missing.

Within a couple of hours it became obvious that a large group of prisoners had escaped. The first report was that as many as sixty might be at large. Since all efforts to locate Colonel Holden, commandant of Papago Park, and his director of security, Major Eugene Tays, proved fruitless, the burden for immediate action fell to Captain Cecil Parshall, provost marshal and assistant to Tays. At six-thirty on December 24, Parshall was beginning a relaxed Christmas Eve round of poker at the Officers' Club. Several days later, testifying before a board of inquiry, he told what happened next.

> Lieutenant Watson called and informed me that at the evening count there had been approximately twenty-five German prisoners of war missing. I instructed him to immediately ascertain the names of the men and told him I would be in my office awaiting this information so that it could be transmitted to the FBI for broadcast. Arriving at the provost marshal's office, I checked with the telephone operator to ascertain whether or not the commanding officer, Colonel Holden, had been called and Major Tays, too. I was informed that she was

endeavoring to locate them. At approximately 7:30 or 8:00, between then, Lieutenant Watson came to my office with a list of prisoners not present at roll call.

After the roster of names of the missing PWs was given to me, I immediately secured their no. 2 forms, called the FBI, and gave them their names and descriptions. In the meantime, while talking with the FBI, I received a call from the sheriff at Phoenix stating that he had one Herbert Fuchs in custody. He stated that Fuchs had hitchhiked a ride with a civilian and the driver had immediately driven him to the sheriff's office and turned him in.

At 1930 a Mrs. Arthur Hunter, Jr., Route #1, Tempe, called me and reported that two PWs had turned themselves in to her at her home. These PWs later developed to be Ferdinand Fuge and Kurt Strehle. At 2030 an unknown Mexican, very excited, called from Tempe and said that two PWs had surrendered to him. He said they were hungry and cold and wanted to return to camp. I immediately called the sheriff's office and asked if they would pick up these men. They were, we learned later, Karl Heinz Frenzel and Hermann Streng.

At 2100 it was reported by an unknown man, believed to be the constable at the Tempe railway station, that another PW had been arrested at that point. This was Helmut Gugger. About that time Colonel Holden arrived back in camp and began organizing search parties, sending them in various directions in the surrounding territory. I spent the rest of the night, until 0830, 25 December 1944, on duty in his office acting as dispatcher and receiving messages from the search parties.

About thirty minutes after Captain Parshall headed for his quarters and some well-earned rest, Lieutenant Watson completed a very careful morning roll call in Compound 1 A. Just as he was leaving, Gerhard Ender handed him a brief note.

On account of the treatment we have been exposed to in PW Camp, Papago Park, and which is against international law, I have decided to withdraw from this treatment through escape. I assure herewith under oath, that I am a defenceless PW, will not resist arrest. I want to point this out because lately escaping PWs supposedly have been shot.
Witnessed by Captain Maus.

Twenty-four names were appended to this statement. For some reason that of Helmut Drescher was missing. Some of those who escaped through the tunnel seem to remember they signed such a message, others are certain they did not. Hans Werner Kraus states emphatically that no such document ever existed. "There was no letter. After thirty years I fear much romance has grown up around our escape."

Nevertheless, even if this statement was concocted by Ender in an effort to create still more confusion, it was like music to the ears of the harassed American command at Papago Park. Clearly, if the prisoners themselves complained of harsh treatment, that POW camp was no slipshod operation.

Gerhard Ender, almost a caricature of a petty Nazi opportunist, was a forty-three-year-old native of Berlin. A man of medium height with an odd, distinctive gait (Palmer says he walked like a monkey), he bragged of having taken part in the Munich "Putsch" of 1923 and of his activities in behalf of the party during succeeding years. In the 1930s he held a variety of lower-echelon government posts and perhaps was a Gestapo finger man. In June 1940 he was assigned to the embassy in Tokyo and three years later joined the *Burgenland*'s crew as a gunner's mate, although Mark and Palmer never saw him in uniform until they got ready to sail for home. As his blockade runner was being scuttled early in January 1944, Ender, on orders of his captain, shot and killed another passenger, a man named Hoffmeyer thought to be a spy and en route home for trial. The captain had been told to liquidate Hoffmeyer if forced to abandon ship.

Shortly after the tunnel escape, Ender was flown to Fort Hunt for questioning. Flattered by this attention, he grew expansive and told of a forbidden camp newspaper he edited and published (no other POW ever saw it), bragged of how, almost single-handedly, he curtailed Papago Park's work program, and heaped praise on Wattenberg's leadership. At Hunt, Ender wrote wild, defiant letters to those questioning him. One interrogator said he was "200% fool and 1000%

Nazi." German POWs with him at Papago Park view Ender as a man of no real importance . . . "only a spinner, a teller of tall tales."

The public first learned of this escape on the morning of December 25. The *Arizona Republic*'s second edition ran a page-one story telling how five "storm-lashed" prisoners of war had appeared in various places near Phoenix and Tempe seeking shelter. According to the *Republic,* an unidentified camp source said they disappeared during a drenching rain storm, "just slithered away like eels." Papago Park authorities, the paper added, informed the Arizona Highway Patrol at 7:17 P.M. on the twenty-fourth that twenty-five prisoners had disappeared five hours earlier, "at about 2:30 P.M." An AP dispatch reproduced in many dailies across the nation said there were rumors that orders for the break were smuggled into the camp in Christmas-tree decorations.

Shortly after noon on Christmas Day, Major Eugene Tays received a call from Lieutenant Colonel B. C. Jones, an internal security officer with the 9th Service Command.

—Major Tays, we want to get some information about that break.

—Yes, sir.

—We got your TWX that gave us no information other than the names. First of all, how did they escape?

—All we know now is that they went over the fence.

—Over the fence?

—Yes, sir.

—How many?

—About twenty-five.

—Well . . . were they all officers?

—No, they were about half officers and the rest enlisted men.

—One half officers?

—Wattenberg is one that escaped. He is one of the officers that escaped.

—I know Wattenberg was one that escaped but how many officers . . . do you know that . . . the exact number?

—Well, there were two officers . . .

—Two officers? Is that all?

—No.

—O.K. There were two officers. Go on from there.

—Wolf Clarus, Helmut Drescher, Fritz Guggenberger, Wilhelm Günther, Otto Hoferichter, Hans Werner Kraus, Jürgen Quaet-Faslem, Martin Peter Reese, Jürgen Schröder, Friedrich Utzolino, Jürgen Wattenberg, and Hans Zundorf.

—Those were the officers? The rest were enlisted men?

—Yes, sir.

—How many have you captured?

—We have captured six. They are all enlisted men, those that have been captured so far.

—Six enlisted men captured?

—Yes, sir.

—Have you any clues on the rest of them?

—No.

—Have you any idea what time they ran away?

—Yes, I believe that they got away Saturday night.

—Saturday night?

—Yes, sir.

—When did you know about it?

—Well . . . I did not know about it until Sunday afternoon.*

—Not until Sunday afternoon?

—Yes, sir.

—I see. Do you know what time Saturday night?

—From all indications it was around 7 or 7:30 P.M., because at that time the compound that two of them escaped from had a demonstration so that it diverted our attention from the principal area involved. We believe that is the time those fellows got out.

—You believe they escaped between 7 and 7:30 Saturday night?

—Yes, sir.

—And you found out yesterday afternoon? You did not report it to us until today though.

—Well, no, we reported it from here right after midnight Sunday.

—At 4:59 A.M. at Phoenix you reported it to us.

—Yes, that is when we sent the telegram. We did not know for sure just how many were out at that time.

* Tays himself did not know about the escape until sometime Sunday evening, perhaps about nine o'clock. What he means is that some officers (Parshall, Davis, Watson, etc.) knew something was wrong late Sunday afternoon. Yet, the truth is, it was early evening—sometime after six o'clock—before the fact of an escape was established.

—Well, that is a pretty long wait for us up here. You see, this is a very important thing because that man Wattenberg is mixed up in it.

—Yes, sir.

—Now, what is the general situation? Have you any ideas . . . any leads?

—No, we have not. We sent out patrols to cover the whole surrounding territory here. We had them out all night. The camp patrols and the FBI have been working together. They are still out, I hope.

—Those six captured . . . now, you said that they got away between 7 and 7:30 Saturday evening and you discovered it yesterday afternoon. About what time did you discover it?

—Around four o'clock, sir.

—Around four o'clock. Was it a check of any kind?

—Yes, sir, roll call at four o'clock.

—I see. Now, is there anything else that we should know about, because General Shedd is very interested in getting all information.

—Well, there is nothing further on the situation except the indications they are going south or southwest.

—Southwest?

—Yes, sir. San Diego. One man had a map of southern California on him.

—I see. Well, Tays, keep us informed. And thank you.

—Yes, sir.

Major Eugene Tays put down the phone and slumped in his chair. Fortunately Jones had not asked what the six men recaptured had in their possession. Tays knew that local reporters were very disturbed by the mass of material they had seen at the Phoenix police station: cartons of cigarettes and various food items civilians had to stand in line to get and for which they sometimes provided ration stamps as well. He leafed through a bunch of papers and found what he wanted: a list of the clothing and equipment that the first three men had with them when apprehended.

FUCHS: 1 filed table knife (taped handle), bandages, mis-
          cellaneous first aid articles, tobacco, shoe strings,
          toilet gear, $4.10 in U.S. coins, 2 hand towels, a

GI raincoat, goggles, 1 wool sweater (brown), a pair of overall trousers, wool underwear, 9 pairs of socks, an English-German language guide, khaki shorts, a haversack made from a barracks bag, GI shoes, a pipe, mess kit, 5 books of canteen slips.

STREHLE: 2 pairs of leather boots, a felt hat, 3 pairs of wool socks, canteen, small German haversack, German infantry pack, 2 suits of woolen underwear, German cotton shirt, cotton undershirt, blue sweater, navy blouse with brass buttons, first aid kit, navy jacket, hand towel, face towel, GI raincoat.

FUGE: shorts, shampoo bottle of schnaps, a wool blanket, 2 white detachable collars, 2 pairs of blue pants, a felt hat, wool underwear, 2 wool jackets, GI raincoat, 2 canteens, wool shirt, wool undershirt, toilet kit, a hand towel, a makeshift haversack, pillow case, mess kit (with knives, forks, spoons), detachable collar shirt, cigarettes, cigarette paper, cigarette lighter, vitamin B powder, toilet paper, tobacco, matches, 2 pairs of socks.

Food taken from the six men included a dozen loaves of German Red Cross bread, ten pounds of pork fat in cans and jars, a can of chocolate cooked solid, four bottles of prepared coffee, a sack of ground coffee, four pounds of bread crumbs in small packages, several bags of rice and sugar, salt, lemonade-powder mix, five cans of pork and beans, and three large packages of chocolate.

Later that same afternoon Colonel Holden met with reporters and told them that the escapees perhaps got out of the camp during a demonstration on Saturday afternoon, "but more likely about 7:30 P.M., Sunday.

"We hesitate to say exactly what happened," the harassed commanding officer continued, "but the break may have occurred during a heavy rainstorm that swept the camp yesterday before dusk. All of them apparently scaled the eight-foot barbed-wire fences and took off." Well-developed U-boat morale and the Rundstedt offensive, he thought, had inspired this desperate exploit. Holden failed to disclose, among other things, the growing concern that this band of naval expertise was heading for San Diego, not Mexico, where the men might seize a ship and set sail on their own.

In the excitement local authorities began arresting anyone who could not explain his activities to their satisfaction. Those ensnared included scores of transients, among them two Mississippi drifters whose drawls sounded suspiciously foreign to Southwestern ears.

During these hectic hours some newspapers promoted Wattenberg to "a *Graf Spee* admiral" and several said Günther Prien of *Royal Oak* fame was among those loose somewhere in Arizona. This erroneous Prien story apparently was based upon a remark by Major Tays, who said, referring to Guggenberger, not Prien, that one of Germany's most decorated U-boat heroes was among the escapees.

After talking with the newsmen, Holden summoned both Major Tays and Captain Parshall to his office. Following a brief conference Tays told Parshall to question three of the men: Frenzel, Streng and Gugger. The first man, Frenzel, refused to give any information other than his name, rank and serial number. The second, Streng, seemed more cooperative and told about his escape Saturday night during the demonstration through a hole which had been cut in the outer fence at the juncture of 1 B and 2. He also proceeded to explain in great detail how the wire was replaced by others after they left. This was, of course, false.

The third man, Helmut Gugger, at first told the same story as Streng, but after he was given a couple of cigarettes it was ascertained that he actually was Swiss, had been drafted into the German armed forces, and would like to return to Switzerland. Following about an hour of intense interrogation Gugger agreed to tell the true story of the escape if he was promised full protection at all times. Why he finally talked is quite obvious: the Americans either beat him up or frightened him in some fashion. (Colonel Holden told his superiors the next day "we worked over some people a bit.") Some of the escapees maintain that the Americans held a fake firing-squad execution of Frenzel which Gugger could hear but not see, and that convinced him to reveal what he knew. Parshall thinks one of his associates probably pulled Gugger's hair until he talked. "Hair pulling was one of his favorite tricks. It doesn't show bruises, you know."

According to Gugger, it took about three and a half months to dig the tunnel. He said it was completed on December 21. Meanwhile, Wattenberg personally selected those who would escape and gave them addresses of friends in Mexico, Panama, Chile and Argentina who would help them. Gugger said Wattenberg, Kraus and Ender were the brains behind the plot. Ender, he emphasized, was the real leader of the camp underground and remained behind to promote further resistance and more escapes. Gugger also told the Americans about the boat made by Clarus, Günther and Utzolino.

Actually, except for disclosing the existence of a tunnel, admittedly a most vital fact, Gugger's story was nearly as far off the mark as that told by Streng. Much of what Gugger said or what the Americans said he said was a mixture of fantasy and falsehood, although as an enlisted man he probably did not know all of the organization and planning involved in this undertaking. His story was, however, precisely what the Americans wanted to hear: Wattenberg and Ender had engineered the escape.

Since it was already dark, Parshall put off searching for the tunnel until the next morning, Tuesday, December 26. So by the close of Christmas Day—a long, harrowing twenty-four hours which were anything but festive for most of the U.S. officers at Papago Park—Colonel Holden, Major Tays, Captain Davis (commander of the stockade which enclosed all of the POW compounds) and the two young lieutenants in charge of 1 A and 1 B, Watson and Boyer, knew that twenty-five German prisoners of war had escaped through a 178-foot tunnel, not over the fence. Parshall and his assistants had squeezed that much out of Helmut Gugger. These five officers also knew something else: they were in deep trouble.

Chapter 9

The next morning, December 26 and the first working day after the long holiday weekend, both the Pentagon and the 9th Service Command headquarters at Fort Douglas, Utah, still were pretty much in the dark concerning developments at Papago Park. At 8:35 A.M. an officer on duty at the Provost Marshal General's Office in Washington made this entry in his log: "Report was heard on radio that twenty-five POWs escaped from Papago Park, Arizona. Five have have been recaptured. No official report received from 9th Service Command."

Twenty-five minutes later he received a telegram from Colonel William Holden sent from Phoenix at 4:59 A.M. on the day before telling of the escape and listing the names of twenty-one German POWs. The names of Palmer, Mark, Schröder and Sternberg were not mentioned in this dispatch. Ten hours after the mass break was detected the American officers at Papago Park apparently still did not know precisely who was missing.

This was simply too much for General Blackshear Bryan,

Assistant Provost Marshal General. Fuming at such bumbling incompetence, he ordered the operations department to contact the 9th Service Command concerning this matter. A few moments later Bryan decided to put in a direct call to Papago Park himself.

—Colonel Holden, this is General Bryan in Washington, what's the dope on that escape out there?

—Well, sir, it was a tunnel job.

—A tunnel job?

—Yes, they tunneled through some 200 feet of solid rock and came out under the high water mark of the Crosscut Canal. It is difficult to figure out just how much start they have on us and so far we haven't picked up anything but small fry.

—Right through solid rock, huh? Do you have any leads on which way they went or anything?

—Last night we worked over some people a bit and we got a tip that one of the high-ranking officers has a collapsible boat he made himself, and the story back of that is he thought there was water in the river down here. It was absolutely dry, before this rain, that is, and we got a road net out here and pick up a little information now and then on some fellows here and there who are probably prisoners. The way it shapes up, sir, is now it looks like we will probably pick up some more enlisted men, but I think Wattenberg probably has a pretty good plan in mind. We are getting ready to start out . . . I was just starting myself, to get down to Yuma and come back up to that river bend. I was going to ask for plane operations as soon as I found out what the FBI was doing. Now the Border Service are quite active with their planes and we might pick up something that way.

—How many men are out now? Twenty?

—No, sir, nineteen. We have caught six enlisted men.

—How many officers are out?

—Twelve.

—Twelve officers? How long after they got out before you discovered the thing out there?

—I think it was Sunday night. Roll call is when the shortage showed up.

—And you don't know just when they got out exactly?

—No, sir.

—They are all from Wattenberg's compound . . . is that right?

—They are all from his compound except two who were from the adjoining compound where we have those belligerent noncommissioned officers.

—And you think Wattenberg is behind the whole thing?

—Oh, yes, sir, there is no doubt about it.

—Well, the FBI knows everything you are doing, do they?

—Yes, sir.

—Well, Colonel, thank you very much. And good luck.

Holden put down the phone very quietly. He stood up and walked to the window. He watched as two captains, Robison and Young, strolled into a nearby building. Perhaps that inquiry board would get down to business today. As required by Army regulations, Holden had convened this group shortly before noon on Christmas Day, the two captains and a young, curly-haired lieutenant named Southard who acted as secretary. It was their duty to investigate the escape and report directly to the 9th Service Command. All they did yesterday, according to Tays, was tour 1 A and 1 B, go up in tower number 3, and adjourn to the Officers' Club for drinks.

What worried Colonel Holden much more than this local board or Pentagon phone calls was a terse telegram from Fort Douglas. General Shedd was dispatching his own pack of personal bloodhounds south to Papago Park: Lieutenant Colonel A. B. O'Rourke and two other officers would arrive the following afternoon, the twenty-seventh, for a four-day visit.

Shortly after Holden completed his brief chat with General Bryan, several of Papago Park's key personnel began searching for the tunnel. Parshall, Davis, Jackson and a handful of enlisted men scoured the banks of the canal along 1 A as the Germans watched intently from inside the fences. To protect Gugger, they ambled about in a desultory fashion for an hour or so, at least that is what inquiry boards were told later. Mirbach says the Americans went *directly* to the exit by the electric-light pole, making it obvious to everyone that one of the six men had talked. Compound 1 A then was cleared out and the search for the entrance got under way. However, it was so cleverly hidden that despite Gugger's help, the Americans prodded the surface in and around the bathhouse for nearly three hours without success.

Corporal Lawrence Jorgensen, a stocky, curly-haired young man, finally found the entrance and immediately volunteered to go through the tunnel. Under questioning, he later described what happened.

> The opening was found before one o'clock and I went through the tunnel shortly after that. I entered at the west end and crawled all the way through. The earth, as far as I could see with the help of the flashlight I had, I believe it is called caliche and it is evidently very hard. The sides of the tunnel may have been brushed with water or else they were rubbed smooth from the PWs working inside of it.
>
> Through the tunnel there were two places, maybe ten or fifteen feet apart, where the tunnel had been cut out a little wider at the sides, making an area maybe four feet across. They may have been used as resting places or places to turn around. Also there were metal spikes driven into the sides of the tunnel at various intervals, some of them maybe three feet, some maybe four feet apart. What those spikes were driven in for I don't know, maybe measurements.
>
> I saw no digging instruments. There was water in the tunnel, possibly two-thirds of the distance, quite a bit of it. I was crawling and my chin was getting wet. At the deepest point, perhaps three feet, my head was rubbing against the top of the tunnel and the water was deep enough to get my chin and mouth wet.
>
> It took me five minutes to complete the trip. I didn't hurry. I crawled several feet and stopped and rested. The air was quite foul down there and I thought it best to take it easy.

Although Jorgensen found no tools, a few days later Master Sergeant Joe Street appeared before an inquiry board and told of discovering several interesting items secreted away in the dispensary of 1 A. These included a pick without a handle, a short-handled shovel, a soot rake and eight feet of electric wire, all obviously used in some way by the tunnelers.

On Tuesday, the twenty-sixth, the day the tunnel was discovered, the Tucson *Daily Citizen* published an angry editorial blasting Holden & Company, a storm-cloud portent of even rougher weather ahead. The *Citizen,* still unaware of the tunnel's existence, said the escape from Papago Park "indicates a looseness of supervision that should be remedied immediately." It was "high time to stop playing 'sucker' to our uninvited guests."

Some one of these days we will discover that these missing prisoners have not escaped with food and bed rolls only but with small arms, or those of larger calibre as well, and they will use them. We are not so well protected in Arizona that a group of defiant, well-armed Nazis might not give us a very merry party indeed.

Did the camp authorities call in the guards to keep them out of the wet? Is it possible that the keepers of the prisoners of war have grown so incredibly soft that they believe a group of German prisoners would forfeit escape because a soft Arizona rain was falling? Are they so dull that they have forgotten the recent Nazi break-through on the Belgian-Luxembourg front in the face of the most disheartening weather conditions? Is it not possible that these men have friends who have prepared the way for them and sent them well on their way to liberty?

We have been guilty of some mighty strange bits of negligence both at home and abroad in this war. We have constantly under-estimated the cunning and daring of the Nazis, whether in prison camp or on the battle field. We have pictured them to be dumkops of the first order, without originality or initiative. We have admired these physical giants and have wondered why the essential brain power was not a natural accompaniment to splendid body-power. And all the time, we have been minimizing the Nazi animal cunning and have relaxed the necessary vigilance to keep him safely within the weakly-fenced prison camps.

Of course there will be the usual investigation, the incident will end there and the public will forget until the next break occurs under the cover of a convenient rain storm on an equally convenient holiday.

Sometime during that hectic Tuesday, the Papago Park command swallowed hard and confessed to reporters that the twenty-five prisoners had escaped through a "200-foot" tunnel. Wednesday's *Arizona Republic* featured a grim front-page headline: ROCK-PIERCING TUNNEL AIDED PAPAGO ESCAPE.

Yet with belated adroitness, camp authorities were developing a systematic story which might, just might get them off the hook. To all who would listen, the Americans began praising the tunnel as an incredible engineering feat through solid rock, at the same time portraying themselves as stern, resourceful guardians. Needless to point out, the tunnel became longer (178 to 200 feet) and was now through granite all the way from bathhouse to canal. The letter presumably left by the escapees deploring harsh treatment was clear proof the American officers were not "softies" (as charged by Tucson's afternoon daily). And as the local inquiry board hearings dragged on into January, those in the line of fire—Holden, Tays, Davis, Watson and Boyer—introduced substantial evidence that visiting brass all the way up to General Blackshear Bryan himself had discounted the possibility of tunnel-digging activity at Papago Park.

On Wednesday, the twenty-seventh, a major at the Pentagon called a colonel at Fort Douglas to ask how the search was going and, with considerable tact since he was outranked, to remind the 9th Service Command to shape up.

—Was that really through rock they went, Colonel?
—Yes.
—They went through rock?
—Through rock.
—I declare. Well, I wondered if there had been any further report with regard to the five that they thought they spotted over near Wintersburg.
—No, that didn't materialize. We had a report but they hadn't gotten them up to five o'clock yesterday. One man, one of the escapees that they captured, claims to be Swiss. He had a notebook and in it a map with all the dope on San Diego. He also said that the party was divided up into twos and

threes. Most of them apparently are headed for Mexico. Some of them are going to try to get to Guayamus, others to a town called Mayarit south of Guayamus. These are places where Chilian boats manned by German skippers come into port. They also found out that traveling with Wattenberg are two men named Kremer and Kozur. Now, just to be on the safe side, we have alerted the Navy and our MPs at San Diego to be on the lookout for anybody that might try to get there.

—That's fine, sir. Please keep us posted. It seems that some-how this thing got out over the radio before we got any official report here and they got a little upset about it . . .

—All right. Now, there is one other interesting development and that is that this escapee reports that the real leader down there at Papago Park is Ender, and this fellow Ender was in the beer hall "push" when Hitler took over and that he is the real boss and that even Wattenberg takes orders from him. Ender is one of those in Compound 1 A.

—Is he still there?

—That's right. He didn't escape. Frankly, I think they are holed up somewhere for a few days waiting for the heat to die down, then they will be on their way. As soon as they begin moving we should be able to spot them.

—Well, please keep us informed. And thank you very much, sir.

On the morning of December 31 Lieutenant Colonel O'Rourke and his associates completed four days of testi-mony and headed back to Fort Douglas. They had heard from the five principals (Holden, Tays, Davis, Watson and Boyer), Corporal Hoya, Lieutenant Jackson (post engineer) and an assortment of other officers. In all, seventeen men were summoned and told under oath what they knew about the escape.

The result of this inquiry was seventy single-spaced typed pages of testimony and a terse ten-page summary which con-cluded that Holden, Tays, Davis, Watson and Boyer were guilty of serious neglect of their duties and should face court-martial proceedings. This report noted that, as claimed, the camp command indeed had used a drill and dynamite to loosen up the soil of Papago Park, but those same officers failed to realize that daily percolation of water from the canal had a definite softening affect which made tunneling possible. Also, the board maintained that these men committed two serious errors in judgment: failure to hold Sunday-morning roll calls and to have a thorough "shakedown" inspection of Compound 1 A for two months prior to the escape on December 23, 1944.

Lieutenant Boyer won slight praise for standing "flatfooted before the ice box where contraband beer was stored by the prisoners of war" and facing an angry mob; but, O'Rourke and others asked, how could such vast supplies of beer be accumulated and remain undetected?

Within a few days copies of this report made their way to Washington, and Major General Archer L. Lerch, Provost Marshal General since June 1944, was very unhappy. This was, however, an "in house" military reaction. Lerch was not as distressed by the escape of twenty-five Germans or their tunnel as he was by the effect a court-martial trial might have on other POW camp commanders.

At 11:38 A.M. on January 4 he called Colonel Jack Nash, a deputy to Brigadier General Joseph E. Battley, the man in charge of all service commands throughout the United States. Lerch stressed that, at first, those commanding prisoner-of-war camps had been too security-conscious. Then the Army instituted its "calculated risk" program. This meant fewer guards, some escapes, yes—but more U.S. servicemen released for overseas duty and much more work out of the POWs, too. As Lerch warmed up to the subject his views became clear.

—Now, if these people out at Papago Park are tried, and this information gets out generally to all the camp commanders, four hundred of them, once again they are going to get so security conscious they are going to be afraid to do nothing else except guard these people, and our work program is completely out the window. It will just ruin it. I know it will.

—Well, remember, the 9th Service Command hasn't done

anything yet. It has not acted. This is just a preliminary finding.

—But it is a matter of much broader interest than the 9th. Shedd agrees Holden may have been a bit careless, but generally he has the reputation of being pretty good. I doubt that Shedd will go ahead and try him unless that is what the War Department actually wants. Now, I think that in the Department we should get together on this matter; and, even though there may have been a little carelessness here and there, the effect on the whole prisoner of war program is going to be . . . Well, all camp commanders are pretty well alerted by the fact these Germans got out anyhow and they are all a little bit worried.

Now, if they go ahead and try Holden and the other people, even though they are found to be not guilty, they are *all* going to be so scared that you are going to get widespread demands for additional guard personnel and the whole labor program is going to end up in the scrap heap.

—Yes, General Lerch, well . . .

—Now, don't get me wrong. If they are really guilty, yes, they should be tried. But if there is any question about it, any question at all, the question should be resolved in favor of not trying them. I am not worried or concerned about these five individuals. I am thinking about the whole program. And I think that if General Shedd tries them he ought to be told that he must be awfully sure that there is a very serious dereliction of duty involved.

—Well, sir, I don't know whether we should tell him that or not. After all, he's . . .

—All right, all right, then. We will ruin the entire work program for the entire United States. The whole thing will go up in smoke.

—O.K. I will speak to Joe when he comes in.

—Now, if a man is guilty, very guilty and it is something that nobody else would have been guilty of under normal circumstances, then we might try him, but if it is merely the fact that there were more prisoners involved in this escape than ever before, and they perhaps were somewhat more desperate characters . . .

—You mean if the trial is sort of a sop to public opinion?

—Precisely. If that is what we are trying them for, then we shouldn't try them at all. Too often that is the case, and we will ruin our work program. We will go back to an extremely security-conscious situation again.

—I will talk to Joe when he comes in.
—O.K. Thanks very much.

Soon even bigger Washington names were getting into the act. On January 5 J. Edgar Hoover wrote the Pentagon expressing deep fears that "certain German submarine commanders now interned in the United States might escape and be returned to Germany." War Department intelligence officials tried to soothe Hoover by assuring him that Günther Prien, who they thought had died three years earlier, never was imprisoned in America. They said nothing, however, about Guggenberger, Kraus, Quaet-Faslem and Wattenberg.

On the same day that Hoover wrote to the U.S. Army he dispatched a long, somewhat inaccurate memo to his boss, Attorney General Francis Biddle, who in turn contacted Secretary of War Henry Stimson. According to Hoover, 1,281 POW escapes had been reported to his bureau. Concerning Papago Park, he said that at six-fifty in the evening on December 23 (should have been 24) the Maricopa County sheriff's office called the Phoenix FBI agent to inquire about German POWs they had in their custody. This, he noted scornfully, was the first the FBI knew of the escape.

Nearly two hours later Papago Park gave the local FBI man a list of twenty-three names and two hours after that, two more. "It is clear," Hoover wrote, "that Wattenberg, an admiral, commander of the *Graf Spee*, led this exploit." He added that these twenty-five men had accounted for thirteen escapes, eight of them from Papago Park. According to an admitted espionage agent, Hoover emphasized, a plan was afoot to get U-boat commanders back to Germany.

On January 10, in an effort to explain what had happened at Papago Park, General Bryan wrote a long memo to Julius Amberg, special assistant to Stimson. It was, he conceded, "not a particularly good camp." Many U-boat crews were interned there intact which meant administration and discipline were difficult at times. His office, he stressed, tried without success to get Wattenberg transferred elsewhere because, in effect, he said that "he was going to get the camp commander." Bryan admitted it was very difficult to understand how such a tunnel remained undetected, but then quickly digressed to brag about U.S. troops in Germany who reputedly dug 121 tunnels in only one month. "One group built a baseball diamond. It is reported that this operation raised the entire field nine inches."

Neither the International Red Cross nor the Swiss legation, he added, had issued any complaints concerning Papago Park, and the latter recognized that Wattenberg was a chronic complainer, a genuine troublemaker. No real lack of cooperation existed between the FBI and the War Department, Bryan continued, acknowledging that some minor personality clashes might erupt from time to time. Neither the navy nor any other source for that matter, he said, had warned the 9th Service Command that a breakout was imminent. The Provost Marshal General also revealed that Holden had been relieved as commander at Papago Park, a statement apparently not quite true, since he continued to sign letters as commanding officer throughout much of January.

Just as Lerch, Bryan and their associates feared, this Papago Park business could not be contained. Most of those who spoke out were irritated by the soft life that enemy prisoners of war seemed to be enjoying on U.S. soil while *they*, the taxpayers, footed the bill. A. F. Wassilah of 1021 East Roma Avenue, Phoenix, sent an irate letter to the *Arizona Republic:*

> Now isn't that a hell of a state of affairs when we, the taxpaying citizens, cannot get a single slice of bacon for weeks on end when we come home from working in a defense plant and then read in the papers that prisoners of war can get away with slabs of it?

W. J. Cummings of Nogales wrote to the War Department on January 4 to express the indignation of border residents. In his opinion, whoever put naval officers with engineering skills at Papago Park was to blame for the escape. What the

Germans found, he knew, was a vein of "self-supporting rock" which made tunneling easy, and once they got across the international boundary—well, it was obvious what would happen.

> In Mexico they will be among people where 50 percent are opposed to us, and where the other 50 percent would do almost anything for a little money. By daybreak men of this stamina could be halfway to Rocky Point on the Gulf of California. Once at the Point they would be able to get boats that are seaworthy for short voyages. The fishermen will rent their boats for *any purpose,* as our officers have reason to know. It would thus be easy for the Germans to meet at any rendevouz on the Gulf.

On December 29 the Casa Grande *Dispatch* commented editorially that putting men who had served on the same ships and U-boats in one camp was a serious error.

> That Papago Park group is made up of real Heil Hitler Huns. They feel they are the superior race. The *Dispatch* would urge that Uncle Sam use a little gumption and split these groups up. Put some of them down here in Pima County. Let the officers and men of the American army teach these babies that "no work, no eat."

Two weeks later the *Dispatch,* alarmed by the capture of some of the tunnel gang in the Casa Grande neighborhood, spoke out much more firmly.

> If a few of the German prisoners who are escaping from camps around here were taken back to their camps in boxes, the escape attempts would no doubt slow down considerably. And believe it or not, many American women are actually fearful with the Huns at large.

Citizens of Chandler, a little town south of Phoenix, were like A. F. Wassilah, incensed to read about the bacon POWs had with them when apprehended. Housewives there were especially angry when they learned that the enemy was enjoying foodstuffs not available in local markets, and their husbands talked of forming posses as rumors spread of guards and POWs drinking together in local bars. On January 12 the Chandler *Arizonan* featured this rather convoluted but certainly explicit headline: GERMAN PRISONER, WITH GUN, AND GUARD ENJOY GLASS OF BEER; PEOPLE BELIEVE PRISONER CODDLING STORIES.

The tunnel at Papago Park had reverberations at the other corner of the United States as well. The *1st Command's Weekly Intelligence Summary* (January 20, 1944) warned that the Arizona escape was fostering schemes, dreams and plans at a large German POW camp in Houlton, Maine, close to the Canadian border. As soon as the ground thawed, come spring, men there were thinking of digging, and other installations throughout the nation should take warning.

Leo J. Donnelly, 8 Maple Avenue, South Glen Falls, New York, offered the War Department some constructive criticism. A World War I veteran who commanded a POW compound in France ("prisoners have to be treated like prisoners and that takes guts"), Donnelly assured authorities in Washington that he was no "crack pot" and would like to help out.

> My old serial number is 1660385 and I belong to American Legion Post #553 in South Glen Falls, and I am superintendent of the Imperial Wallpaper Company in Glen Falls. If you wish to check on me, I am at your service.
>
> I would like very much to look over some of the camps and perhaps suggest changes. Maybe I'm talking out of turn, but someone is damn slack somewhere.

Of much greater concern to the United States Army than what Wassilah, Cummings, Donnelly and scores of newspapers had to say about Papago Park was an incipient congressional outcry which, within a few weeks, would erupt on front pages across the nation.

On January 4, the same day that Major General Lerch pleaded with his superiors not to endanger the POW labor program by disciplining Holden and his associates too severely, members of Tucson's Kiwanis Club held a luncheon meeting at the Pioneer Hotel. Their scheduled speaker, Captain Homer Davis of Papago Park, already recommended for court-martial, was unable to attend "because of the pressure of military business." Instead, the Kiwanians saw two short war films, one on the Normandy invasion, the other depicting the exploits of the U.S. Navy. Like Lerch, Davis was busy answering questions, but unlike Lerch, he was much more nervous, unaware that those in the mysterious upper echelons of the United States Army already had pretty much concluded, regardless of what various inquiry boards might say, that there would be no courts-martial.

During the last few days in December most of the escapees
continued to hide out by day and hike each night as far as
they could, always heading south toward Mexico. On the
afternoon of December 31 Hans Werner Kraus and Helmut
Drescher lay stretched out on the ground in a tangle of salt-
bush and greasewood not far from a highway near Casa
Grande, forty-three miles south of Papago Park. Their food
was dry and plentiful, their camping site ideal. A hot winter
sun warmed their bodies. Kraus found this landscape beautiful in a wild, untamed sort of way. One always seemed to be
on flat land, yet high mountains continuously rimmed the
horizon, the highest of them usually blocking the path ahead.
Even during the day the desert was quiet, the sun blazing
and brilliant, nights cold and even quieter, if that was possible. In some stretches the country was cluttered with enough
bushes and low undergrowth to conceal a hundred men, then
suddenly for several miles there was nothing, not even a stray
cactus to hide behind.

The first four nights they had traveled eight, nine, even
ten miles, but now they had to make a decision. Drescher

spoke first, interrupting Kraus's reverie. "Frankly, Hans, I can't go on. This foot of mine has gotten worse today, not better. It is more swollen than ever. Rest just doesn't seem to help much. You go on alone. I'll simply go to the police tomorrow and they'll give me a ride back to Papago Park."

Kraus made no reply, simply smiling as he raised up on one elbow and stared through the bushes at a lone auto as it disappeared in the distance toward Casa Grande. "Listen to me," Drescher continued, almost as if issuing an order to his former U-boat captain. "It is only a hundred miles or so to Mexico. Go on without me."

But Kraus refused to do so. That evening the two men ate a large meal of bacon sandwiches, coffee and chocolate. After a sound sleep and a leisurely breakfast they abandoned most of their gear and headed for a small group of buildings about a mile away. They traveled very slowly, Drescher leaning heavily on a forked stick which served as a crutch. As the two men approached the ranch house they heard a dog barking, but fortunately the animal was inside.

Kraus knocked several times, very forcefully. Finally the door opened slowly. He looked down into the eyes of a twelve-year-old boy. Behind him were two much younger children and a small dog, still barking quite loudly. Kraus explained that they were unarmed German officers who had escaped from Camp Papago Park near Phoenix and wished to surrender to the local police. He then introduced Drescher, who smiled at the children and bowed slightly.

After a few moments of confusion amid constant reassurances that they meant no harm, the youth finally stepped aside and let them walk into the kitchen. His parents were away, he said, but would be back in an hour or so. Then his father could take them to Casa Grande.

Within a short time, conversation became more animated as Kraus and Drescher began to tell their young host about U-boat life. The two officers made coffee, shared the last of their chocolate with the three children and relaxed in the warmth of the kitchen.

At about eleven o'clock Newfield S. Cooper and his wife stepped through the door, their arms filled with late Christmas gifts from relatives who lived in a town. "It's okay, really it is," the boy said with a grin. "These are two German U-boat officers who escaped from the camp near Phoenix and they are telling us war stories."

Cooper said nothing, just staring in amazement. His wife dropped some packages on the table as the two youngest children ran to greet her. Reaching in his back pocket, Cooper pulled out a folded sheet of the Phoenix *Gazette* containing photos of the Papago Park escapees. Wetting a pencil stub in his mouth, he glanced first at Kraus, then at Drescher. Then, with studied precision he drew a large X across their pictures in the paper.

The return of Kraus and Drescher, the first officers apprehended, produced yet another rhubarb between the Pentagon and the 9th Service Command. Fort Douglas, it seems, again was slow in reporting what had happened, and on the morning of January 2 a major on Bryan's staff once more called a high-ranking officer in the 9th's security and intelligence section.

—But you see, Colonel, the capture of these two officers got into the papers and that was our first notice of it. And as I indicated to you before, it is a little embarrassing for us to get such news through the papers because, you know, people read it and call us up.

—Frankly, Major, I had a call in to you when you called me just now.

—Uh huh. Well, if they get any more back I wish you would instruct them to call us on it, sir, rather than TWX.

—All right.

—Because this thing is pretty damn hot, and we would like to be informed immediately of any new developments.

—Well, you see, all this happened out in the desert and the FBI is on the job and they probably released it and Phoenix didn't report it, Papago Park didn't report it, I mean, until they got some confirmation, see.

—Uh huh.

—They had to make a check, you know.

—Yes, sir, all right. I think if we can get this straightened out why then we will move along O.K. Can I ask you a bit about the tunnel? We are all intrigued by it here. Just how in hell did they ever hide the entrance right in the camp itself?

—Well, they would fill it up, that's how. They would fill up the entrance with bags of dirt. You could walk right over it apparently and not even know it was there. In fact, it is reported that Colonel Barber and one of our men, while making a check, stood right on top of the entrance. Every time they stopped working they leveled off the top of the ground so it couldn't even be seen at all.

—Uh huh. Was the entrance inside a building?

—No, there was a small building, a wash house, I believe, then there was a coal bin and it was between them. Then the tunnel went out under this drainage ditch and came out near the canal. And there was brush all around and everything, so you couldn't see the exit either.

—I see.

—Look, I mean you could walk right by it and not see it.

—Yes, well, will we be getting a copy of that preliminary report soon?

—Yes, of course.

—We are anxious to get it here, you know. The chief of staff is asking about it and that was why I wanted to check with you. Do you think I might tell him that he will get it this week?

—The men just made a verbal report and now they are writing it up. So, I imagine we would be able to get it there by Friday or Saturday.

—Will you see that it is airmailed, Colonel?

—Yes, of course.

—All right, sir, and then you have no more information other than the recapture of the seventh and eighth man?

—That's right. Now, Colonel Holden was just talking with me on the phone, and he was a bit disturbed because the newspapers are saying that we are coddling prisoners out here. You know, I know, and probably the press knows, too, that simply is not true. Those men even signed a statement before they got out that they were leaving because the treatment was so severe. There is no coddling down there at Papago Park. There is none in this entire command.

—Uh huh.

—And your friend, what's his name?

—Wattenberg?

—No, no. That radio broadcaster fellow?

—You mean Walter Winchell?

—Yes, Winchell. Winchell says we were coddling prisoners. So, the question Holden raised was do we want to . . . do you think it would be advisable to make a release of the fact we definitely are not?

—Well, Colonel, we will think about it back here. And thank you so much. Remember, we will be looking for that O'Rourke report.

"We will creep up very quietly. You hold the canteens and I will pump as fast as I can. Then we'll run. We have simply got to have water. That is all there is to it."

Mark nodded in agreement and followed Palmer through the shadows toward a small pump about fifty feet from a low adobe structure. This was their second assault on the pump. An hour before, it had creaked and wheezed so loudly that a light went on in the nearby building and they fled in terror. Palmer grabbed the pump handle, working it up and down furiously. The sound seemed deafening, but no lights appeared and in a few moments they were on their way once more.

Although this was a strange way to celebrate New Year's Eve, both men were happy. They were only thirty-one miles from Mexico and making excellent time. All that marching, jogging and running certainly was paying off. Three hours later, five miles south of Covered Wells, they decided to make camp. Just as Palmer put down his pack he heard a strange noise not too far away, several snorts and squeals. Before the two men had time to reflect upon whether they were in danger, thirty or forty wild horses swept past them, a swirl of dust and fury coming out of the night and then being swallowed up by it again just as suddenly as it had appeared. "That was a remarkable experience, something I will never forget," Mark recalls. "And those wild horses had red eyes. They really did. I suppose it is a reflection of some sort that gives that impression."

The next night the two men continued south, following a dirt highway but keeping it at a safe distance. Just before sunrise they crossed it so as to reach a clump of bushes. Near the road Palmer found a jack rabbit recently killed by a vehicle. "Reinhard, do you know what? We are going to eat rabbit. We are going to have ourselves a feast."

While Palmer skinned the animal and cut it up, Mark made a small fire out of twigs and bits of wood, and pulverized some salt tablets for seasoning. "It really was excellent," says Mark. "The best meal we had during the whole trip." Then, thoroughly contented, they curled up and went to sleep.

About two hours later Juan Sam, a Papago Indian living in Kaka, was walking along the road leading to Sells. Suddenly something in the underbrush caught his attention. Drawing closer he made out two sleeping figures. Sam returned to the highway and soon caught a ride to Sells, where he went straight to the office of the U.S. Customs Service.

Palmer heard the truck stop and knew some men were approaching. It was much too late to run, and besides, that would be dangerous. So he pretended to be asleep as fifteen men, most of them Indians, surrounded them.

"That customs official was a very good man, a kindly man. He simply woke us up, took our things away from us and then padded us down. You see, they saw the rabbit skin and thought we had shot it. They failed to detect the small compass I had in a trouser pocket. It was from a U.S. Army truck and was very helpful during the first day or two when it rained so hard. Fearing I might be charged with stealing government property if it was found, I suggested to the Americans that I cover the ashes of our small fire with sand. They agreed. As I knelt down, into the fire went that small compass."

Mark also had something he wished to get rid of. "We had to walk about a hundred and fifty meters to the highway and en route cross a wire fence. Everyone else went over, I went under, and while close to the ground, I jettisoned that highway map we had been using. I did not want to have it on me when we got thoroughly searched. Then they put us in a small cow carrier behind a truck, the men all piled into the truck, and we rode into the village of Sells.

"We were allowed to wash up, get some warm food and something to drink, and then practically the entire village swarmed into the home of the customs official to have a look at us. One white lady stared and gasped, 'Why they look just like our boys!' What in hell did she expect, horns? We really were treated like guests, though, not criminals, which, of course, we weren't.

"Then a very strange thing happened. The Americans brought in a crippled boy who asked if either of us could play chess. The poor devil had no one to play with there in Sells. He was very nervous, I recall, much more than we, the prisoners, were. Anyway, Palmer told me to go ahead and begin a game, so I did."

As Palmer tells it, Mark started out much too strongly. "You must remember, this was that poor kid's first international chess match. For all we know it was his last, too. And we were escaped German prisoners of war only recaptured a short time before. So, in German, I quietly cautioned Reinhard to, for Christ's sake (and ours), use his head and let the young man win. He did."

Shortly after midnight two men showed up from Papago Park, a lieutenant and a German-speaking corporal. Both of the escapees saluted smartly. The officer said they could sit in the back seat of the car without handcuffs if they gave their word of honor they would not try to escape. Mark and Palmer assured him one escape attempt was enough.

After an hour or so the party came to a junction and the Americans did not know which way to turn. Palmer, who had studied maps of the area very closely, was able to give them directions. As they drove through Tucson the American officer said he would like to buy them a drink but he didn't think they were dressed well enough to go into a tavern. According to Palmer, this was true. He had on German navy trousers, a blue sweater, GI boots. Mark also was wearing U.S. Army shoes, a faded green shirt and leather pants.

They thanked the lieutenant for his kind thoughts. Then he asked if there was any favor he might be able to grant. "Well," Mark asked, "could we perhaps drive through the city again to see the lights?" The officer told the driver to turn around, so once more, like two country yokels, they stared at the people and the bright lights. After prison camp and nine days in the desert, running, hiding, sleeping under bushes, that was, they recall, a real treat.

When the group got back to Papago Park, Mark and Palmer were put in the guardhouse. An FBI man who said his name was Brown questioned each of them for an hour, especially concerning any civilians they might have known in Arizona and Mexico. Then they had to explain their luggage to him. Why did they have this, where did they get that, and so on. Eventually Palmer got back his $20 tube of shaving cream. (The Americans never found the money.) Mark even gave "Mr. Brown" some pumpernickel bread as a souvenir.

"Actually, the hiking was a lot of fun," Palmer says with a shrug. "We enjoyed it. It was a fine outing. Mark was the 'baby' of the escapees, you know. He was only twenty-one. The affair did no one any harm. And we went the farthest the quickest of any group. That shows the benefits of physical conditioning, doesn't it?

"Do you know how much those Indian scouts got for tracking us down? Fifteen dollars. That's not much for a man, is it?"

On January 5 Papago Indians living in the Sells area earned some more bounty money when they caught up with Martin Peter Reese and Jürgen Schröder. These two men, well outfitted with food and clothing, were apprehended by a group led by Fred H. Claymore and Dewey Jose as they slept in the desert not far from the border.

That same day a patrol from the POW camp at Florence surprised Sternberg, Mohrdieck and Karstens at nine-thirty in the morning near Rillito, about a dozen miles north of

Tucson. This trio was dressed in GI boots, dyed U.S. Army trousers, American broad-brimmed campaign hats cut down to look like civilian clothing, and a collection of unmarked shirts and jackets. None of these men spoke English. They had only $3.33 in U.S. currency in their possession, no papers, no maps. Six hours later they were back at Papago Park.

On New Year's Eve, Guggenberger and Quaet-Faslem walked partway up a mountain near Fresnal. They finally decided they could not make it over the top to a safe hiding place by daylight, so reluctantly they dropped their rucksacks (which Guggenberger says were unbearably heavy during the first few rainy days), rested, ate some chocolate, wished each other a happy, prosperous 1945, and trudged back down the mountainside.

"We were extremely careful during the first week," Guggenberger recalls. "After that we let our guard down a bit. We saw searchers from time to time, true, but we never thought the whole region—police, Army, border patrol, customs agents, FBI, Indians—would turn out to get us. We didn't think we were that important. Even women fliers in small aircraft were hunting for us. We met some of them later. They were youthful, slim, beautiful, astonished to discover they had flown right over us many times.

"One night, I remember, near an Indian village a pack of dogs started toward us, barking and yelping as they ran. Jürgen and I froze. Then it turned out they really were not after us. They had not even seen or smelled us. They were after a trapped coyote which lay in our path. That was another close call.

"Jürgen and I tried every trick we knew. Remember, in a hunt he who is moving has the advantage; the choices are his, not the hunter's. We walked backward in the sand, the way Karl May says the Indians did. The best water holes—and getting water was a key problem—were those near windmills. Some water holes were dry, others dirty and muddy and soft around the edges. We always boiled the water. Once, again remembering what we had read in May, Quaet-Faslem cut into a cactus to get water. All Jürgen did was slash through a wren's nest. A bunch of startled birds flew out, no water.

"There was no drama in our capture. A group of Indian scouts found us during the day as we were sleeping. It was January sixth. We were less than ten miles from Mexico. The first thing I heard was this deep voice: 'And Captain Quaet-Faslem, did you have a good sleep?' Hard to believe, but it was one of the same men who had captured Jürgen eleven months earlier.

"They put us in a small jail in a little village. There was an Indian in there, too. Through the back window, when the guard was busy, we talked with a kid who bought some food for us. After a few hours a truck, several GIs and an officer showed up from Papago Park. It was a long, boring trip back. The Americans had big lunches, but all of our food was gone. After eating, they went to sleep, and as we bounced along, I reached out with my foot and pulled the lieutenant's bag toward me. Jürgen and I were able to get his sandwiches and some cake, too. One or two of the enlisted men must have known what we were up to, but they said nothing. When we got back to camp the officer was astonished to find his bag so light."

At four-thirty on the afternoon of January 8, Joe Bodillo of Three Points and Sergeant Herbert Stockton of the POW camp at Florence arrested Hans Zundorf and Otto Hoferichter near Sasabe. This pair, whom the Americans had been tracking for several days, planned to use the Gila River as their guide but got lost in the heavy rains, and having no map, simply wandered in a southerly direction toward the border. They had two handmade compasses in their possession, $6.39 in U.S. currency, and an assortment of Italian lire and French francs. Both men were back at camp five hours later.

With the capture of Zundorf and Hoferichter, only six men still were not accounted for: Wattenberg and his two aides, and the three boatmen. After leaving that schoolhouse near Phoenix, Clarus, Günther and Utzolino continued west toward the Gila. Early on the morning of December 28 they reached its banks. They were somewhat disappointed. The river was not as large as they had hoped. It looked much bigger on maps but obviously would have to do. Just after sunrise they waded out to a small island and made camp.

"It was a very pleasant spot," Clarus says. "A fine place to hide. After sleeping, we tried to put the boat together, and it was then that we discovered the skin had shrunk. So we lost six or seven hours shortening all of the struts."

There was a yet more pressing problem. The waters of the Gila were falling rapidly. Eventually the three men decided to remain on their "island" one more day, but by the evening of the twenty-ninth, when they tried to set out, where they had waded twenty-four hours before there was no water at all, just mud.

Several miles downstream from their "island," now no longer surrounded by water, they tried to launch the boat, but once they put their gear in, it just sat there, resting on the bottom. "There simply was not enough water in the mighty Gila to float our tiny craft," Clarus recalls with a grin. "It was one of those frustrating moments in life when you don't know whether to laugh, cry, swear or kick the ground in disgust. All that work for nothing!"

During that night and the next they tried to use the boat, tugging it along behind them like some huge toy. Occasionally they would find a short section of the river with sufficient water to float the craft, then they would have to carry the boat, their packs, everything, around a dam to another stretch of water, often too shallow for their purposes. At last they gave up, destroyed the boat and set out on foot for Yuma. "We should have known," Clarus says, "that the Gila wasn't much of a river. Of course, everyone who lives in Arizona knows that. We didn't."

One day they lay near a single railroad track close by a

turnout, watching as trains went by, trying to figure out where they stopped and when. However, there did not seem to be any pattern and they were unable to get aboard any of them.

At first, food was no problem. They had bread crumbs, milk, chocolate and coffee, and found some grapefruit and oranges as they hiked along. One night near a ranch house they caught a duck and roasted it. "*That* was the best duck I ever tasted," Clarus says.

Shortly after dawn on the eighth of January, still following the river, such as it was, they set up camp near Gila Bend on the bank of an irrigation canal in the midst of some tall grass. It was warm and dry and Utzolino decided to wash out his underwear. Günther told him to wait until it was dark. They were still talking as Clarus dozed off. "The next thing I knew," he says, "all hell had broken loose. It must have been sometime after noon. There were cars, people, soldiers all over the place. Despite Günther's warning, Utzolino, he was a stubborn man, went ahead and washed his clothes. Some cowboys saw him and called the police.

"By the time I realized what was happening a GI had spotted me. He was perhaps a hundred meters away, so I pretended to be a member of the search party, walking along, trying to maintain that distance as long as I could. 'Where is your car?' he asked. I replied that it was over there along the road. The soldier nodded and suggested we go to it. 'I want to see your license.'

"When we got near a car—he was then about fifteen meters away—I shrugged and said with a grin, 'I think, sir, I am perhaps one of those you are looking for.' The soldier was stunned. He almost dropped his rifle. Of course, that was the end of my escape.

"They wanted to know if there were others. Since our food was nearly gone, there seemed little reason to hide the existence of Günther; they would have flushed him out anyway, I suppose. So I led them back to our little camp and they had to wake him up! He had slept through the entire uproar. That man could sleep anywhere and under any conditions."

By January 9 only the "big boy"—Wattenberg—and Kozur and Kremer still were at large. During the preceding eight days Indian scouts and various search parties had tracked down sixteen of the escapees, each capture being duly noted by a flurry of telegrams from Colonel Holden to his superiors at Fort Douglas and in Washington. Then, for nearly a fortnight, nothing happened. There were no arrests, no telegrams, nothing, except that this tunnel escapade suddenly took an extremely bizarre turn, one of those unforeseen developments which no one, be he American, German, Indian, Mexican, guard, prisoner or civilian, could have anticipated.

Fritz Snobeck, a twenty-year-old youth captured in North Africa, yawned and scratched his new beard as the truck rolled along the highway toward Papago Park. He had traveled this same road several times. There was nothing much to see except a few houses, cacti, dust, sand and bushes. Another prisoner, Heinrich Schmidts, sat beside him, and a German doctor, Frithjof Breidthardt, also a POW, rode in the cab with the driver, Corporal Nathan Stafford. There were no guards.

It was Saturday, January 20, a bright, warm morning, and these men had left Eleven Mile Corner Camp near Casa Grande at nine o'clock, bound for Papago Park. Snobeck, who complained of chest pains, and Schmidts were to have physical checkups. Eleven Mile Corner, a branch facility under Papago Park, housed four hundred German POWs, most of whom picked cotton six days a week.

Snobeck, who had been at Papago Park until three months before, did not like Eleven Mile at all, nor did he like picking cotton. It was a dirty job, something he heard only black people did in much of America. Besides, most of his friends were at Papago Park and the recreation facilities were much better there, not to mention the work details. Not just cotton, cotton, cotton. Eleven Mile, in Snobeck's opinion, was a dump, a dirty, primitive, poorly run dump.

Shortly before noon Stafford deposited his three charges at the base hospital at Papago Park. A sergeant told him the men would be ready for the return trip by four o'clock. He drove off to a mess hall and had lunch, then began to pick up beer, Coca-Cola and food for Eleven Mile Corner. Meanwhile the three prisoners ate bologna sandwiches prepared back at camp, washed down with some soft drinks Stafford had bought for them at a gas station on the way to Papago Park.

A few minutes after two o'clock an Army surgeon finished examining Snobeck. He could not find anything wrong with the man, but was not really satisfied. He did not think Snobeck was faking, so he decided to take a blood sample and a spinal tap to be analyzed. At three-fifteen Fritz Snobeck was dressed and sitting on a bench near the hospital entrance, right where Corporal Stafford had told him to wait. Five minutes later he was gone and no one on the hospital staff saw him leave.

Considering that Papago Park recently had lost twenty-five men through a 178-foot tunnel and testimony before the major inquiry board looking into that fiasco had ended only forty-eight hours earlier, on January 18, the reaction to Snobeck's disappearance was casual indeed. Hospital personnel assured Corporal Stafford the man must be "around here someplace." He could not have gone far. The corporal also stopped by the office of Major Tays, told his staff what had occurred, and ascertained that no pass had been issued which would have enabled a prisoner to go from the hospital to a compound.

When Stafford got back to Eleven Mile minus one POW, he told the camp commander, Captain Nathan S. Hale, what had happened. Hale said the matter was not especially serious; a man could not hide inside a camp for very long.

He ordered Stafford to check again when he went up to Papago Park for supplies on Monday. Perhaps by that time Snobeck would turn up. But he didn't, and early Tuesday morning, January 23, some sixty-five hours after this prisoner of war had disappeared, Captain Hale officially informed Major Tays that Friedrich Snobeck (8WG 2648) was missing.

That afternoon Papago Park authorities held a shakedown in Snobeck's former compound and shook "Snobeck" out of a library ceiling where he had been hiding. So the incident was closed—that is, except for a brief, routine investigation. Tays called Eleven Mile at eight o'clock on the evening of the twenty-third, told Hale the good news, and asked both him and Lieutenant Robert L. Smoak, the man in charge of Snobeck's compound there, to be at Papago Park at 1600 on the twenty-fourth for the inquiry. "It won't take long, just a formality. There are some papers to sign," he said. "You both have been through these things before, I'm sure."

The next morning Fritz Snobeck was a prime topic of conversation as word of his capture quickly spread throughout the camp. Then, at about eleven o'clock, Captain Edmund Chase, the officer in charge of Compound 3, heard a disturbing rumor. Several of the prisoners told him that they did not believe the man taken from the library actually was Snobeck, but when queried, they conceded they did not know who he was. Fully aware that this might be a trick to cause a bit of trouble and have some fun at his expense, Chase decided nevertheless to report this gossip to his superior, Captain Homer Davis. When he got to stockade headquarters, Davis was not there, so he told Master Sergeant Lawrence Strange what he had heard. Strange simply smiled and shrugged, and, as Chase recounted later, merely muttered, "How strange!"

Yet the rumor would not go away. An hour later Technical Sergeant Joe Street appeared at stockade headquarters and told Strange he was certain that the man they thought was Fritz Snobeck actually was Johann Kremer, one of the three missing tunnel escapees. Street added that he had worked with Kremer from time to time and that the prisoner over in the guardhouse was Kremer.

This time Strange reacted, telling Street to report this information to Tays or Parshall at once. Street followed this suggestion and immediately talked with one or perhaps both of these officers. The records of this very confusing day fail to make clear what transpired, but a short time later Strange again ran into Street.

"Well, did you tell them about Kremer?"

"Yes, I did."

"And what did they say?"

"They didn't believe me. They said that was simply impossible."

Meanwhile, perhaps even before this brief exchange took place, Corporal Theodore Davidson, interpreter for Tays and Parshall, began hunting for his superiors. Davidson had received a strange message from Helmut Gugger, the POW who had first disclosed the existence of the tunnel. Gugger, he was told, wanted to speak to him at once, said it was "very urgent." Davidson finally located Major Tays as he was conducting a shakedown in Compound 4 and informed him of Gugger's unusual request. The major ordered Davidson to go see the prisoner at once and report back to him as soon as he could.

Within fifteen minutes Davidson returned to Compound 4. "Gugger," he said, "claims to have some information of great importance which he wishes to reveal."

"What is it?" Tays asked.

"He won't say. He wants to talk to both of us."

Irritated by this mixture of rumor and mystery, Tays told Davidson to bring Helmut Gugger to the Internal Security office. Once the three men were together, Gugger reported that the man the Americans thought was Fritz Snobeck actually was Johann Kremer. And even more startling, he related how Kremer had told him that both Wattenberg and Kozur were living within a very few miles of Papago Park. A key question was, of course, *how* had Kremer gotten into camp? Gugger said he really didn't know.

By four o'clock that afternoon Parshall and Tays concluded that Street, Gugger and others were indeed telling the truth: Fritz Snobeck was Johann Kremer. Tays first notified various authorities of this extremely embarrassing development, then he belatedly told the officers from Eleven Mile (who had already arrived at Papago Park) that the inquiry into the disappearance of Snobeck had been canceled. Meanwhile the Internal Security staff began an intense interrogation of both Gugger and Kremer in an attempt to learn all they could about the whereabouts of Wattenberg and Kozur.

Shortly after dark that same evening Walter Kozur left the mountain cave where he, Kremer and Wattenberg had been living for the past month, a spot from which they could almost see Papago Park. He carefully made his way down the trail toward an abandoned car where men on work details from the camp sometimes left food for them.

They had worked out an unbelievably successful routine. Every few days Kremer had gone back into camp with a work party, found out how the search for them was going, picked up some food and then returned. Sometimes he just changed places with one of their friends, that man staying out in the cave overnight and going back to camp when Kremer came out. If a work party was large, one could melt into the group and get past the guards easily enough. Sometimes when the risk seemed too great, Kremer would send out food by one of their friends.

Wattenberg said they would head south as soon as the excitement of the tunnel escape died down. But he kept putting off their departure and now they would have to wait until Kremer returned from Papago Park once more.

The three men had made several forays into Phoenix, about a three-hour hike away. Kozur and Kremer even went into a bowling alley one night and had a couple of beers. Kozur was fascinated by the huge American bowling balls.

Now he approached the car very cautiously, looking in all directions before leaving the shelter of the rocks and bushes.

He opened the door slowly, but there was nothing there. No food. Kozur heard a slight noise behind him, turned and discovered that he was facing three American GIs. One held a large flashlight, the others two rifles pointed right at his head. Now only Fregattenkapitän Jürgen Wattenberg, former skipper of the U-162, was unaccounted for. And, oh yes, Fritz Snobeck, too.

The following day, Thursday the twenty-fifth, the *Arizona Republic* featured a strange, confusing (and eventually false) page-one story: THREE NAZIS FLEE CAMP. The FBI told reporters that Papago Park notified them on Tuesday afternoon that Fritz Snobeck was missing and on Wednesday that two other prisoners had escaped from the Mesa branch camp. Sometime that same day, however, Papago Park reported that Snobeck had been found hiding within the camp, but then reversed field. No, Snobeck had not been found, after all, and camp officials conceded he "may have been gone since Saturday."

Late editions of Thursday's *Republic* muddled this tale still further by informing readers that Walter Kozur had been apprehended some twenty-four hours earlier on McDowell Road two and a half miles from Papago Park. Army authorities and the FBI stated, with obvious relief, that now only two of the tunnelers still were at large: Wattenberg and Kremer.

The Snobeck incident and the capture of both Kozur and Kremer (despite what that page-one story said) greatly increased pressures on Jürgen Wattenberg. He had very little money and no longer could be sure of getting food from inside the camp. Papago Park officials knew he must be close-by, perhaps even in Phoenix itself. Additional patrols scoured the area without success.

On Saturday morning, January 27, the Fregattenkapitän ate his last bit of food. He did not dare go near the old auto. Failure of Kozur to return indicated that the Americans undoubtedly would be watching it closely. That afternoon Wattenberg heated some water, shaved carefully, washed, put on his last clean shirt, a brilliant yellow plaid cotton, and like scores of Americans, headed for a Saturday night in town. The rest of his wardrobe consisted of wool trousers, GI shoes, a Navy jacket and a dyed coat. He also carried a small bundle of clothing.

Wattenberg had only seventy-five cents in U.S. coins. This meant he could perhaps get a cheap room or a meal, not both. After some reflection he found the prospect of a good night's sleep more enticing than food. However, he was unable to find a room in the sea of servicemen and war workers crowding the city for the weekend and spent much of the evening lounging around the lobby of the Adams Hotel. Shortly after midnight, a bit wary of a desk clerk who began examining him intently, he went to a nearby Chinese restaurant and spent nearly all of his money on a bowl of oatmeal with raisins, a soft-boiled egg, toast and tea. Then he began to walk the streets of Phoenix, still trying desperately to somehow ward off the inevitable.

At three-thirty in the morning he approached Charles V. Cherry, a foreman of a street-cleaning crew near the corner of West Van Buren and Third streets, and asked where Van Buren Street was. (Later he told Kozur he was trying to locate the Japanese colony in Phoenix or at least find out if one existed.) Somewhat taken back by this question, Cherry told Wattenberg he already was on Van Buren Street, one of the city's principal thoroughfares. The Fregattenkapitän thanked him and strolled on.

His suspicions aroused by Wattenberg's accent and obvious ignorance of his surroundings, Cherry told a passing police officer what had happened. Sergeant Gilbert Brady, who was on the night-desk duty and had stepped out for a sandwich, quickly caught up with Wattenberg.

"Excuse me, sir, where do you live?"

"I am a rancher in town for the weekend."

"Yes, sir, but where do you live?"

"In Glendale."

"Glendale, California, or Glendale, Arizona?"

"Why, Glendale back East."

"I see. Sir, could I please see your Selective Service registration card?"

Wattenberg smiled, looked down at the American, shrugged and said with a sigh, "I might as well tell you. I am the man all of you fellows are looking for. I am Captain Jürgen Wattenberg, the escaped prisoner of war from Papago Park." Since Van Buren leads to Papago Park, it is possible that even if Brady had not found Wattenberg, this German officer had decided to give himself up. With no money, no food, there really was no other choice.

Wattenberg was taken to police headquarters, where the FBI queried him closely about many aspects of the escape, including a list of items found on Kozur. Agents were especially disturbed by a request for "a hose with a screw attachment," fearing he might have been thinking of siphoning gas for a stolen vehicle. No, the prisoner replied, he merely wanted a means of drawing water without making a noisy splash. Wattenberg refused to say where he and his aides had been hiding, and despite a thorough search by scores of soldiers, their lair never was found.

By nine in the morning on the twenty-eighth the man the Americans thought had devised and led the great tunnel escape was back at Papago Park, and readers of the Monday edition of the *Arizona Republic* learned of the capture of this "internationally known" German naval officer. They also were told that "Johann Kremer, the twenty-fourth missing prisoner to be returned, was picked up last week near Phoenix." This was, of course, an essentially true statement. Compound 4 of the Papago Park prisoner-of-war camp was "near Phoenix."

The twenty-five tunnelers were now back, including the "big boy," and there were only a few loose ends to be taken care of. On January 26 Gerhard Ender left the interrogation center at Fort Hunt but did not return to Papago Park. Instead he was shipped to Camp McCain, Mississippi, where, within two weeks, he was up to his old tricks. The commandant of that base soon placed Ender on a special detention list, noting that the man was "thoroughly uncooperative in every way."

Meanwhile, shortly after fingering Johann Kremer, Helmut Gugger was transferred to Florence, Arizona, and from there to Camp Ruston, Louisiana. In mid-February, authorities at Ruston dispatched this brief memo concerning Gugger to Washington:

> P/W searched and all clothing and evidence of naval connections were destroyed. P/W fully instructed prior to his assignment to an anti-Nazi compound away from German naval personnel.

The scheduled inquiry into Snobeck's disappearance, finally held on Saturday, January 27, developed into a heated exchange between Papago Park and Eleven Mile, each trying to prove the other was at fault. Tays conceded he was told informally on Saturday, January 20, that Fritz Snobeck was missing but received no official statement on his disappearance until three days later. When asked about cross-over roll calls at Eleven Mile, the officer in charge of Snobeck's old compound said none were ever held. "No, sir. We always had the right number of men and did not have any roll calls."

Under intense questioning Captain Hale, commandant at Eleven Mile, admitted there really was no positive means of identifying prisoners held at his camp. Each man's record folder was retained at Papago Park. They had some photographic equipment there, yes, but were so busy with work details, day-to-day business and picking cotton that it was never used.

> —How many men do you have at Eleven Mile Corner, Captain?
> —Three hundred and ninety-seven, of whom nine are up here in the hospital right now.
> —Couldn't almost any man have taken Snobeck's place on the 20th and come up here on that truck?
> —Yes, I suppose that is true.

—And you and your men probably wouldn't have known the difference?
—Yes, sir.

Not long after five o'clock on January 29, Lieutenant Edgar Pilschke was driving past Compound 4 at Papago Park. He glanced at a group of prisoners and was certain he saw Fritz Snobeck standing among them. A short time later Pilschke and a corporal walked through a mess hall and spotted Snobeck eating evening chow. This POW's only request (which was not granted) was: Could he please finish his meal before being sent to the guardhouse?

Snobeck refused to say precisely where he had been hiding for nine days but boasted that he had merely left the hospital and walked through the unguarded gates leading into his old compound. Why did he do it? To be with his friends and because he did not want to pick any more damn cotton. Besides, Eleven Mile Corner was "a dirty, filthy, cold place."

Friedrich Snobeck, now a resident of the Ruhr city of Essen, proved to be the undoing of Major Eugene Tays, who was removed from his post as Papago Park's director of intelligence and security on January 28, the day before Lieutenant Pilschke spotted Snobeck in Compound 4. These were the specific charges leveled against him:

1. Tays should have begun the search for Snobeck on January 20 when he disappeared, not seventy-two hours later.
2. He developed no positive means of identifying prisoners held at branch camps.
3. To January 28 no record was kept at the stockade gate of individual prisoners entering and leaving, only work party groups.
4. To January 28 it was possible for a prisoner to go freely from the hospital to other parts of the stockade, just as Snobeck had done.

In short, Fritz Snobeck and the twenty-five tunnelers proved something which Colonel William Holden, Fort Douglas, the Pentagon, Walter Winchell and scores of Arizona citizens feared was indeed true. Papago Park was a very poorly run prisoner-of-war camp. The place leaked like a sieve, and there were a lot of questions to be answered.

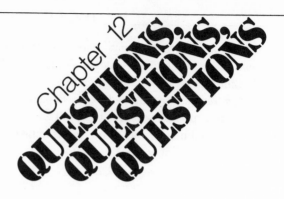

Chapter 12

The local inquiry board established by Colonel Holden sat for seventeen days, heard some fifty witnesses and compiled nearly two hundred pages of testimony. Unlike the investigators from Fort Douglas, this group tried to explain and rationalize what had happened, not fix blame. Yet, like the O'Rourke panel, they obviously had to deal with the same facts, and query after query probed at one crucial point: Why was no roll call or head count held in 1 A and 1 B on Sunday morning, December 24, especially after the uproar of the previous day?

Another matter of special interest was dirt which was or was not hauled into Compound 1 A to help the "troublemakers" build their faustball field. Lieutenant William Watson, the man in charge of that area, and the Germans themselves maintained that no dirt ever appeared, none whatsoever. Other officers—Holden, Tays and Jackson among them—testified just as convincingly that many loads of soil were taken into that compound.

Some of the most interesting testimony was heard on January 5 when six of the escapees appeared. Gugger, the first to be called, was the only one who readily agreed to be sworn in. He credited Kraus, Günther and Spehr with organizing the tunnel work, gave the impression he was "halfway" ordered to escape, and told how Wattenberg distributed names and addresses of South American contacts and made a little speech before they went out through the tunnel.

Gugger was followed by one of two men captured the previous day near Sells. The official transcript identifies the prisoner as Jürgen Schröder, but testimony indicates Martin Reese actually was speaking, not Schröder. Whoever it was, he was extremely uncooperative and simply refused to talk much of the time.

—Will you answer any questions at all?

—I am willing to answer why I escaped and what I have answered so far.

—Well, then, why did you escape?

—I think it is my duty to help Germany as much as possible. I could not stand any longer the insults which were brought upon me by the Americans.

—What insults do you have reference to?

—First of all, I was transferred to the guardhouse without reason. I was called by Colonel Barber a "no human being" and a "cut throat." A further transfer was to 1 A where there is no opportunity to study anything or to attend sports and where nearly everybody is sleeping in one room, which is not for an officer.

—When did you make up your mind that you couldn't stand any more of this and that you should escape?

—I will not say.

—Have you received any insults recently?

—Not recently, but the treatment in Compound 1 A is insulting by itself.

—In what way?

—Because we have not got the same treatment as other officers. We cannot go to the show and we have to be in a small compound.

—You haven't been forced to work, have you?

—No.

—Have you been required to perform any labor by anyone?

—No.

—Did you perform any labor of your own accord?

—I was working in there for the compound in cooperation with the whole group.

—What were you doing?

—We were building chairs and things like that.

—Did you do any digging?

—I will not say.

—Did you find any fault with the food you received?

—We got less than in the rest of the compounds.

—Did the fact that you saved up food for the escape have anything to do with the shortage?

—Not on account of that.

—How do you know that Compound 1 A received less food than other compounds?

—We compared the charts with other compounds.

—Where did you get the food charts?

—I will not say.

—Is Colonel Barber the only officer or American personnel who has insulted you?

—A direct insult, yes. There has been an order by Colonel Holden that we have to attend count for any American, whoever he is, and this is an insult to a German officer. In Germany any falling in ranks shows honor to the person who calls the men out and for whom they stand formation and we do not do that for just a noncommissioned officer or a soldier. Only for officers.

—Since Colonel Holden read you the order have you stood formation?

—First I got a written order and we would not follow that, so they took off our rations and after this Colonel Holden came in and read the order to us and from that time we are falling out in formation.

—But at the time your rations were reduced you stood a few formations . . . did you stand those formations to get food?

—No. We just fell out when there was an officer present, not in order to receive food.

—Where were you captured?

—Near Sells.

—How did you get to Sells?

—I cannot say.

—Did you walk?

—I will not say.

—Did you surrender yourself or were you captured?

—I would not give myself up.
—Who captured you?
—A civilian patrolman.
—Who was recaptured with you?
—Schröder.
—Is he a navy man, too?
—Merchant marine. I am navy.
—Why did he escape?
—It is the duty of every German prisoner to try to escape, that is one reason. The second reason is on account of the treatment in Compound 1 A.
—Were you treated badly?
—I do not want to talk about it, enough is proved by the complaints coming out of the compounds.
—But those complaints do not come to this board.
—It would take much too long to talk about the complaints.
—How much food did you take with you?
—Anything connected with the escape, as I have indicated, I will not talk about.
—How long did you work on the tunnel?
—I will not say.
—Did you do any digging or supervising?
—I will not say.

Strehle, Frenzel, Streng and Fuge were equally uncommunicative, each stressing their dislike of the treatment they received in 1 A and belief in their duty to try to escape. Strehle, asked if calluses on his hands came from digging, replied, "No, that comes from sport."

—And did you consider the digging of a tunnel sport?
—That is also sport, yes.
—You must have worked at it pretty hard, too.
—I have plenty of time. If I do anything voluntary it goes easy.

Frenzel, who refused to comment upon his own rough hands, stoutly maintained that enemy soldiers held in Germany lived much better than the men at Papago Park. "I have seen in Germany how the American prisoners of war are treated. I know."

Streng added a strange, poignant note to this dry, repetitive recitation:

—But you surrendered, didn't you? Why did you surrender?
—Because I wanted to come back.
—Well, then, why did you go out in the first place?
—I did not want to have this kind of treatment at Christmas time.
—But did you fare any better over Christmas outside?
—Three of my brothers have died in this war, two of them in Russia. I could be together with them.
—Then it wasn't your intention to stay out?
—Only over Christmas. I just did not want to be behind barbed wire over Christmas.
—How far were you from camp when you gave up?
—Near Mesa. I left the camp, celebrated Christmas outside, and then came back.
—Was there any disturbance in the compound when you went out through the tunnel?
—Maybe. I did not pay much attention. I could not say.
—When you worked on the tunnel did you work at night or in the day?
—I never said that I worked on it.
—Where did you spend Sunday?
—Off the road. There were some kind of bushes and we were sitting there and celebrating Christmas.
—Drinking beer?
—I do not drink beer.

Fuge, who traveled with Strehle, answered very few questions. However, before lapsing into surly silence, he blurted out several very obvious truths.

—Why did you escape?
—As long as there will be prisoners of war there will be some escapes and some tunnels.
—Did you have any special reason to escape?
—I do not like it here anymore.
—Why did you surrender?
—Because the food was spoiled.
—It didn't last twenty-five days, did it?
(No answer.)

—Did you escape on Friday?
(No answer.)
—Did you got out through the tunnel?
—I will not say.
—What course did you take when you left Papago Park?
(No answer.)
—How did you travel? Did you walk?
(No answer.)

During the last two days of testimony, January 17 and 18, four men were given an opportunity to present witnesses and defend themselves against accusations of negligence and dereliction of duty building up against them. Before appearing, each was informed by letter concerning the precise nature of these "prejudicial allegations." The officer in the most trouble, perhaps the man who, somewhere along the way, the others decided could be thrown to the wolves, so to speak, was Major Eugene Tays. Tays called Lieutenant William R. Hill, once an assistant in his office, Captain Parshall, his current deputy, and Lieutenant Jackson, the post engineer. Through interrogation he sought to prove that no one thought prisoners held in the Phoenix area could dig a tunnel and that inspections of the compounds at Papago Park therefore were infrequent. Tays concluded his defense with this statement:

So, because of the conditions brought out by the testimony of these witnesses, which were known to me, and because of the "calculated risk" policy which was definitely impressed upon the minds of all concerned with the management of prisoners of war, it was not deemed advisable to establish an elaborate system of detecting tunnels, which in my opinion would have been the only effective means of discovering tunneling activities. During a conference held at Fort Douglas of all commanders and other officers connected with prisoner of war work, this statement was made by one of the instructors, General Blackshear Bryan: "Don't be too alarmed over escapes. They are to be expected and remember no escaped prisoner ever has committed an act of sabotage."
This is a general statement, of course, and refers to all types of escapes. In my estimation the only system which

would have prevented tunneling would have been to post two guards in each compound around the clock. These guards to be continually on the move all over the compound. This would have required thirty-six additional guards which we did not have.

Since I once made a special trip to Fort Douglas to try to retain the number of personnel I thought adequate and since I was unsuccessful and our complement was reduced in spite of all my efforts, therefore, I was convinced that it would be futile to ask for the thirty-six men needed to inaugurate an adequate plan of detecting tunneling activities.

Captain Davis, who called Colonel Holden as his only witness, stressed that to his knowledge, no Sunday-morning head counts were ever held at Papago Park until December 31, 1944, regardless of who the commanding officer was. Boyer, the man in charge of 1 B, tried to prove that upon orders of Davis he changed all roll calls so as to conform with the routine practiced in 1 A. The purpose was, he emphasized, to achieve more accurate counts by holding them simultaneously.

Lieutenant William S. Watson came up with a strange collection of defense witnesses: Corporal Gebhardt and two German POWs, Ferdinand Fuge and Helmut Gugger. Watson considered calling August Maus but later decided not to. With the assistance of this trio he endeavored to show that his inspection of 1 A on the afternoon of December 23 was both thorough and complete.

After considerable soul-searching, the board suggested that three of the men involved—Davis, Boyer and Watson—merely be admonished for so-called dereliction of duty under the 104th Article of War, which stipulates that a commanding officer may impose disciplinary measures without court-martial proceedings unless those reprimanded request trial. On January 24 Colonel Holden, soon to retire for "reasons of health" (both a discreet way out of this dilemma and a true cause for stepping aside), approved most of the board's findings; however, he adamantly refused to sanction one conclusion absolving Major Eugene Tays of any blame.

A detailed program for detection of tunnels was considered by the Director of Internal Security, but due to the difficulties of placing such a program in effect, he decided to apply the principle of "calculated risk," supplemented by irregular inspections. Although there might have been an error of judgment, the board finds no dereliction of duty.

Holden's objections were of no consequence. The inquiry into the Snobeck affair (that board also headed up by Captain Robison) ended Tay's career as chief of security and intelligence at Papago Park. So the Pentagon ultimately received two reports, one recommending court-martial trials for five officers, the other a tap on the wrist for only the three junior men who had let twenty-five German POWs escape through a "200-foot, solid rock" tunnel.

During February the antics of the high-spirited prisoners at Papago Park stirred up such a reaction on Capitol Hill that the U.S. Army could no longer keep the lid on what was becoming a source of considerable embarrassment. Strangely, it was not the tunnel or the Kremer-Snobeck mix-up that made a handful of legislators see red, but a Nazi flag flying in the brilliant Arizona sunshine, not once but twice in the same day.

At nine-thirty on February 7, POWs heading out to pick cotton unfurled a swastika banner as their truck passed through Chandler, a small community just south of Phoenix. Roy Wolf, city marshal, stopped the vehicle and tried to search the men, but an American officer said the incident was military business and the Army would take care of it. According to the *Arizona Republic* of February 8, Chandler citizens were "further incensed" when the men flew the same flag as they went through the city en route back to camp that evening. Friends of Otto Reuter who were on the truck told him later that the flag became a neckerchief, and although a guard conducted a perfunctory search, it was never found.

On February 12 Arizona's Ernest W. McFarland, a Navy man in World War I, rose in the U.S. Senate to discuss this latest bit of affrontery and read angry words from aroused constituents. For example, Arthur Morton of Phoenix was very upset by what was going on:

> From what I hear it is time that prisoners of war at Papago Park were made to realize that they are *prisoners*. When escaped prisoners are caught with bacon and cigarettes that does not go down good. We do not object to going without bacon and cigarettes when the armed forces need them. But I do not consider that American citizens should have to do without so that the Germans can have them. The secretary of war stated that the prisoners were not being pampered, but were being strictly treated according to the Geneva Convention rules. Let someone investigate some of the camps who is not connected with the armed forces. Congress can do it.

W. J. Eden, president of the Phoenix Central Labor Council, had sent Senator McFarland a formal resolution also calling for an inquiry, noting that members who had worked on the construction of the camp at Papago Park and knew something about mining thought Holden's tale of a tunnel through solid rock "fantastic and highly improbable." Judge Howard C. Speakman, a personal friend of McFarland's, blasted the "soft" treatment of prisoners of war in the Phoenix area.

> You probably read of the numerous escapes. In fact, they are not escapes, the Germans just walk off from the job. They roam the neighborhoods, steal from people in the vicinity, pilfer houses where no one is at home. They seem to do it at will. I presume you read of their displaying a Nazi swastika in Chandler as a truckload of prisoners drove through the town. Upon being stopped by the constable he was prevented from searching them by the guards. People are sore and disgusted, especially men who have sons overseas; when armed guards stand with rifles and prevent red-blooded American people from searching the damned Nazis to take from them a swastika, I think the War Department deserves condemnation. The army now insists that no civilian accost a prisoner for any matter whatsoever. The army is lucky half of them haven't been killed or lynched. They say that this kind of treatment is given the Nazis because Germany has lived up to the

Geneva Conference. I guess they failed to see the pictures of dead American boys in the snow in Germany recently, killed immediately after their capture.

On February 19 Richard F. Harless, a Texas-born Democratic congressman from Arizona, carried this battle to the floor of the House of Representatives. In extensive remarks Harless told how "twenty-five hardened Nazis led by the notorious Captain Wattenberg dug a tunnel some 200 feet long and made a rather spectacular escape." He then proceeded to call for formation of a special committee to investigate "the prisoner of war problem" and formulate general policies. Although some "facts" presented by Harless were inaccurate, his outrage was genuine and sparked comment by three other lawmakers, Gordon L. McDonough, a California Republican, John R. Murdock, an Arizona Democrat, and Dewey Short, a Republican from Missouri.

According to Harless, Colonel Holden, too arthritic to be stationed anywhere but Arizona, headed up a staff of inept, limited-service officers and guards. He questioned use of the "calculated risk" policy "where desperate and fanatical Nazis are stationed" and told his colleagues that even though Papago Park was known as "the Alcatraz of all camps, only one out of every four guard towers was being manned." Harless called for less pampering of prisoners, indoctrination of democratic principles, and segregation of rank Nazis. "With regard to food," this congressman noted scornfully, "I suggest that some POW menus might make you think you are in the Waldorf-Astoria."

Unaware that isolating the so-called troublemakers in Compound 1 A had made tunneling possible, and confused concerning the true role of Gerhard Ender (whom he apparently credited with the murder of Werner Dreschler), Harless forged on:

> I am told that in the camp near Phoenix there is no proper segregation and that installation is in the grip of fanatical Nazis who actually run the place. A man named Ender, holder

of the coveted "order of the blood" insignia, is the dictator. He even tells Captain Wattenberg what to do.

This man Ender is so powerful that he even holds secret trials within the camp and has executed at least one prisoner of war. Yet nothing has been done to bring these executioners to justice. Who knows but what we are harboring another Hitler in our camps now?

I think we must establish a policy which is firm and fair. Radio commentators, newspapers, and the public at large, standing on the streets, are talking about the POWs and the mismanagement of their camps. It is high time the Congress should do something and check up on conditions in them.

Congressman Dewey Short agreed wholeheartedly that the situation was very bad and demanded attention.

I think the gentleman from Arizona is right to point out that our psychological warfare has been the weakest and poorest perhaps in all the world. The best way to make converts is through fair but firm treatment.

Also, we should not forget that escaped POWs are potential saboteurs. Last night, in his radio broadcast, Walter Winchell said a huge powder factory may be built in the state of Oklahoma near a POW camp. I do not know just where it is but I plan to check on it. I do not think we should blame the prisoners for our own stupidity. One man who gets out, with the light of a match, perhaps could blow the whole thing to smithereens.

The United States Army fought back, of course, denying some assertions, ignoring others, and stressing positive aspects of its POW program. Enemy labor, various generals testified, had saved American taxpayers perhaps as much as $100 million. It was, in fact, like transferring the work force of a city such as Cologne or Leipzig to this side of the Atlantic.

Fair treatment of 350,000 Germans on U.S. soil was the best means of assuring similar conditions for nearly 80,000 Americans living behind barbed wire in the Third Reich. Indoctrination in democracy was desirable, they agreed, but it must come more from example than through classrooms, movies, books and lectures. Whatever prisoners absorbed as they lived and worked in American communities was the best training. Formal propagandizing would provide Herr Goebbels with valid reasons for teaching his brand of dictatorial rule to our boys.

As for escapees—General Lerch preferred to call them "absentees" whenever he talked with congressional committees— their ranks were thin; only 1,354 men had escaped by February 26, 1945. The rate of escapes was about equal to that from federal penitentiaries, and since all of the POWs were intent on trying to get home or lost in a large city, none had committed any acts of sabotage.

One local Arizona weekly, Florence's *Arizona Blade-Tribune*, failed to jump on the anti-POW bandwagon, perhaps for very selfish reasons. Instead of talking about escapes, the *Blade-Tribune's* editor stressed how many pounds of cotton the prisoners were picking. During the last five days of 1944, men at the local camp harvested 1.295 million pounds. A short time later they picked 2.699 million pounds in one week in the Casa Grande–Eloy neighborhood, and on January 19 the Army said POWs quartered at Florence had accounted for over 20 million pounds during the last three months of 1944.

Quite clearly, not everyone in Arizona was willing to jettison this ready supply of labor just because a few Germans dug a tunnel and got away. If some of them got treated a bit too well, so what? Cotton was needed in the war effort. If the Germans didn't pick it, the crop would rot and do no one any good. The *Blade-Tribune* suggested that each POW donate a pint of blood every month to help their wounded countrymen in Europe. "At least indirectly," the editor wrote, "the good food given to these prisoners then would become a valuable asset to our nation."

Some of this outcry against coddling of prisoners arose because of an ill-conceived program for Italian prisoners in America. After Italy switched sides in September 1943, some 30,000 young men willing to help the Allies were organized into Italian Service Units (ISU), given special privileges and second-hand GI uniforms, and were even allowed to go on leave in groups to cities and towns near their camps. Dances were frequently held for them on various bases, and once these often good-looking youths met Yankee signorinas starved for male companionship, trouble erupted.

Major Cecil Parshall says he never had any problem with Italian and German POWs molesting women, but the reverse actually was true. "Those Germans out at Papago Park were a fine bunch of men—smart, good-looking, well-built. Hell, down at Florence we had to put machine guns on top of the trains to scare off the women when those Italians arrived. Says something about our patriotism, doesn't it?"

Girls who dated ISU men frequently were assured that if they got pregnant, then marriages could be arranged. This was not true. No POW was permitted to marry, although a few zealous ISU took advantage of liberal state laws and did just that. Eleanor and Franklin Roosevelt, the Secretaries of State and War, congressmen, Pentagon brass, camp commanders and priests all received scores of angry letters from distraught females and distressed parents. In July 1945 General Brehon Somervell blew up: "One would think from the volume of this correspondence that one of the Provost Marshal General's prime functions is to conduct an 'advice to the lovelorn' bureau!"

During the last twelve months of World War II, U.S. newspapers, magazines and radio waged a sometimes spirited homefront battle over the treatment of enemy prisoners held in America. Bill Cunningham, a well-known Boston *Herald* columnist, and Walter Winchell, a man most deskbound generals feared more than Hitler, were among the U.S. Army's severest critics. In time, *Business Week, Life, American, Newsweek, Reader's Digest, Time* and *Collier's* joined in the fray, assuring their readers that the Army was or was not coddling POWs.

Of course, this Italian Service business had nothing to do with Germans. No German prisoners of war were ever dressed up in GI uniforms for an evening on the town or enjoyed prearranged dates and dancing in their camps. Yet Americans found it difficult to tell the difference between Germans and Italians. In their eyes, prisoners were prisoners, enemy were enemy, and many knew that their sons were dying in Italy. If these ISU men were helping us, if they really were our allies, why didn't they go home and fight? If they were prisoners, why didn't they stay behind barbed wire where they belonged?

By early March of 1945 Gerhard Ender and Helmut Gugger had been dispatched to other camps, the tunnelers and their buddies put in a new isolation compound a few hundred yards from the Papago Park stockade, and the Pentagon was trying to resolve conflicting reports from the two inquiry boards that looked into the tunnel affair. On the morning of March 3 Lieutenant Wendell Phillips, a member of the Provost Marshal General's staff in Washington, called Colonel Charles K. Wing at Fort Douglas, director of security for the 9th Service Command.

—Colonel, I have been asked to find out about this thing at Papago Park. We are very anxious to proceed cautiously and we are just a bit in between because one investigation apparently says there was no serious dereliction of duty and another, from higher authority at Fort Douglas, says some corrective action should be taken.

—I think that corrective action has been taken, Lieutenant. Holden and Tays both have stepped aside. I do not know what has happened to the others. If they haven't already done it, I believe those men, the three junior officers, are to get administrative reprimands.

—Then that is the status of things now?

—Yes. But, of course, you cannot give a man an administrative reprimand if he demands a trial. And whether or not any of them have asked for trials, I don't know. I will try to find out.

—Well, I wish you would check on it and let us know, Colonel. We need all the information we can get if we are going to continue to get questions from congressmen and the press.

—What on earth do those Arizona people have against Holden? I understand the man saved their cotton crop.

—That's true. Of course he did, and I'll tell you one of the funniest twists in this tale, Colonel, some folks down near Yuma wrote to their senators to this effect: "We think this Papago Park thing is making a mountain out of a mole hill and for God's sake shut up about it before you cost us our chances at some prisoner labor to save our crops down here." This gave us swell ammunition to use in answering those men up on Capitol Hill. Anyway, we could give them a good rounding answer, you know, but the damage was done. Their words about Holden and his men being unfit got into the *Congressional Record*. They said Holden had arthritis.

—That's not true, although he does have a weak heart.

—Well, of course, they don't always get things right, these senators and congressmen. And there there are radio men like Winchell and civilians in general. They feel free to speak out and object to nearly everything and, well, the condemnation is becoming pretty general, I fear. They just say the staff and guards at Papago Park were incompetent and inefficient and so on, and this talk gives all POW camps a bad name. But if you'll give us the full information as soon as possible on what action has been taken there, we would appreciate it. Also, it might help us blunt some of these questions.

—All right.

—Thank you very much, Colonel.

A few hours later Lieutenant Phillips called again and Wing repeated much of what he said before, adding that higher authorities in Washington had concluded that no courts-martial were warranted. Instead Davis, Watson and Boyer would be admonished by administrative reprimands. One board, Wing reminded Phillips, originally recommended trials on two counts. One was not discovering the tunnel, but upon reflection, the Pentagon decided this actually was not a "triable" offense. The tunnel was so well disguised that conviction seemed very doubtful. The other count was Sunday-morning roll call, and Wing conceded that Colonel Holden was negligent to that extent, not holding such roll calls, true. But Holden was now in the hospital, would soon retire, and there seemed no good reason to proceed further with this matter.

Davis, Boyer and Watson, Wing continued, still were at Papago Park awaiting new assignments, as was Major Tays. The tunnel crowd was in a separate area called Pima Camp, a safe distance from the Arizona Crosscut Canal, and a new spokesman, Colonel Horst von Pflugk-Harttung, would presently arrive at Papago Park. Pflugk-Harttung, the colonel added, was a trusted army man whom they could count on to be cooperative.

By mid-February, men in the South Pacific knew about Papago Park and its tunnel. Bill Hill, a native of Bisbee, Arizona, serving in that area, wrote to his hometown paper, the Bisbee *Review*, suggesting that troublesome POWs be shipped across the Pacific. "It looks like the boys at Papago Park can't handle them. I don't understand why. Men overseas don't like to hear that kind of talk. I also see in the papers they are bringing Japs back to California. It looks like bad business to me."

The tunnel story even reached the Third Reich. Late in February 1945 a small item in an Erfurt newspaper caught the eye of Frau Kraus: "Twenty-Five Germans Escape Through Rock Tunnel." Reflecting upon this news for a moment, she smiled and then picked up the phone.

"Frau Quaet-Faslem, please . . . Ruth, I have just read in the paper about a tunnel some naval POWs dug in America. Do you think Jürgen perhaps was mixed up in this?"

"It would not surprise me if he were. Of course, we do not know precisely where our men are. They were moved west about a year ago, somewhere beyond Texas but not near the ocean."

"Yes, and we know Hans is in the same camp. If one went out through this tunnel, I am sure the other did, too. One thing we can be certain of is this: if they were involved, we will undoubtedly hear the story of their exploits many times."

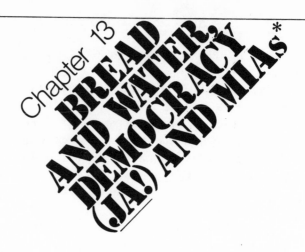

Chapter 13

BREAD AND WATER, AND DEMOCRACY (JA!) AND MIAs*

After each tunneler returned to Papago Park he spent a few days in the guardhouse, where he was questioned by G-2 officers and FBI agents, and then went back to Compound 1 A to be greeted by his friends. "It was a great time for the telling of stories," Clarus recalls. "And some of them probably improved considerably each time they were told. But that tunnel, conceiving of it, digging it, getting out, getting back, telling about our adventures, finding out what happened to the others . . . why, it covered a year or more and was our great recreation. It kept our spirits up even as Germany was being crushed and we worried about our parents and our families.

"Of course, we all wondered what was going to happen to us. What punishment was in store for the 'troublemakers'? Then, early one morning we were told to pack our gear and put it on trucks. Everyone who had gone out through the tunnel was to move. Heavily armed guards were all over the place.

"So out we went through the gates, the Americans all

* Missing in America.

around us. The men in Compound 3 started to jeer as we marched past but then became silent. For as two trucks with our belongings drove by, so did another truck loaded with caskets.

"None of us spoke. But I found out later everyone had the same thought: if the Americans try to shoot us, we are going to make a break for it and die running, or if that is not possible, at least take a few of them with us. I had already picked out the man I planned to lunge at and grapple with, if I could. Guggenberger, Kraus, Günther, all of us had selected our targets. There were rumors that American POWs recently had been shot in retaliation for air raids on Dresden, and that worried us."

The prisoners marched out to the old guardhouse area just outside the camp, now somewhat enlarged. An officer ordered them to form two ranks and a sergeant started calling out their names: "Wolfgang Clarus, 4WG 19183. Lieutenant Clarus, you were absent from roll calls in Compound 1 A, Papago Park, for sixteen days, 23 December 1944 to 9 January 1945, and therefore, by order of Colonel William A. Holden, commanding, will be confined to Pima Camp on a restricted diet for sixteen days, that sentence to begin immediately and to be carried out strictly according to the rules of the Geneva Convention."

As the sergeant began to read Drescher's name and number, the Germans suddenly realized what was happening: bread and water for the number of days they had been out! It became virtually impossible to hear the rest of Drescher's sentence—they were all laughing too hard. It was pandemonium for several minutes as their captors, completely baffled by this strange behavior, tried to restore order. Apparently the truck loaded with caskets had passed the prisoners by accident and none of the Americans realized what was on their minds. Hence the wave of hysterical relief and nervous laughter was, to the guards and their officers, utterly incomprehensible.

The Pima Camp diet was not restricted solely to bread and

water. It was impossible to stop a little food from being smuggled in by various details, and even the guards helped out at times, especially the Negroes, who often gave them cigarettes. (Black GIs frequently told the Germans, "We're prisoners just like you guys are.")

Once the restricted diet was ended, the men held in Pima Camp were sometimes deluged with food, much more than they could eat. Since the United States Army tends to think only in round figures, food for up to a hundred men was shipped there each day, even though they were far fewer in number. Eventually nearly all of the men once held in 1 A ended up in Pima Camp—Maus, Mirbach, Kaiser and the others. And that became their home for the rest of their months in Arizona. According to Clarus, Pima Camp was a pleasant enough place, but they dug no more tunnels. One, he emphasizes, was enough.

Unlike the other escapees, Reinhard Mark and Heinrich Palmer went back to Compound 1 B. And had Mark kept quiet, they might never have had to endure ten days of bread and water.

"A month or so went by and Hein and I really were puzzled, wondering why nothing happened to us, no punishment, nothing. One day we were having new photographs made and I spotted one of the intelligence officers who had questioned us when we were brought back. I asked him why all of the other tunnel escapees were over at Pima Camp and not us. It was a bad mistake. He laughed and said he forgot. I think he forgot on purpose. We were very cooperative when caught and interrogated, less arrogant I believe than some of the men from 1 A.

"Other officers heard this conversation and the next day we ended up in Pima. Each morning at 11 A.M. Hein and I got a loaf of American white bread and, you know, each loaf has seventeen slices in it. We immediately would eat half of them, then dry the rest in the sun. That American bread somehow is more filling when dry. Then we ate one slice every two hours.

"We got cigarettes from the guards at times. It was not a bad experience, just boring. After ten days we both went back to 1 B again."

A U.S. State Department official and a Swiss legation representative who toured Papago Park in January 1945 noted that general conditions were "very poor." The installation obviously had not recovered from a bad case of jitters and numerous repercussions created by the tunnel affair. No spokesman could be found who was acceptable to the faltering Holden administration, recreation facilities were shut down, educational programs curtailed, canteens "very poorly stocked," and the work output (perhaps because little incentive to work existed) was only 40 percent of the average elsewhere.

The Swiss diplomat criticized the curtailing of so many necessary activities, despite the celebrated tunnel escape, observing tartly that such measures did little for morale. He also expressed regret that supervised weekly walks and occasional beers no longer were permitted. At that time the compounds and branch camps contained 3,419 prisoners of war.

COMPOUND/CAMP	OFFICERS	NCOS	EMS	TOTAL
1 A	0	0	0	0
1 B	0	279	0	279
2	0	23	246	269
3	0	58	636	694
4	0	225	543	768
5	141	3	39	183
Company 10 (QM)	10	2	148	160
Mesa	1	34	568	603
Eleven Mile	1	23	376	400
Pima	31	7	25	63
TOTAL	184	654	2,581	3,419

These visitors also met with Lieutenant Colonel John B. Madden, the executive officer who had replaced Barber three months earlier, indicating that Holden may have been hospitalized at that time. Meanwhile Tays, Boyer, Watson and

Davis drifted off to other duties and other camps. Apparently, whatever reprimand or punishment they finally received, if any, was not severe. William M. E. Rachal, a Virginia officer stationed at Papago Park for several months in mid-1944, met Davis at a Judge Advocate General's school in Texas early in 1945, and by June of that year, the former commanding officer of the stockade at Papago Park was in charge of a small POW installation near Tucson.

The Casa Grande *Dispatch,* bitter critic of Holden, hailed the arrival of his successor, Colonel Verne Austin, with a few words of blustery advice.

> Those hog-wild "supermen" must be taught their place in the scheme of things. The mothers, the sisters, the brothers, the other relatives of American soldiers who have been given foul treatment in Hun camps are insisting that this wet-nursing of the blond-haired gorillas be halted, and at the point of a gun. It only remains for some escaped Hun to rape a woman or assault a citizen, to have old bloody Hell on our hands.
>
> These snarling, surly Hun "supermen" need to be taught the only way they understand. Colonel Austin may expect his little charges to seek every means to discredit him. The citizens of Arizona will back him to the hilt, if he really shows these vandals what the American system actually means.

The impact of this tunnel escape extended far beyond Papago Park and the 9th Service Command. Sensing a hot issue, one that intrigued a civilian public angered by alleged military incompetence, rationing, shortages and tales of Nazi cruelty, various congressmen, news reporters and men such as Walter Winchell turned their attention to conditions in other POW compounds throughout the nation. On February 27, 1945, citing the necessity to conserve food on the home front, the Army directed all commands to feed prisoners of war only cheap cuts of meat and meat substitutes.

Reacting to a fiasco at a Florida camp, Army generals said prepared POW menus would no longer use phrases such as "à la king" and "parsley potatoes." "Simple phraseology will be used to describe simple fare." Seven weeks later, practically all meat was eliminated from POW meals. Also, cigarette consumption officially was cut to three packs a week and canteens were forbidden to stock leading brands eagerly sought by civilians. In practice, most POWs got no cigarettes whatsoever and had to "roll their own" or go without.

The final outburst of trouble at Papago Park occurred on Hitler's last birthday, April 20, 1945, when Wattenberg and some of his friends, despite specific orders forbidding such levity, staged a small celebration in honor of der Führer. Guards eventually broke up the affair, seized a large picture of Adolf that Wattenberg tried to protect, and roughed up the Fregattenkapitän somewhat as they took him from one isolation area to yet another.

A few weeks later, as Americans learned the full horror of the Third Reich's concentration camps, public outcry concerning lenient treatment of POWs escalated dramatically, and soon all prisoners, not just those who dug tunnels, were being punished for the sins of the Fatherland. American vengeance took several forms. The POW diet was cut even more drastically. No Germans starved, but nearly all of them lost weight. An "intellectual diversion" program—the Geneva Convention specifically required combatants to stimulate the intellectual life of POWs—became a high-gear cram course in democracy. And the United States began loaning millions of prisoners to France, Britain, Holland, Belgium and other war-ravaged countries so they could rebuild after five and a half years of bombing and devastation.

As soon as fighting ceased in Europe, Washington issued new food regulations cutting out all meat except bologna and sausage stamped in purple FOR POW ONLY. Many camps began serving vegetable sandwiches: chopped cabbage, cabbage and carrots, carrots, carrots and onions, carrots and prunes, carrots and mixed fruit, and so on. A 9th Service Command officer told the Pentagon in firm terms that such meals were totally unsatisfactory. "They chop up carrots and various things and put them between bread. As a matter of fact, about the only sustaining food in those things is the bread itself."

By summer, farmers, contractors and even the military feared the prisoners were losing too much weight and would not be able to work. Many farm wives supplemented slim Army lunches with their own sturdy chow. In small branch camps it was difficult to maintain a separate GI mess, and where this was done, the Germans were further embittered when they learned how well their captors were eating.

Prisoner-of-war morale sank to an all-time low. No mail from home, defeat, the Fatherland divided and occupied by various powers, work hours increased, no longer did they get even ten cents a day for incidentals, nothing to eat but soup, soup, soup, vegetable sandwiches and sausage made from God-knows-what. The Americans had treated them so well until May 1945. To make matters worse, canteen shelves in many compounds contained nothing but hair oil, soap and toilet articles, no food whatsoever. Thus there was little incentive to work even if one felt able to do so.

Ironically, some months earlier—at the worst possible moment, under puzzling conditions and at first largely in secret —the United States Army had begun efforts to de-Nazify its charges. This move represented a distinct reversal in War Department thinking. For more than a year all proposals by educators and congressmen to indoctrinate prisoners of war in the ways of democracy had been rebuffed, U.S. government officials fearing such proposals might stimulate Nazi propaganda among American servicemen in Germany. Since the Army had at least three general service companies of pseudo-Nazis tucked away somewhere out of sight, it realized that despite impending defeat, words of Goebbels and Hitler still could have appeal, especially to men held in German compounds, if the rewards for cooperation were substantial enough.

Many U.S. camp commanders were not sympathetic to this "re-education" effort, fearing that movies, lectures and courses extolling American virtues would disrupt work schedules and lower monthly production totals so dear to General Lerch and others. But despite some opposition from Army brass and considerable from the Germans themselves, on March 1, 1945, *Der Ruf* ("The Call"), a national POW newspaper conceived and published by the U.S. Army with the assistance of sympathetic prisoner personnel, made its appearance. Purportedly, "the call" came from the Fatherland for young men who could provide democratic leadership in a defeated Germany, although some of its columns seemed to be strangely militaristic and Nazi-like in tone:

> DER RUF, sounding its call from camp to camp in America, will not silently fade into oblivion, let us make certain of that. Our country must know that she can count on us to answer the call with a strong echo. Although we are prisoners, we will not be forgotten. They will know at home that we are preparing ourselves for the future by building our mental and physical strength. They will know that we have used the time during our imprisonment to become self-thinking, ripe men. Our country counts on us. Listen to the call.

Not everyone listened. In some camps *Der Ruf* was burned and those who read it beaten up. Perhaps it is unnecessary to point out that this publication (it cost five cents) was not a best seller in Papago Park. But on July 4, 1945, opposition suddenly ceased. In a stern front-page statement Provost Marshal General Lerch bluntly told readers that if they did not discard their Nazi ideology and become more cooperative, it might be months or even years before they saw their homeland again. This threat was contrary to the Geneva Convention, which stipulates that prisoners are to be returned to their homes as soon as possible after the cessation of hostilities.

In addition to *Der Ruf*, Germans held at Papago Park could now read the *Papago-Rundschau* ("Papago Review"), a ten-page item with a decorative masthead featuring an Indian, a horse and a mountain. First a monthly and then a weekly, this publication became a high-class newspaper under the leadership of Rolf-Kurt Gebeschus. Although it contained the standard helping of sports, movie news, English lessons, cartoons and articles praising America and bemoaning the fate of German democracy, the *Papago-Rundschau* scored a dramatic coup in Christmas 1945 when Gebeschus asked Thomas Mann to write a foreword to a special issue. Mann responded with a five-page lecture on government which, interestingly, included some lines favorable to the U.S.S.R.

Movies which became an integral part of this de-Nazification process included *The River, Abe Lincoln in Illinois* and *Woodrow Wilson*. And all POWs were forced to see many reels depicting concentration camp atrocities. Papago Park reaction to these horrors at first was a mixture of incredulity, revulsion and disbelief. Many thought the scenes impossible, just another Yankee trick to break down whatever spirit remained. Slowly, however, as the prisoners talked things over back in their barracks and A remembered something he once heard, B recalled how a neighbor disappeared, C told of a train he had once seen, they gradually concluded that this devastating film footage might be all too true.

Loan of prisoners of war to Allied governments was perhaps the most frightening decision of all. In October 1944 the French had asked General Eisenhower for 50,000 German POWs to be used as laborers. With firm assurances that the Geneva Convention would be obeyed to the letter, a few weeks later the Pentagon told Eisenhower to begin turning over captured Germans to the French government, a move which eased POW pressure on American troops somewhat. By May 1945, just as hostilities ceased, U.S. authorities were expressing concern that French civilians, not army personnel as required by the Geneva rules, were guarding many of these men. Nevertheless, Eisenhower shortly released still more Germans to the Belgians, Dutch and other European allies, and on August 20, 1945, the United States formally agreed to turn over 1.3 million to the French, who, by that time, had 562,000 of Hitler's former warriors in their grasp.

Within a few weeks, however, this program was terminated as the result of formal complaints by the International Red Cross and considerable unfavorable publicity. The IRC said the United States, as captor, still was responsible for the welfare of these men. The French, IRC officials charged, were not maintaining camps properly and were diverting food and supplies intended for captives to their own use.

Of course, Europe in 1945–1946 was a chaotic, dog-eat-dog world as hordes of homeless, both victor and vanquished, roamed across the continent. The specter of concentration camps and Nazi cruelty to numerous nationalities, including the French, embittered daily relations to a marked degree. But stowaways appearing in U.S. ports, both Germans and Italians telling of mistreatment at French hands, gave credence to IRC charges and led to the demise of this ill-conceived loan arrangement.

Yet the damage had already been done. Word of the transfer of POWs to America's allies sent shock waves through every compound in the United States. If Uncle Sam could hand over their comrades to France, Belgium, Holland, Britain, why not Russia? Could they look forward to years on the upper Volga eating still more soup and cabbage? Perhaps cabbage without even prunes and white bread? Perhaps just soup?

Camaraderie and close rapport created by the tunnel adventure did not last long in Pima Camp, since U-boat, merchant marine and coast artillery men and officers quickly reverted to their own little groups once more. Also, concern for the future, for their families at home as the Allies overwhelmed their shattered homeland weighed heavily on all of their minds. Nevertheless, it was possible to laugh at times. One subject of universal amusement was the "mad" dogs guarding the compound perimeter. Within weeks these vicious animals were eating out of their hands and knew the prisoners much better than the guards who were supposed to be their masters. This resulted not from any deep-seated knowledge of canine behavior, but from the simple truth of familiarity. Guards were changed every four hours, prisoners were always there.

In time those held at Pima, both enlisted men and officers, were encouraged to volunteer to work about the compound and eventually trusted to do farm labor, too. Kraus, for one, picked dates. Guggenberger, Quaet-Faslem and others tried their hand at cotton. Like nearly all of their compatriots they detested the job and soon quit, or at least tried to. Palmer and Mark protested to no avail that cotton was used in bombs and thus by the Geneva rules they should not pick it.

Both officers and NCOs discovered that if they volunteered for work details after May 1945, it was almost impossible to "unvolunteer." However, their cumulative record of escapes, noncooperation and irascible behavior was so impressive that this made little difference. They were marked as rank Nazi troublemakers no matter how many pounds of cotton they picked.

Guggenberger, Quaet-Faslem and Maus took up cardplaying once more. Kraus took advantage of extension courses offered by UCLA. Clarus, who also spent some weeks in the cotton fields of Arizona, devoted three hours each day to translating David Dallin's *Russia & Post-War Europe* into German. "It was excellent training, informative, educational, even enjoyable at times."

During these months, pressures were building up which would send these POWs home much sooner than they expected. Public demand resulting in the release of thousands of GIs from service created a huge labor supply for which jobs had to be found. By late 1945, strikes were occurring in some plants across the nation where POW labor still was being used, civilians insisting that jobs go to returning servicemen, not to the defeated enemy.

From time to time the men in Pima Camp were told they soon would be shipped to the Nazi camp in Alva, Oklahoma. They were also assured they would be the last, the very last group of German POWs to sail for Europe. One day early in February 1946 two guards came into Pima Camp and told the troublemakers to pack. Yes, they were leaving for Alva that evening. At about midnight trucks picked them up and took them to another camp seventy miles away at Florence. Two days later they were told, no, they were not going to Oklahoma after all . . . they were going to Europe! The men were delirious with joy. Guards gave them new clothes and ordered them to paint "PW" on them. Some men used toothpaste at first but the guards insisted on oil paint, so they complied. It was much too late to cause trouble, not when bound for home.

Clarus recalls that just as he was boarding the train in Florence a motorcycle roared up and the rider handed a letter to an American officer who, in turn, gave it to him. "That was the first, the very first and the only letter I received from my wife while I was in America. I knew she was safe, well, waiting for me to come home. I was so impressed. After barbed wire, lousy food, picking cotton, months of dreary days and lonely nights, that the Americans would dispatch a motorcycle rider to deliver a single letter to me, an unknown German officer who was leaving for home . . . well, I have never forgotten it."

Most of the men in the Pima Camp group, still classified as rank troublemakers, went to Camp Shanks, New York, departure point for several hundred thousand POWs. A few days later they were aboard ship in the Atlantic Ocean, and within two weeks, behind barbed wire in yet another compound located near Münster in the British zone.

"We sat around for days," Guggenberger says, "and did nothing. I am convinced our records simply never caught up with us, so after about a month, the Brits got tired of us and let us go. To our amazement some of the more cooperative men at Papago Park were not released until months later."

As Guggenberger says, others were less fortunate. Kozur was quartered for several months in Belgium before being released in June 1946. Palmer and Mark also spent a few weeks in Belgium. Their camp was awful, wet tents and truly miserable living conditions. Those who preceded them had even eaten the grass in the compound area. Then one day they were taken by train to Antwerp and put on a ship. Where were they bound for? Hamburg? Bremen? Home at last?

No, England! Palmer was so furious that he almost attacked an interrogation officer who asked him why Germany started World War II. This outburst put him back in solitary confinement once more. Within a few days Palmer realized he must change his ways. To fight back was both impossible and stupid. From that time on, until released in September 1947, he was a model prisoner, quickly adapting to camp routine. He even became a trusted employee of the administrative command; in this capacity he "pinched," as he puts it, a substantial number of documents from his personnel file and today, of all the tunnel crew, has the most complete dossier on his wartime experiences.

By March of 1946 Papago Park had joined a growing list of deactivated POW camps as thousands of Germans, men very much like Clarus, Guggenberger, Kozur, Mark and Palmer, climbed aboard trains bound for Camp Shanks and troopships which would take them, if not home, at least thousands of miles closer to it than Arizona.

On July 23, 1946, the last group of German prisoners of war held in America sailed for Europe. A few days later the War Department triumphantly announced the findings of a survey which, based on a sampling of 22,153 prisoners who had departed from Shanks, showed that 74 percent of those held in the United States were at least "partially" re-educated and now had some appreciation for democracy and the American way of life. Since they had been told more than twelve months earlier that the only way to get home was to reject Hitler and Nazism, these results are not surprising.

Younger men, the Army conceded, still tended to admire certain features of the defunct regime, and many professed approval of the way Hitler had brought order out of chaos, created jobs and bestowed numerous economic and social benefits on the average worker. In general, those surveyed agreed that Germany was responsible for World War II, expressed disapproval of some aspects of National Socialism (lack of freedom, exaltation of the party, too much discipline), thought anti-Semitism hurt the Third Reich, yet still blamed Jews for the troubled times of the 1920s which led to Hitler's rise to power.

Some of the questions posed in this survey were, to say the very least, phrased in a manner to elicit the desired response.

> Hitler taught that the state is everything and that the individual exists to serve the state. Americans are taught that the state exists to serve the people. Which do you believe to be more democratic?
>
> What type of government would you prefer in the future Germany?
>
> Do you believe that Jews were the cause of Germany's troubles?
>
> Knowing what you know now, if Germany could fight the same war over tomorrow and win, and you knew you would not come out alive, would you be for it?
>
> Check the statement you believe to be true:
> _____ Germans are not suited for democracy.
> _____ Germans must be educated to democracy.
> _____ Germans are entirely capable of democratic government.

Only 36 percent of those surveyed thought concentration camps actually had existed in the Third Reich. Almost as many believed this was enemy propaganda, and an equal number declined to comment on the matter. Answers to a query as to whether Germany should help rebuild France were so varied that the Army could not formulate a cohesive, meaningful response. In general, when asked what impressed them most in the United States they replied (dutifully) democracy, freedom of the press, and freedom of speech, although many were dismayed, they said, by the absence of public welfare programs and by the evidence of widespread poverty. A Papago Park prisoner once remarked to William Rachal that he hoped, when it came time to go home, that they could travel across America by bus. Trains only went through slums, he said, and he would like to see the better sections of our nation's cities and towns. On one occasion a group of POWs in the Deep South decorated their mess hall with paintings of Negro shacks and clear evidence of racial prejudice, paintings which were soon removed.

Interestingly, this survey revealed that when they arrived in America, 80 percent of the POWs knew no English whatsoever. Now, as they departed, 50 percent had some knowledge of the language, a development of considerable import in decades to come, perhaps of much greater significance than anything learned in those democratic cram courses.

There were POWs who did not return to Europe willingly, although nothing prevented them from coming back to America as immigrants if they could get legal visas. The last group sailing from Camp Shanks included a German youth who searched in vain for his father, supposedly living in Manhattan, and several of his comrades said they were eager to return at once and work on farms and ranches in the West.

Some three hundred prisoners, most of them Italians, tried to establish that they actually were American citizens. A Los Angeles woman even instituted habeas corpus proceedings in an effort to keep her son, Gaetano Territo, in the United States. Territo and his mother based their appeal on the grounds that he was an American citizen (born in West Virginia in 1915) and not legally a prisoner of war. This case was eventually decided by the Ninth Circuit of the California Court of Appeals. The court held that Territo was a POW, that neither American citizenship nor his presence in an Italian Service Unit affected that status, and that under the terms of the Geneva Convention it was incumbent upon the United States of America to return him to Italy.

Citing a decision relating to Americans residing in Cuba during the Spanish-American War, the court ruled that residents of an enemy country, regardless of citizenship, are enemies. Since thousands of Japanese-Americans spent several years behind barbed wire during World War II, many of them not far from where Gaetano Territo was working on the West Coast, apparently the converse of this argument—those on friendly soil, regardless of citizenship, are friends—is not true.

Actually, even after that last shipload of Germans sailed from Camp Shanks, a handful of prisoners still remained behind in America after July 1946: 141 Germans, 20 Italians and a single Japanese soldier, all serving time for crimes committed in various camps. There were also 28 Germans and 15 Italians at large somewhere, men neither the United States Army nor the FBI could account for, who apparently now believed firmly not only in free speech and a free press but in freedom of movement as well.

During the remainder of that year the FBI tracked down a few of these individuals, and on December 29 the United States government wrote an official end to the POW story in America with payment of $200 million to prisoners of war or to their dependents for work done in the United States during World War II. This sum represents credit earned either through daily labor or in salaries not spent in camp canteens, often because after May 1945 shelves were bare and there was nothing to buy, no way to spend canteen chits.

In all, over 425,000 of the enemy came to the United States during the war years. Of that number, 735 Germans, 99 Italians and 24 Japanese died, most of natural causes, although a few were shot while trying to escape. In the summer of 1945 a Colorado GI killed three Germans he said he thought were about to "rush" him, and a Utah guard killed nine Germans and wounded nine others in a burst of gunfire, by far the worst incident of this kind.

There are many more stories, in fact they are countless, of prisoners of war returning rifles to guards who misplaced their weapons or of men on work details hiding a GI's gun and then bargaining with him for it at the end of the day. At most installations, as one would expect, there was a widespread, tit-for-tat sub rosa agreement: if you, the prisoners, will not give us, the guards, any trouble, then we will reciprocate in kind.

In June 1947, the day after the Marshall Plan for the recovery of Europe was unveiled at Harvard University, American authorities announced that 5,308 POWs held on the continent would be released by the end of the year, making the United States the first major power to set loose all of its European captives. During that same year the FBI picked up two or three more escaped POWs, among them a Munich youth found in Troy, New York, Martin Eppich. Eppich, it turned out, had escaped from a camp in England, not the United States, and made his way across the Atlantic as a stowaway on the *Queen Mary*.

Then, six years later, in March 1953, the FBI captured the most celebrated of these illusive Germans, Reinhold Pabel. Pabel, thirty-eight, was a prosperous, highly respected independent book dealer living in Chicago. He was married to an American girl; they had one child and were expecting another. A former seminary student, this Russian-front veteran had been captured on Sicily and taken first to North Africa, then in June 1944 to a camp in the Midwest by way of Norfolk, a route followed by thousands of his comrades.

All went well enough for a year or so. Work details, which Unteroffizier Pabel joined voluntarily, gave him a chance to get out of drab compound surroundings, see the country and chat with American farmers and their families. Some American officers, he says, used POWs as baby-sitters. After V-E Day, however, his situation changed dramatically. Petty officers such as Pabel were ordered to work or exist on a diet of herring and milk. Pabel, who sincerely believed that any "re-education" had to "come from within," was disturbed by tensions which the intellectual diversion program created within his camp and disgusted by the U.S. Army's campaign to win converts to democracy through varied inducements such as transfer to better camps, supervised visits to towns and cities, and similar special privileges. He also was alarmed by the Morgenthau Plan, designed to strip Germany of all industry.

One morning, while on garbage detail, Pabel found an old issue of the *American Magazine* (April 1944) containing J. Edgar Hoover's "Enemies at Large" article. "It was a gift from heaven," he says with a broad smile, "a complete blueprint telling how to escape. Do it alone. Do not talk any more than absolutely necessary. Go as far as possible as quickly as you can. Have some cash."

By August 1945 "Operation Vapor," as Pabel dubbed his plan, was in full swing. He had accumulated $15 in American money through sale of a carving, medals and souvenirs, and had put together an outfit which, he hoped, could pass for civilian clothing. Early one morning when the guards at his small camp near Peoria, Illinois, were momentarily distracted by a brawl, Reinhold Pabel rushed into his tent, grabbed his do-it-yourself escape kit, rolled under a fence and was gone.

After changing clothes, he walked along a highway singing "Cuddle Up a Little Closer" until a farmer gave him a ride to town where he caught a bus to Chicago. There he got a job as a dishwasher. When told to get a social security card, Pabel went to a local office and said he was "Phil Brick," a Dutch refugee. No one asked any questions, so "Phil Brick" he was until 1953, when the FBI showed up. How did federal agents find him? "I got overconfident, careless. The book business was going so well that I asked my sister in Hamburg to open a bank account in my real name to facilitate payment for German books I was importing. The FBI showed up a few weeks later. What infuriated me was they took up an hour of my time before telling me who they were. They at least could have bought something."

Despite efforts in his behalf by neighbors and two American officers who captured him on Sicily, Pabel was officially charged with illegal entry and deported following a formal inquiry. He returned to his native Germany, eventually got a visa and came back to a new child, to Dave Garroway's

Today show and to another flurry of publicity. This remarkable odyssey is delightfully detailed in Pabel's *Enemies Are Human,* published in 1955. A decade later this one-time POW decided to return to Germany and today operates yet another rambling little bookshop on Hamburg's oldest street, a narrow alley in the shadow of a magnificent eighteenth-century church, St. Michael's.

A small, slim man with hair now white, Pabel recalls his "Brick" career with good humor and twinkling eyes. "And I am especially indebted to Mr. J. Edgar Hoover, the man who made it all possible. Without his assistance I could never have spent those wonderful years in America."

Publicity surrounding Pabel led to the capture in 1953 of yet another ex-POW, Polish-born Harry Girth, a house painter– interior decorator who recently had announced his engagement to an Atlantic City girl. At that time the FBI said four more Germans still were loose somewhere in the United States. One of these men, Kurt Rossmeisl, a multilingual officer who had escaped from Camp Butner, N.C., in August 1945, was found in Chicago in 1959 operating an elevator at the Union League Club. Like Pabel, both of these men were deported. Girth apparently returned to America, Rossmeisl did not.

Since 1946 hundreds of former POWs, especially Italians, have come back to the United States to marry, raise families and become citizens of the land which once kept them in barbed-wire enclosures. Yet it is possible that a handful of their comrades, a few of the forty-three "MIAs" unaccounted for in 1946, are still here today, having achieved much the same status without any transatlantic voyage to tidy up legal niceties.

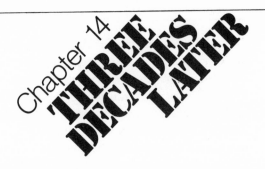

Over thirty years have passed since Colonel William A. Holden discovered that twenty-five Germans had dug a 178-foot tunnel through "solid rock" and fled into the Arizona desert. Some of the men involved in this drama are now dead, and Papago Park, bearing few reminders of its exciting World War II days, has become a gigantic complex of city, state and national facilities. That expanse of rolling, scrub-covered land and huge red rocks located on the borders of booming Phoenix and its well-manicured satellite, Scottsdale, today includes, among other things, two golf courses, the Phoenix Zoo, picnic areas, lakes, bicycle trails, water-treatment plants, an amphitheater, a botanical garden, headquarters of the Arizona National Guard, a blood bank, a trap-and-skeet club, a riding academy, and a U.S. Army Reserve Training Center.

The northeastern corner of this area, what was once Compound 1 A, the home of the troublemakers, has been transformed into Hy-View Subdivision, a collection of rather modest, rambling one-story homes. Most have carports stuffed to overflowing with boats, trailers and bicycles, and proudly flaunt other accouterments of middle-class America such as TV aerials, basketball hoops, fenced-in backyards and air conditioners. A few lawns feature crushed green stone and cacti, not grass, Arizona's unique contribution to the world of twentieth-century landscape architecture.

Hy-View community, apparently so named because one can look up to mountains and buttes in the distance, is criss-crossed by several pleasantly named streets: Cambridge, Virginia, Lewis, Wilshire, Sheridan and Vernon, each running east-west between 64th and 66th streets, the latter curving along the edge of the Arizona Crosscut Canal much as two eight-foot wire fences once did. The tunnel exit was on that water-way's west bank close by the corner of Wilshire and 66th.

Near Oak and 64th streets, approximately the center of the old prisoner-of-war camp, there are four or five low structures bearing telltale Army designations, such as S-106 ,T-104, and a few concrete foundations, sole reminders of this region's exotic past. The best preserved of these buildings, the American officers' club, where Captain Cecil Parshall was playing poker when informed that perhaps as many as sixty Germans had vanished, now is the home of the Scottsdale Elks Club, Lodge # 2148. This structure, added to a bit but essentially unchanged, has several large windows looking out toward picturesque Camelback Mountain, which dominates the northern skyline. The club, ably managed by Dick Bales, serves both lunch and dinner and stages bingo games each Thursday night at seven-thirty.

Service Command Unit # 84 has largely been forgotten by most area residents, except perhaps Lawrence Jorgensen, the ex-corporal who went through the tunnel after it was discovered. Jorgensen, now retired, married a vivacious secretary who worked at the camp, and they now live only about six blocks south of the old stockade. Cecil Parshall, who after the uproar at Papago Park rounded out his exciting military career as a major in occupied Germany, also is retired and resides in nearby Glendale, a suburban area lying north-west of Phoenix. It was Glendale that Wattenberg tried to use as his American address when apprehended near Third and Van Buren in downtown Phoenix in January 1945.

At least three members of the tunnel crew—Helmut Drescher, Wilhelm Günther and Jürgen Quaet-Faslem—are dead, perhaps others as well. Some may have strayed into East Germany, although their former comrades think this highly improbable. Unlike Parshall and Jorgensen, most members of the 1 A "troublemaking" contingent have not quite reached the age of retirement.

Finding these former POWs presented both problems and surprises and, in time, developed into a true detective hunt. National Archives records in Washington, D.C., occasionally contained clues to the addresses of some of the men circa World War II, but changes which have occurred in Germany since that time often rendered such data obsolete. The most fruitful sources were Deutsche Dienststelle (a records center in West Berlin), German telephone books at the Library of Congress, and the men themselves, who, when contacted, sometimes knew the whereabouts of a few of their wartime buddies.

In this hit-or-miss fashion, aided by considerable luck, seven men who went out through the Papago Park tunnel eventually were tracked down: Wolfgang Clarus, Fritz Guggenberger, Walter Kozur, Hans Werner Kraus, Reinhard Mark, Heinrich Palmer and Jürgen Wattenberg. All of them, except Wattenberg, readily agreed to talk about that adventure. The captain, now seventy-eight years of age and formerly manager of the Lübeck branch of the Bavaria & St. Pauli Brewery, first answered in English saying he was very busy. Then, on November 26, 1975, although he once told a Phoenix resident he would cooperate on the tunnel tale for a fee, the captain wrote (in German) that he did not think the Papago Park story had any historical significance. Besides, sometime he himself might like to disclose what actually happened. Then, Wattenberg proceeded to make his views crystal clear.

Aus wohlerwogenen Gründen muss ich es ausserdem ablehnen, mich auf einen umfangreichen Schriftwechsel über eine "story of German POWs in U.S.A." einzulassen. Auch möchte ich darum bitten, von einen späteren persönlichen Interview Abstand zu nehmen.

Mit freundlichen Grüssen,
*Jürgen Wattenberg**

Ruth Quaet-Faslem, widow of Jürgen Quaet-Faslem, who now lives on the shores of the breath-takingly beautiful Starnberger See south of Munich, was a key figure in this search, providing much information on her husband and the addresses of Emmerich von Mirbach, August Maus, Fritz Kaiser, Fritz Guggenberger and others. Yet it is apparent that imprisonment and the tunnel fostered few close personal relationships. Thirty years later, U-boat officers often knew where their own kind were living, especially members of their "crew" or class at the naval academy. NCOs such as Palmer and Mark, the two men from 1 B, had maintained loose ties through the decades (occasional Christmas cards, etc.), and Walter Kozur, an enlisted man and the only individual interviewed who was not conversant in English, was certain Johann Kremer was living in Cologne but did not know his precise whereabouts. Probably the closest friends today are Maus, a well-to-do Hamburg businessman, and Guggenberger, a retired naval officer. Quaet-Faslem clearly was a member of this same intimate circle until his death in the early 1970s.

The experiences of these men and their families mirror those of their homeland since 1945. All went through extremely harsh times during the late 1940s, especially individuals such as Quaet-Faslem, Maus, Kraus, Walther and Mirbach who abandoned homes in the Russian-held zone to begin life

---

* "For well weighed reasons I must decline to enter into a lengthy correspondence about a 'story of German POWs in U.S.A.' Also, I must ask to be excused from a later personal interview.
"With friendly greetings,
"Jürgen Wattenberg"

anew in West Germany. Since their nation had no navy for a decade or so, they also had to seek out new careers.

Quaet-Faslem went into the family road-building business with an uncle, Guggenberger studied architecture, Kaiser and Mirbach became engineers; yet, in one way or another, most of them eventually tied their hopes and fortunes to West Germany's industrial miracle or made good use of their nautical knowledge. Clarus, Kozur, Mirbach, Kraus, Walther and Kaiser are among those who became employees or executives of large companies and multipurpose conglomerates. Mark, Palmer, Johanssen, Mirbach (for a time) and especially Guggenberger have made excellent use of their seamanship skills. Mark and Palmer work on ferries and waterways that dot northern Germany. Johanssen, never a resident of Compound 1 A or Pima Camp, was an official on the Kiel Canal until his retirement several years ago. Mirbach, now a projects engineer with MAN in Augsburg, taught at Colombia's naval academy for some years before joining the diplomatic corps, subsequently entering private business.

Fritz Guggenberger, still trim and youthful, lives in the Alps south of Munich, enjoying what one is forced to call "semiretirement" after a distinguished naval career which saw him rise to the rank of admiral and hold NATO posts in both Washington and Oslo. Ironically, while in America in the late 1950s and early 1960s, he attended the Naval War College in Newport, Rhode Island, and lived for several years in Bethesda, Maryland, not far from the hospital where he was held prisoner in 1943. In Oslo his statuesque, very attractive Lilo became enamored with Norwegian sweaters and now distributes them to select boutiques located in several European countries, a thriving operation which keeps her husband, ex-Admiral Guggenberger, her special assistant as it were, busy indeed.

Of all the tunnelers, Wolfgang Clarus, a Klöckner executive who lives in a tiny village in the hills rising above the Rhine near Coblenz, probably has the most explicit recollections of

Papago Park. Perhaps this is because he was not a member of the select U-boat circle dominating camp life in Compound 1 A and thus was often merely an observer, and an excellent one, of what was happening around him. Thirty-two years later he can still relate in detail the frustrations of boating down the Gila River and describe how hard, how very hard it is to pick cotton.

Hans Werner Kraus, resident of yet another tiny community located between Hanover and Göttingen and a man much like Clarus with keen memory and almost total recall, made an unusually trenchant observation while discussing Papago Park and its tunnel. After reviewing various documents and photographs, his face suddenly lit up when he spied a map of the entire camp detailing various compounds. "There! That is what we needed in 1944. We could get maps of the surrounding countryside, Arizona, even Mexico. But nothing on Papago Park itself, nothing at all. We had to guess, improvise, measure with string, just hope we were doing the right thing. If only we could have gotten a copy of that map, our task would have been so much simpler!"

Papago Park obviously was the home in 1944 of a group of smart, even shrewd POWs who had another advantage as well. "It is easy, very easy indeed for a prisoner to go on the offensive," Fritz Guggenberger remarked as he reminisced about those days. "He has the time to plot, scheme, plan. If a guard permits any 'human life' to exist within a compound, then a prisoner naturally will use it as best he can. And, of course, that is precisely what we did at Papago Park."

Cecil Parshall puts it more succinctly: "They were a damn good bunch of men. Top-flight. They were just doing their duty when they dug that tunnel. And it was a superb job, beautifully constructed. You have to hand it to them."

Guggenberger concedes that, in theory, there should be no rapport, no comradeship between prisoner and guard, since both may lose an awareness of their true status. The prisoner becomes less of a prisoner, the guard less of a guard. Several Papago Park alumni who later spent time in East German compounds report that the Russians clearly understood the full meaning of Guggenberger's words.

If Americans harbor an innate streak of humanity and curiosity which trips them up and ill fits them to be guards in wartime, if they permit what Guggenberger calls "human life" to exist within their prisoner-of-war compounds, this character defect has paid manifold benefits since 1945. Thousands of Germans returned home able to speak some English, and for the most part, favorably impressed by their treatment in America. Unwittingly, although perhaps bumbling, even stupid at times, thousands of GIs much like those who made up the guard details at Papago Park and their officers, too, laid the groundwork for a swift postwar rapprochement.

During the past three decades that good feeling has fostered innumerable ties between diplomats, generals, businessmen and rank-and-file citizens once separated by bullets, bombs and war. Scratch many an influential West German today and you will find an ex-POW who learned his basic English in Texas, Virginia, Oklahoma, or perhaps even Papago Park. If this tale has a moral, it clearly is this: if you are a guard, treat your wartime prisoner with tact, care and correctness . . . tomorrow you may need his help and his friendship. Certainly the flip-flops of postwar diplomacy, cold wars and hot, reveal that this dictum has considerably validity.

The 178-foot tunnel at Papago Park was, of course, just one incident, albeit an intriguing one, in the great adventure of imprisonment in the United States of America during World War II. This tale still has some loose ends and raises questions which only a handful of ex-servicemen and a few residents of the Phoenix area may be able to answer.

Did anyone ever find that schoolbook in which Heinrich Palmer brazenly wrote "This is a nice house for a prisoner of war on his way back to Germany"? Palmer would like to know. Wolfgang Clarus, by the way, says he is sorry for any damage he and his companions may have done to the school while hiding there. Palmer, Kraus and others would like to know if the men who captured them remember what happened. The customs officer in Sells, the chess player, the Cooper family . . . more than thirty years later, do they recall these escaped German prisoners of war? Palmer would also like to know where a certain Captain Cheese is. Does he still have the small model torpedo boat that Palmer gave him when he departed for Camp Shanks?

Walter Kozur is positive he left a small bottle of schnaps in the cave which was home to him, Wattenberg and Kremer for five weeks. "When I win at Lotto, my wife and I will go to Arizona and I will find that bottle. I am sure it is still there. The Americans never found our hideout."

Fritz Guggenberger would like to know the identity of the interrogator who quizzed him at Bethesda Naval Hospital. "Of course, he used a false name, and being weak, I made mistakes. Lonely, eager for companionship, I talked a bit too much. I learned later that the most innocent comment can be used to an adversary's advantage. Spin out a few disjointed facts to another prisoner of war, and naturally enough, he concludes that if the enemy knows those details, he must know the big picture as well."

But these are trivial matters. Who questioned whom? Did anyone find a textbook with a strange phrase scrawled in it? Does a U.S. officer still have a model boat? Is there a little bottle of citrus-fruit schnaps aging in the hills north of Phoenix?

What is really significant is the fact that a group of German prisoners of war, holed up in a dreary, sun-baked compound, dug a 178-foot tunnel through supposedly impregnable rock and dirt—right where Cecil Parshall predicted trouble might erupt—and tried to make their way across 130 miles of wild desert country to Mexico, an audacious undertaking which even today prompts Arizona natives who know that region to shake their heads in disbelief.

At a time when Adolf Hitler's Third Reich clearly was stumbling toward certain defeat, why did they do it?

"Damned if I know," Palmer admits. "I guess we were just young and foolish enough to think we might actually succeed."

"It was a challenge and an adventure," Guggenberger says with quiet but firm conviction. "The tunnel became a kind of all-consuming sport. We lived, ate, slept, talked, whispered, dreamed 'tunnel' and thought of little else for weeks on end."

"The entire operation," Clarus recalls, "became our great outlet for exercise, both physical and mental. Planning, digging, scheming, getting out, running, hiding, getting captured, coming back, telling our tales, piecing the whole exploit together—why, it occupied our time for nearly one year. I only wish the Gila really had been a river. If it has no water, why do the Americans show it on their maps?"

"Why dig a tunnel? Why escape?" Kozur stares into his beer for a moment, then smiles broadly. "The Americans would not let us work. They said we were Nazi troublemakers. They locked us up in 1 A with our U-boat comrades and officers who had both engineering and organizational skills. They did not specifically forbid tunneling, since they believed it was impossible to do it . . . so, why not?"

Sources

This story is based largely on reports issued by the U.S. Army inquiry boards which investigated the Papago Park tunnel and interviews with men involved in that remarkable episode. Newspapers, a few books and an occasional magazine or journal article helped round out the picture somewhat. The conclusions of the investigating panels can be found in Record Group 389 (Office of the Provost Marshal General) at the National Archives, Washington, D.C. These PMG files also contain numerous letters, memos and telephone transcripts describing various aspects of the tunnel and the hell it raised in Arizona, Utah and Washington. The National Archives, the Department of the Army's Center for Military History and the U.S. Navy's Operational Archives have a substantial body of material relating to submarine warfare, U.S. intelligence activities, and the care and treatment of prisoners of war during World War II, each an integral part of this Papago Park adventure.

Of special interest are these files: Record Group 165 at the National Archives (War Department General Staff) detailing secret interrogations at Fort Hunt; four volumes on

Prisoner of War Operations at the Military History Center; and the Navy's four volumes on *United States Naval Administration in World War II: Office of Naval Operations,* as well as assorted action reports on submarine sinkings and "Post Mortems," booklets describing very minute facts concerning the life and death of various German U-boats.

Details relating to German POWs in America in World War I can be found in the National Archives: Records Groups 60 (Department of Justice), 165 (War Department General Staff) and 407 (Adjutant General's Office). The Arizona Department of Library, Archives and Public Records has a few random letters and reports relating to the prisoner-of-war camp at Papago Park.

INTERVIEWS: *West Germany*—Wolfgang Clarus, Leuterod; Rolf-Kurt Gebeschus, Mühlacker; Fritz Guggenberger, Garmisch-Partenkirchen; Hans F. Johannsen, Kiel; Fritz Kaiser, Bensburg; Gerd Kelbling, Ammerland; Walter Kozur and Gerd Kutscha, both of Dortmund; Hans Werner Kraus, Duingen; Reinhard Mark, Heiligenhafen; August Maus and Reinhold Pabel, both of Hamburg; Heinrich Palmer, Münster; Ruth Quaet-Faslem, Ammerland; Otto Reuter, Barsbuttel; Emmerich von Mirbach, Augsburg; Berndt von Walther und Croneck, Bremerhaven. *Arizona*—Dick Bales, Phoenix; Charles C. Colley, Tempe; Lawrence Jorgensen, Scottsdale; Bill Lagattuta and Steven Talley, KOOL-CBS, Phoenix; Cecil Parshall, Glendale. *Virginia*—William M. E. Rachal, Richmond. *Georgia*—Joseph O. Baylen, Atlanta; Nancy Lancaster Robertson, Athens.

NEWSPAPERS: Ajo (Arizona) *Copper News* (1945); *Arizona Blade-Tribune* (Florence) (1945); *Arizona Republic* (Phoenix) (1944–1945, 1971); Atlanta *Constitution* (1917–1918); Atlanta *Journal* (1917–1918); Boston *Herald* (1944–1945); Casa Grande (Arizona) *Dispatch* (1944–1945); Chandler *Arizonan* (1945); Chattanooga *Times* (1917–1918); Louisville *Courier-Journal* (1944); New York *Times* (1915–1918, 1942–

1948, 1953, 1959); *Papago-Rundschau* (1945–1946); Phoenix *Gazette* (1944–1945); Tucson *Daily Citizen* (1944–1945).

BOOKS: Kurt W. Böhme, *Geist und Kultur der deutschen Kriegsgefangenen im Westen* (Munich, 1968), and Hermann Jung, *Die deutschen Kriegsgefangenen in Amerikanischen Hand: USA* (Munich, 1972), two volumes in *Zur Geschichte der deutschen Kriegsgefangenen des Zweiten Weltkrieges*, edited by Dr. Erich Maschke; Paul Brickhill, *The Great Escape* (London, 1951); Lothar-Günther Buchheim, *The Boat* (New York, 1975); *Congressional Record* (Washington, 1944–1945); Herston Cooper, *Crossville* (Chicago, 1965); George C. Lewis and John Mewha, *History of Prisoner of War Utilization by the United States Army, 1776–1945* (Washington, 1955); Reinhold Pabel, *Enemies Are Human* (Philadelphia, 1955); Jürgen Rohwer, *Die U-Boot-Erfolge der Achsenmächte, 1939–1945* (Munich, 1968); A. I. Schutzer, *Great Civil War Escapes* (New York, 1967); J. P. Mallmann Showell, *U-Boats Under the Swastika* (New York, 1974); Glendon Fred Swarthout, *The Eagle and the Iron Cross* (New York, 1966); Edward P. Von der Porten, *The German Navy in World War II* (New York, 1969); Richard Whittingham, *Martial Justice: The Last Mass Execution in the United States* (Chicago, 1971); Eric E. Williams, *The Wooden Horse* (New York, 1958).

ARTICLES: Heinz Ludwig Ansbacher, "Attitudes of German Prisoners of War: A Study of the Dynamics of National-Socialistic Followership," *Psychological Monographs* (1948); Jessie Ash Arndt, "Prisoners of War on the Kansas Prairies," *Christian Science Monitor Magazine* (October 16, 1943); Ralph O. Busco and Douglas D. Alder, "German and Italian POWs in Utah and Idaho," *Utah Historical Quarterly* (Winter 1971); F. G. Alletson Cooke, "Nazi Prisoners are Nazis Still," *New York Times Magazine* (November 21, 1943); Robert De Vore, "Our Pampered Prisoners," *Collier's* (October 14, 1944); J. V. Dillon, "Development of Law Relative to Treatment of Prisoners of War," *Miami Law Quarterly* (December 1950); Henry W. Ehrmann, "An Experiment in Political Education: The Prisoner of War Schools in the United States," *Social Research* (September 1947); Ernest O. Hauser, "German Prisoners Talk Your Ears Off," *Saturday Evening Post* (January 13 and 20, 1945); J. Edgar Hoover, "Enemies at Large," *American* (April 1944); E. J. Kahn, Jr., "Annals of Crime: The Philologist," *New Yorker* (March-April 1950); William E. Kirwan, "Escape Tactics of German War Prisoners," *Journal of Criminal Law and Criminology* (January-February 1945); Werner Knop, "How Do the Germans Feel Now," *Saturday Evening Post* (May 22, 1943); Arnold P. Krammer, "German Prisoners of War in the United States," *Military Affairs* (April 1976); Robert Lowe Kunzig, "360,000 PW's—the Hope of Germany," *American* (November 1946); Archer L. Lerch, "The Army Reports on Prisoners of War," *American Mercury* (May 1945); Maxwell S. McKnight, "The Employment of Prisoners of War in the United States," *International Labour Review* (July 1944); Betty Fible Martin, "The Crops Come In," *New York Times Magazine* (September 23, 1945); John Brown Mason, "German Prisoners of War in the United States," *American Journal of International Law* (April 1945); John Hammond Moore, "Hitler's Afrika Korps in New England," *Yankee* (June 1976); "Italian POWs in America: War is Not Always Hell," *Prologue* (Fall 1976); "Hitler's Wehrmacht in Virginia, 1943–1946," *Virginia Magazine of History and Biography* (July 1977); Reinhold Pabel, with Bill Fay, "It's Easy to Bluff Americans," *Collier's* (May 16, 1953); James H. Powers, "What to do with German Prisoners: The American Muddle," *Atlantic* (November 1944), condensed in *Reader's Digest* (January 1945); Walter Rundell, Jr., "Paying the POW in World War II," *Military Affairs* (Fall 1958); Gaetano Salvemini, "Italian War Prisoners," *New Republic* (January 10, 1944); Beverly Smith, "The Afrika Korps Comes to America," *American* (August 1943); Jake W. Spidle, Jr., "Axis Invasion of the American West: POWs in New Mexico, 1942–1946," *New Mexico Historical Review*

(April 1974); "Axis Prisoners of War in the United States, 1942–1946: A Bibliographical Essay," *Military Affairs* (April 1975); Robert Warren Tissing, "Stalag–Texas, 1943–1945: The Detention and Use of Prisoners of War in Texas during World War II," *Military History of Texas and the Southwest* (January 1975); Martin Tollefson, "Enemy Prisoners of War," *Iowa Law Review* (November 1946); Michael Walzer, "Prisoners of War: Does the Fight Continue after the Battle?," *American Political Science Review* (September 1969); Terry Paul Wilson, "The Africa Corps in Oklahoma: Fort Reno's Prisoner of War Compound," *Chronicles of Oklahoma* (Fall 1974); David G. Wittels, "Are We Coddling Italian Prisoners?," *Saturday Evening Post* (March 3, 1945).

Index

About the Author

JOHN HAMMOND MOORE was born in Maine in 1924. He has worked as a newspaperman, editor and textbook salesman (McGraw-Hill), history teacher, "Nader Raider" and very briefly as press aide to a congressman. Educated at Hamilton College and the University of Virginia, he now resides in Washington, D.C.

Moore has published some sixty articles in magazines and journals such as the *South Atlantic Quarterly, Proceedings of the US Naval Institute, Smithsonian Journal of History, Yankee* and the *Virginia Magazine of History & Biography.* His books include four published by Southern university presses (Georgia, South Carolina, Virginia and LSU) and three written while teaching American history in Australia 1968–1971: two paperbacks, one dealing with the pre-Hollywood life of Errol Flynn, the other with Australian-American relations (1940–1970), and a hard-bound collection of Australian impressions of America (1876–1976).

His research on German POWs in America grew out of (a) discovery while writing *Albemarle: Jefferson's County, 1727–1976* (U. P. of Va., 1976) that a small POW camp was located in that region, (b) knowledge that his father used them on his Maine potato farm, and (c) curiosity as to how many Germans were held in America during WWII. That curiosity led to a book.